A PICTORIAL HISTORY OF ARKANSAS'S OLD STATE HOUSE

A PICTORIAL HISTORY OF ARKANSAS'S OLD STATE HOUSE

Celebrating 175 Years

Mary L. Kwas

The University of Arkansas Press
Fayetteville • 2011

Manufactured in the United States of America

ISBN-10: 1-55728-955-7
ISBN-13: 978-1-55728-955-1

15 14 13 12 11 5 4 3 2 1

Text design by Ellen Beeler

⊗ The paper used in this publication meets the minimum requirements of the American National Standard for Permanence of Paper for Printed Library Materials Z39.48-1984.

Library of Congress Cataloging-in-Publication Data

Kwas, Mary L.
A Pictorial History of Arkansas's Old State House : Celebrating 175 Years / Mary L. Kwas.
pages cm
Includes bibliographical references and index.
ISBN 978-1-55728-955-1 (casebound : alk. paper)
1. Old State House (Little Rock, Ark.)—History. 2. Old State House (Little Rock, Ark.)—History—Pictorial works. 3. Little Rock (Ark.)—Buildings, structures, etc.—Pictorial works. I. Title.
NA4412.A8K88 2011
725'.110976773--dc22
2010043114

Support for this project was provided by private donations to the Old State House Museum.

In memory of my great-grandmother
Essie Dill West Tucker
and her daughters
Ruth, Nelle, and May,
who knew the Old State House some 75 years before I did,

and for my sister,
Susan Estelle Kwas

CONTENTS

Construction of Arkansas's Old State House began in 1833, and it was declared finished in 1842. In 1836, however, it was sufficiently complete to serve as the seat of the newly formed state government. It was originally designed and constructed in the Greek Revival architectural style, but its curving central stairway and ornate exterior ironwork are evidence of a later and substantial Victorian era renovation.

The Old State House was the home of Arkansas state government for seventy-five years, a period that saw ratification of the state's first constitution, a fatal knife fight in the House of Representatives chamber, the 1861 Secession Convention, and armed occupation during Reconstruction's Brooks-Baxter War. Over time the structure deteriorated, and with little funds available for repair, it became a near ruin in the heart of downtown Little Rock. State government eventually moved to a newly constructed capitol building in 1911.

After 1911 the Old State House hosted various government offices and was the home of civic and patriotic organizations. The Medical Department of the University of Arkansas and the Arkansas Board of Health occupied much of the building beginning in 1912. Had the structure not been in use, it very likely would have been demolished despite intensive lobbying by Arkansas preservationists.

Arkansas's Old State House is the oldest standing state capitol building west of the Mississippi River and is listed on the National Register of Historic Places. In 1997 the structure was also designated a National Historic Landmark. It earned this last honor not because it was a Greek Revival temple symbolizing democracy on the American frontier nor was it for Bill Clinton's association with the building during his successful U.S. presidential campaigns in 1992 and 1996. Instead, Arkansas mosquitoes enabled the Old State House to be recognized as a site worthy of special status. Headquartered at the Old State House, Rockefeller Foundation workers and state public-health officials began their efforts to control malaria by eradicating the disease-carrying mosquitoes. The highly successful Crossett Experiment dramatically reduced the number of malaria cases reported at the test site of Crossett, Arkansas, and served as a model worldwide for control of the disease. For its role in the Crossett Experiment, Arkansas's original statehouse was granted Historic Landmark status by the National Park Service.

Mary Kwas, Research Associate for the Arkansas Archeological Survey, has written a much-needed history of Arkansas's most recognizable artifact. Her research includes evidence retrieved from disparate archival and architectural sources as well as archaeological excavations at the site. The talents of an archaeologist were needed to dig through the convoluted layers of the Old State House's history and then tell a coherent story. Ms. Kwas has done this in language appealing to all readers.

Willard B. Gatewood III
September 2010

ACKNOWLEDGMENTS

The project to write a history of Arkansas's Old State House began in 1996 when the Department of Arkansas Heritage provided funds for the Arkansas Archeological Survey to investigate archeological deposits around the perimeter of the Old State House, prior to the commencement of work to underpin the foundation of the building. As both archeological and architectural work progressed through 1997, I undertook a search for information on the construction and physical changes to the building in the archival record. Out of that modest beginning grew the desire to present a book to the public, in an accessible and well-illustrated form, that celebrated the long and interesting history of the Old State House.

My thanks goes, first and foremost, to Bill Gatewood, the director of the Old State House Museum, who believed in this project and provided tangible support with both staff and resources. He has always provided a warm welcome on my visits to the museum.

Among the Old State House Museum staff members who contributed directly to this project, I especially would like to thank Gail Moore Stephens, exhibit director, who worked closely with me to locate illustrations, obtain permissions, and track down odd bits of information. Bill Reames, exhibit specialist, drew several fine illustrations, and Rita A. Wilson, exhibit specialist, prepared photographs for publication. Jo Ellen Maack, curator, and Danyelle Fletcher, registrar, selected and provided photographs of objects from the museum collection and closely examined objects to answer my nit-picky questions.

Several researchers in the 1970s undertook studies of Old State House history that, unfortunately, did not result in more widely available publications, but their work did contribute to this one, and the authors are deserving of recognition. Susan Smyer produced an unpublished, in-house manuscript in 1976 on the early years of the Old State House, which resulted in the exhibit "First State Capitol in Transition: 1833–1885." Ned Shank picked up the thread in 1977 with *Arkansas' First State Capitol, 1885–1947*, and Donald Richard Brown, Marvin Ray Franklin, and Michele Roussel Wasson concluded the story in 1978 with *The Old State House: Its Survival and Contributions, 1911–1947*. The latter two works were printed for limited distribution by the Arkansas Commemorative Commission.

Archeologist Randall Guendling of the Arkansas Archeological Survey conducted the archeological research at the Old State House in 1976 and 1977. I worked closely with Randy during those years, comparing archival information with field discoveries and examining artifacts. For this book, Randy discussed with me his interpretations of the archeological features and made available field and artifact photographs.

I would like to thank Robert Mainfort, archeologist at the Arkansas Archeological Survey, for his assistance in digitizing slides, cleaning up images, and consolidating artifact photos. He also has been a long-term supporter of this project. Thanks also to historical architect Charles Witsell for his support and continuing interest in this project, as well as to William N. Banks, Dorothy Hinkle, Virginia Mabry, James J. Holmberg, Robert T. Chapel, and numerous archivists and librarians who assisted me in gathering research materials and photographs.

Finally, I thank Thomas Green, director of the Arkansas Archeological Survey, whose continued support helped make this publication possible.

Fig. 0.1: The Old State House as it is seen today. *Photograph by Greg Hursley, 1992, Old State House Museum Collection.*

INTRODUCTION

FROM 2008 TO 2017, the Old State House celebrates the 175th anniversary of its construction. This venerable building already has spanned three centuries, being born in Arkansas's territorial period of the nineteenth century, continuing to serve the state in changing capacities throughout the twentieth century, and now beginning life in the twenty-first century as a symbol of Arkansas's history.

The Old State House has witnessed as much of Arkansas history as anything can. It has served as the state capitol, a state office building, a war memorial, a shrine, and a museum. Its history is a fascinating one. The story presented in this book goes beyond the building's life as the Arkansas capitol. Rather than examining the political scene and the laws that were enacted in the building during the capitol years, this book explores the original architecture, the physical changes, and the changing purposes of the building. It also brings to light the stories of the many Arkansans who shared parts of their own histories with that of the building. This book is, in a very real sense, the biography of the Old State House.

In order to adequately cover a complex history, the book is divided into four sections. Section 1 is set before the Old State House came into existence and describes the process that led to the construction. Chapter 1 explores territorial governor John Pope's efforts to secure the money and select an architect to design and build a state house for Arkansas. While it is common knowledge that Gideon Shryock was the architect chosen for that purpose, little about Shryock beyond that fact is known in Arkansas. Chapter 2 remedies that omission by tracing Shryock's life and work. Because Shryock's plan for the Old State House was modified by Governor Pope and supervising architect George Weigart in order to keep costs within means, chapter 3 attempts to recreate what Shryock's original plan might have been.

Section 2 traces the 175-year history of the Old State House, beginning with the construction years in chapter 4. Work on the Old State House began in 1833 and the first state General Assembly met in the building in 1836, but the construction wasn't considered complete until 1842. Work progressed in fits and starts during those nine years, and numerous setbacks contributed to the length of the project. Chapter 5 covers the first period in which the building served as the Arkansas state capitol, spanning over 40 years. By the end of that time, state government had grown to the point that the building could no longer accommodate all the offices needed. Chapter 6 deals with the expansion of the Old State House, when the building took on the form we see today. Chapter 7 follows the next 25 years of the enlarged State House, up until the year when state government moved to the new Capitol it currently occupies. During this period, the Old State House was looked upon as an old office building that had outlived its usefulness, and there were calls for tearing down the building and selling the valuable land. But Arkansans with foresight knew that the Old State House was more than just an office building. In chapter 8, which covers 40 years, the gallant efforts to preserve the building and the variety of uses it was put to are examined. Beginning in 1951, the preservation of the Old State House was secured and it began a new life as a museum of Arkansas history. Even that role, however, was not a stagnant one, and chapter 9 explores the 40 years of growth and changes as the Old State House Museum. Finally, chapter 10 and chapter 11 bring the story up to the present through the archeological work, another restoration, and the building's meaning to today's Arkansans.

The physical structure of the Old State House in the years when the building was the seat of state government merely served as a background to the business of the state. It was the work of the legislators as they grappled over bills and debated laws that was the focus of newspaper reports and later memoirs. Thus, in

Fig. 0.2: Early reports of Arkansas's secretaries of state include information on the condition and upkeep of the Old State House. *Photograph courtesy of Arkansas Archeological Survey.*

the early years, especially before 1885 when an expansion was undertaken, there is little in the way of written descriptions or visual records of the building. Most descriptions during this period come from the reports of the secretaries of state, who were charged with the upkeep and care of the building. When the building was in good condition, there would be little or no mention of it in the secretaries' reports, but as the building aged and repairs became increasingly necessary, more details would be included. The reports were prepared every other year, and because the secretaries were trying to make the case for adequate funds, the reports also tend to focus on the negative. Continuity could also be a problem, as some secretaries served only for one 2-year term, while others had multiple terms, leading to sparse or rich descriptions depending on the years of service.

Around the beginning of the twentieth century, as the Old State House outlived its usefulness as a capitol, the future of the building began to be discussed in the newspapers. The reuse of the building, the fight for its preservation, and its rebirth as a museum all contributed to newspaper coverage and more material from which to reconstruct its story. Thus, as this biography of the Old State House progresses, the early chapters will seem lean by comparison to the much-richer accounts in the later chapters. This is simply the nature of the historic record.

The story of the Old State House, however, is not just one of bricks and mortar. The inanimate building is infused with life through the people who have interacted with it over the years. Arkansans have taken care of the building, fought for its preservation, battled on its grounds, and even died within its walls. The stories of those people add vivid color to the history of the Old State House. But the point where their lives come together with the building is a moment out of context, leaving us to wonder, who were these people? What did they do before and after their time at the Old State House? Section 3 offers the answers to those questions by providing biographical sketches of the many people who were touched by the Old State House. Arranged in alphabetical order by last name, readers can find information on the secretaries of state who served as caretakers, the governors involved with the construction, legislators who fought in the hall, preservationists who saved the building, and a museum director who brought the building into a new life. Their stories are just as fascinating as that of the Old State House.

Rounding out the book, section 4 provides an image gallery of illustrations and artifacts from the history of the building. Because the Old State House always was and still is a public building, its visual image has interested illustrators, artists, photographers, and tourists down through the years. Images from the nineteenth century are rare, but the numbers and kinds of images grew throughout the twentieth century and continue today. In addition, there are many historic objects associated with the building and grounds. Successive renovations to the building eliminated early physical features and substituted later additions, while numerous public activities added to the artifactual record. We are fortunate that the Old State House Museum actively collects examples of the historic images, as well as artifacts of the physical history and use of the building and grounds. Section 4 illustrates many of these images and artifacts, arranged in groups by architecture, postal commemoratives and postcards, souvenirs, political memorabilia, historical images and activities, and artists' interpretations.

The story of the Old State House, in both text and image, celebrates this splendid building, which has weathered 175 years of struggles to survive as a symbol of Arkansas's history. I hope this story will continue to endear Arkansans to the Old State House so that it will always embody Arkansas's past and remain vital for future generations.

SECTION 1

Designing the Old State House

CHAPTER 1

Governor Pope's Lofty Ideas

IT WASN'T UNTIL 1836 that Arkansas became a state, operating prior to that as a territory, although by the time John Pope began his first term as territorial governor in 1829, the eyes of Arkansans were firmly fixed on statehood. As third territorial governor of Arkansas, appointed by President Andrew Jackson, Pope served two terms, the first from 1829 to 1832 and the second from 1832 to 1835, during which time the wheels were set in motion to procure money and land for a territorial assembly building. Before construction was completed, the building had become Arkansas's first State House (Carter 1954; Flynn 1971:130).

An amusing legend has it that Pope made his inaugural address to the Territorial Legislature in 1829 during a rainfall. The roof of the building leaked, causing Pope to move from side to side to keep his papers dry, thus setting his resolve to work for a permanent assembly building (Herndon 1933:89; Kennan 1950:35). It is more likely, however, that because the Territory had no building for the express purpose of conducting its business, acquiring one was an obvious next step. There had been some discussion of the need for a permanent building prior to Pope's appointment, and as soon as he took office Pope began his campaign to secure just such a building. He began by suggesting to the General Assembly that the U.S. Congress might be persuaded to come up with the needed funds (Eno 1945:241; Flynn 1971:131; White 1964:90–91).

The General Assembly liked that idea and addressed a Memorial to Congress on the subject. Pope, who knew many of the congressmen from his stint as senator from Kentucky, went to Washington to plead the case, along with Ambrose H. Sevier, delegate to Congress from the Arkansas Territory. The two men were successful in their cause, and on March 2, 1831, President Jackson approved the act of Congress that appropriated ten sections of public land for the purpose of raising money for the erection of a government building. Not long after that, in June 1832, Congress granted another 1,000 acres for the erection of two more buildings—a county courthouse and a jail. From the very beginning, the proceeds from the sale of both land grants were combined, and the courthouse was considered as part of the whole construction (Carter 1954:108–109; Eno 1945:242; Ferguson 1968:3; Flynn 1971:131–132; More 1837:202).

Unfortunately Congress left the business of selecting and selling the ten sections to the General Assembly. The legislators were persuaded by former secretary of the territory Robert Crittenden to trade the ten sections to Crittenden for his house, and the General

Fig. 1.1: Arkansas territorial governor John Pope. *Courtesy of Arkansas History Commission.*

Assembly passed an act in October 1831 to that effect. The Crittenden house, built during the 1820s, was Little Rock's most elegant home at the time. It was a large and fashionable brick house, with a main section containing four large rooms separated by a wide central hall, as well as an additional rear room and a two-story wing. Two of the rooms in the main section were 22 feet square and the other two only slightly smaller. It probably would have served adequately for the purposes of the Territory, but Pope had a higher vision—and he vetoed the act (Flynn 1971:131–132; Roy and Witsell 1984:33–34).

Pope saw the new state house as something that would "command the admiration and respect of the passing stranger" as well as have a "moral and political influence on the whole community," and he wanted it to be built "with taste and elegance." A building such as that, Pope asserted, "would give an impulse to the general improvement of the country," and "better houses would soon appear through out the land" (Roy and Witsell 1984:47). Pope was looking to the future statehood of Arkansas and wanted a state house that would be an inspiration to its people.

Fig. 1.2: Arkansas territorial secretary Robert Crittenden wanted to trade his house for the ten sections of land given by the U.S. Government to raise funds for a State House. *Old State House Museum Collection.*

Fig. 1.3: Crittenden House. *Courtesy of Arkansas Historic Preservation Program.*

Fig. 1.4: Artist's conception of Little Rock in 1836 shows a sparsely settled frontier town. *From the collection of the* Arkansas Democrat-Gazette.

He was also concerned with selecting a proper site and wanted it, if possible, to be in view of the Arkansas River, then the major transportation route to the city (Roy and Witsell 1984:47). Pope described the site that was finally selected: "The situation, moreover, is commanding, having a street on every side, and a view of it can never be obscured by any advance in improvement or population of the town" (*Arkansas Gazette,* November 20, 1833). Pope's ideas for the building and the site matched well the feelings of the time. Like a Greek temple high on a commanding location, the building would reflect the ideals of Greek democracy and culture and inspire the new state to rise to those ideals. What better architecture to embody those ideals than the new architecture being seen in the land—Greek Revival.

Crittenden's supporters were so angry at Pope's veto that they attempted to have him removed as governor but were unsuccessful. The U.S. Congress put an end to the political squabbling and passed another act authorizing Pope to handle the sale of the land and the erection of the building. Pope's stand on the matter was supported by the *Arkansas Gazette* as well as by many residents of Little Rock. In the end Pope's wisdom and business sense proved correct. The ten sections of land brought in $31,722, while the Crittenden house sold for a mere $6,700 (Flynn 1971:132; Hempstead 1911a:116).

Pope selected blocks 80 and 81 in the heart of Little Rock, right on the river, for the site of the new state house. Chester Ashley, David G. Eller, and William Russell donated part of the land, and the remainder was purchased from Russell for $800, in part from money donated by a number of Little Rock residents (Eno 1945:242–243; Ferguson 1968:5). Then Pope selected an architect—the young Gideon Shryock.

The Greek Revival Period in America

The Greek Revival period, falling roughly between 1820 to 1860, was a time during which interest in the classical world flourished. The period was inspired by archeological discoveries and pictorial recordings of ancient Greek and Roman ruins, as well as Greece's fight for independence. Literary and artistic interest abounded. This interest seemed to rivet the identity of young America. Having turned away from England during the Revolutionary War and its aftermath, the people were filled with a fierce spirit to be American, full of confidence in the success of their great experiment in government and their conquering of a continent (Arnaud 1944:xv–xviii; Hamlin 1944:1–9; Sutton 1992:15–17). With their democratic ideals, Americans felt their country was the spiritual successor of ancient Greece and expressed these feelings in ways that included naming newly established towns after Greek cities (Poppeliers et al. 1983:36). What better way to express these lofty ideals than in the public architecture of America's towns and cities—especially in government buildings—and what better examples than the noble, temple-like, and artistically inspiring architecture of ancient Greece? It was a perfect fit.

The period of Greek Revival, however, was not just a time of copying Greek buildings. On the contrary, the best of Greek Revival used Greek architecture as inspiration, but adapted it to the needs of the client, creating an architecture uniquely American. That architecture, in which structure and design were thoroughly integrated, sought to express the ideals of democracy and the exuberant hopes Americans held for their country. The Greek Revival period was also the time when professional architects came to the fore, bringing with them experimentation and changes in style (Hamlin 1944:88–89).

The birth of Greek Revival in America was embodied in the Bank of Pennsylvania, designed in 1798 by Benjamin Henry Latrobe (1766–1820). Latrobe, an Englishman, had traveled extensively in Europe observing ancient antiquities, before returning to London and receiving training in architecture and engineering. He left an established practice there after the death of his wife and found fame in America, which quickly accrued with the success of his Bank of Pennsylvania (Hamlin 1944:63; Newcomb 1927:175; Sutton 1992:18). Sutton describes the work, as follows:

> The basic form was derived from the Greek Ionic temple on the Ilyssus near Athens, but the

Fig. 1.5: Architect Benjamin Henry Latrobe. *Courtesy of White House Historical Association (White House Collection).*

Fig. 1.6: Benjamin Latrobe's Bank of Pennsylvania, South Second Street, Philadelphia, from the fourth edition of William Birch's *Views of Philadelphia,* 1827–1828. *Courtesy of Philadelphia Print Shop of Philadelphia, Pennsylvania.*

> low central dome, broad wall surfaces, arched windows, central skylit vaulted banking hall, and simple finishing treatment throughout were his own innovations—inspired by his grand tour of the antiquities. His bank established a precedent for later American Greek Revival efforts. (Sutton 1992:18)

Latrobe designed a number of other public buildings as well as residences for notables of the time, but is probably best known, after his Bank of Pennsylvania, for his contributions to the U.S. Capitol. Latrobe, one of several architects involved with the project, was hired by President Thomas Jefferson in 1802 as surveyor of public buildings that included as a major duty completion of the Capitol. While basing his ideas on classical examples, he wove American symbols into the design, such as using images of cornstalks and tobacco leaves on the capitols of columns in the Senate and House of Representatives (Hamlin 1944:32–36; Sutton 1992:32–33).

Besides the inspiration Latrobe provided for other American architects, he was also instrumental in training a number of young men, the two most notable of his students being Robert Mills and William Strickland, both of whom practiced in Philadelphia (Hamlin 1944:66). Strickland's influence is important since he served as Gideon Shryock's mentor.

Strickland (1788–1854) was the son of a carpenter working on the Bank of Pennsylvania and came to the attention of Latrobe as a 14-year-old. He worked for Latrobe on and off as a young man and came into his own in 1818, when he won the competition—even over his mentor Latrobe—to design the Second Bank of the United States in Philadelphia. The bank was designed as an eight-column Parthenon Doric, with interiors that were efficient and well proportioned. The bank impressed observers both in America and abroad and influenced American architecture. By the 1840s Greek Revival–style banks were prevalent throughout the country (Gilchrist 1969:1; Hamlin 1944:74–77; Newcomb 1928a:227; Sutton 1992:25–27).

Strickland designed a number of other public buildings as well as residences throughout his time. The one considered to be his Philadelphia masterpiece is the Merchants Exchange building (1834), in which he utilized a triangular-shaped lot to great success by placing a rounded Corinthian portico and tower at the narrow end. As his final project, he accepted the invitation in 1844 to design and build the Tennessee state capitol in Nashville. He died before the work was completed, leaving it to be finished by his son, and his body is interred in a vault in the capitol specially designed for that purpose (Gilchrist 1969:18–19; Hamlin 1944:59–60, 79–80; Sutton 1992:28–30).

When Gideon Shryock was 21 years old, he spent a year studying under Strickland, thus receiving professional training and influence that descended from Latrobe through Strickland, and which prepared him to make his mark on Greek Revival architecture in the middle west.

Governor Pope Chooses an Architect

While it may have been that Pope's vision for a state house reflected the mood of the times, his personal taste in architecture was not lacking in an experienced eye. Pope served as Kentucky's U.S. senator from 1807 to 1813, during the time that architect Benjamin Henry Latrobe was supervising work on the U.S. Capitol, and Pope could not have been unaware of the beauty and symbolism of the building. What was more, Pope must have known Latrobe personally, for it was Latrobe who drew the plans for Pope's Lexington, Kentucky, residence in 1811. The house was built in 1814 after Pope finished his term in Washington and returned to Kentucky (Baylor 1943:37–38, 59; Flynn 1971:45; Newcomb 1953:51–53).

Pope's knowledge of Kentucky architect Gideon Shryock had to be from personal experience as well. Shryock won the commission for the design and construction of the Kentucky State House in the spring of 1827 and completed the work in the fall of 1830. This was during the period Pope served as state senator, his term running from 1825 to 1829, in which he would have been involved in voting on business regarding the new State House (Baylor 1943:194, 266–267). When Pope arrived in Little Rock in late May 1829 to begin work as territorial governor, he was fresh from the Kentucky Senate. What he knew of Kentucky's new State House undoubtedly influenced his choice of an architect for Arkansas (Baylor 1943:340).

Although contractor Thomas Thorn later wrote that Pope contacted other architects about providing plans (*Arkansas Gazette*, May 23, 1837), Pope's own words describing the process give no indication of this:

> After selling about six sections of the land, on the terms of my Proclamation, and being assured

Fig. 1.7: Architect William Strickland. *Courtesy of Charles Henry Hart Autograph Collection, 1731–1912, Archives of American Art, Smithsonian Institution.*

that I should have the means to progress with the building, I thought it necessary and expedient to procure a skillful Architect to plan the State House and superintend and direct the work. I applied, by letter, to a Mr. Shryock, of Lexington, Ky., of much fame as an Architect, who has planned and superintended the erection of the Capitol of that State, to repair to this place and direct our operations. He declined coming, owing to his engagements in Kentucky, and other considerations; but sent on a Mr. George Weigart with a strong recommendation of his fitness for the undertaking. He furnished, also, a splendid plan of the building, but on too large and expensive a scale, for the fund placed at my disposal. Mr. Weigart and myself, after much consideration, abridged so far as to bring it within the means applicable to the object. (*Arkansas Gazette,* November 20, 1833)

Shryock couldn't come to Arkansas because he was in the midst of work on Morrison College at Transylvania University in Lexington, Kentucky, and it is unlikely he would have been interested in leaving his home state as long as commissions for his work in Kentucky were forthcoming. Nonetheless, as Pope explained, Shryock did draw plans for the Arkansas State House and sent them with George Weigart,

Fig. 1.8: Strickland's Second Bank of the United States in Pennsylvania. *Courtesy of Historic American Buildings Survey, U.S. Library of Congress, Frederick D. Nichols, Photographer.*

Fig. 1.9: George Weigart served as supervising architect for the construction of the Old State House until 1834. *Old State House Museum Collection.*

whom he recommended to superintend the work.

We know very little about Weigart because of his early death. He may have been a young architect apprenticing under Shryock, but it was more likely that he was one of the many competent builders active at the time who were more than contractors but not trained as professional architects. He was about 26 years old when he came to Little Rock, and it is obvious that his early death prevented him from establishing himself and his work.

Weigart was from Lexington, Kentucky (*Arkansas Gazette*, July 29, 1834). An interesting footnote in a work on Transylvania University places him there in 1829 when the university's main building burned. The trustees rewarded Weigart with a four-year scholarship for one of his sons for his "extraordinary exertions and eminent services . . . on the night of the 9th of May, 1829, in preserving the library and property of the University when the building was on fire" (Peter and Peter 1896:159). This was the building that Shryock's Morrison College was to replace, and considering that Shryock was occupied with its construction when the request for building plans from Arkansas arrived, it is likely that Weigart was employed on Morrison College as well.

It is not known what Shryock's original plans for the State House looked like or how Weigart abridged them as neither set of plans have survived. Governor Pope, however, did provide a verbal description of his plans for the building to readers of the *Arkansas Gazette.* Although brief, he described all the main features:

> The house will present two fronts, one to the river, the other to the town, of four columns on each front, eleven feet in advance of the building. The Legislative rooms will be on the second floor, and Committee rooms below. The Courthouse will be near forty feet east of the Legislative house; and the Office wing, having room for Auditor, Treasurer, Secretary of State, and Land office, will be placed the same distance on the west of the centre building; and each wing to be connected to the centre building by dwarf colonnades. (*Arkansas Gazette*, November 20, 1833)

CHAPTER 2

Gideon Shryock, Architect

ALTHOUGH IT IS COMMON knowledge in Arkansas that Gideon Shryock was the architect of Arkansas's Old State House, writings on the history of the first capitol generally offer little more than the architect's name. Despite the implication that little is known of the architect, a number of studies of Shryock's life and contributions have been published. This chapter examines Shryock's life, his place in American Greek Revival architecture, and the research efforts that have explored his life and work.

Who Was Gideon Shryock?

Gideon Shryock was born on November 15, 1802, in Lexington, Kentucky, the son of Mathias Shryock and Mary Elizabeth Gaugh, who came from Frederick County, Maryland, in the late 1780s. Mathias was a contractor and builder and made his living constructing homes in Lexington. Among his eight children who lived to maturity, all three sons followed in their father's footsteps. After Gideon, who was the oldest, Montgomery became a civil engineer, while Cincinnatus became an architect practicing in his hometown of Lexington (Field 1952:111–112).

Shryock was educated in Lexington schools and attended Mr. Aldridge's Lancastrian Academy for boys before apprenticing with his father. From Mathias Shryock it is presumed that Gideon learned sound construction methods and developed skills as a supervisor of work. He also would have had access to his father's library, which undoubtedly contained the architectural works of the day, such as the guidebooks of architectural design by Asher Benjamin (e.g., Benjamin 1969). At age 21 it was decided that Shryock would spend a year in Philadelphia studying with the renowned architect William Strickland. The fact that Strickland accepted him as an apprentice suggests that Shryock's training and talents were more than adequate. Shryock arrived in Philadelphia—the cultural metropolis of young America—in late 1823 (Field 1952:12; Newcomb 1928a:229). Although two letters Shryock wrote to his parents from Philadelphia still exist (Flynn 1971:205–208), they give no indication of the method of his training under Strickland, but it is assumed he made good use of his year of study.

In 1824 Shryock returned to Lexington and embarked on his career, bringing with him from Philadelphia an "enthusiasm for Greek detail and a creative proficiency in using it that made him one of the most skillful of all the earlier Greek Revival architects of the country" (Hamlin 1944:244). He probably began his

Fig. 2.1: Gideon Shryock, architect of Arkansas's Old State House. *Courtesy of Kentucky Historical Society.*

career working with his father (Flynn 1971:8). The same year that Shryock returned to Kentucky, the State House at Frankfort was destroyed by fire, leaving only the two separate brick office wings. In 1827 a bill was approved for rebuilding the capitol, offering a premium for the best design. The 25-year-old Shryock had no intention of submitting a plan, but was encouraged to do so by his friends so that, at least, the public would be introduced to him as an architect. To Shryock's great surprise he won the commission, tradition having it that all the other contestants, upon seeing Shryock's plan, immediately and unanimously agreed it was the best (Field 1952:114–115; Flynn 1971:21–22; Hamlin 1944:245; Newcomb 1928a:231).

Wasting no time after winning the commission, Shryock packed his bags and moved to Frankfort to superintend the building of the new capitol. The Greek Revival building was patterned after the temple of Minerva Polias at Priene in Ionia; it featured a six-column Ionic portico, a dome and lantern (or windowed cupola) to light the interior, and a magnificent self-supporting stairway. During the construction years of 1827–1830, Shryock's life must have been charmed, for the work went smoothly and he completed the capitol in under four years. His building, which introduced Greek Revival architecture into Kentucky and was the first state capitol built in the new style, spread the young architect's fame (Collins 1877:247–248; Field 1925:117; Floyd 1978:110; Flynn 1971:22, 24–25; Newcomb 1928a:231–232).

During construction of the Kentucky capitol, life was promising for Shryock in other ways as well. In 1829 he married Elizabeth P. Bacon

Fig. 2.2: Kentucky State House, front view. *Courtesy of Historic American Buildings Survey, U. S. Library of Congress, Theodore Webb, Photographer.*

Fig. 2.3: Kentucky State House, side view shows the dome and lantern. *Courtesy of Historic American Buildings Survey, U. S. Library of Congress, Theodore Webb, Photographer.*

of Frankfort, and eventually the two of them had ten children (one son becoming an architect) (Newcomb 1928a:231). He also prepared plans for what was to become his second commission for the design of a prominent building. That year the main building of Transylvania University in Lexington burned (Flynn 1971:31), and Shryock submitted a plan for the new building that would be known as Morrison College. The building, with its six-column Doric portico, was patterned after the Parthenon. The building committee received proposals from several architects and also consulted Benjamin Henry Latrobe, but finally decided on the plans submitted by Shryock, approving them in October 1830 (Andrews 1944:74; Field 1952:119; Flynn 1971:31).

With the work on the Kentucky capitol completed, Shryock returned to Lexington to begin supervising the construction of Morrison College. Unlike his experience with the capitol, however, the Morrison College project caused much mental and financial suffering on Shryock's part. Problems included interruptions caused by having to re-site the building after the foundations had been dug, a lack of funds and workmen, and a cholera epidemic in the summer of 1833 that killed several hundred people in two months including Shryock's father (Andrews 1944:72, 1945:35; Field 1952:120; Newcomb 1928a:233). In addition, the Transylvania trustees were difficult to deal with and very slow to come through with promised money. Shryock pleaded with the trustees in 1835:

> I hope the Trustees will make arrangement to pay . . . me immediately . . . the law suits, perplexities, and other difficulties, I have been involved in on account of it, have been the means of alienating from me my friends; destroying my credit; agitating my mind, and disqualifying me, for all the purposes for which my genius and talents had fitted me. (Andrews 1945:36)

Fig. 2.4: Morrison College, Transylvania University, Lexington, Kentucky. *Courtesy of Historic American Buildings Survey, U.S. Library of Congress, Lester Jones, Photographer.*

Despite the ongoing problems with Morrison College, Shryock continued to submit designs for other projects. In 1832 he submitted plans for a courthouse for Franklin County, and in early 1833 he drew plans for the Arkansas State House and sent them to Little Rock with George Weigart (*Arkansas Gazette,* November 20, 1833; Haggard 1971:59; Kennan 1950:36).

By August 1833 the Franklin County building commission was getting antsy to start construction on the courthouse, but Shryock was still tied up with Morrison College. When the site for the courthouse was finally purchased in late 1834, although matters were still unresolved in Lexington, Shryock moved to Frankfort to begin work on the courthouse and supervised the last of the Morrison College construction from there. Work on the Franklin

Fig. 2.5: Franklin County Courthouse, Frankfort, Kentucky. *Courtesy of Gail Moore Stephens.*

Fig. 2.6: Orlando Brown House, Frankfort, Kentucky. *Courtesy of Historic American Buildings Survey, U.S. Library of Congress, Lester Jones, Photographer.*

County Courthouse sailed along smoothly, and less than a year later, in November 1835, the building was far enough completed to allow the county to occupy it (Haggard 1971:54, 60–61). In general, 1835 was another good year for Shryock. Besides finishing the courthouse, Morrison College was also completed and he was paid the remainder of what he was owed for the job. He also designed at least one private residence in Frankfort, the Orlando Brown House, although he did not supervise the construction.

What must have appeared in 1835 to be his most exciting opportunity—his design for the Jefferson County Courthouse in Louisville was accepted in September and he was subsequently appointed as the city's architect in November—ultimately would prove to be his downfall (Flynn 1971:52–53; Haggard 1971:54, 72, 74). Upon accepting the appointment Shryock moved to Louisville, but work on the courthouse did not begin immediately. He filled his time serving as supervising architect for the construction of the Bank of Louisville (a.k.a. the Southern National Bank), leading to the confusion among his family in later years that he was the bank's architect. The bank was actually designed by New Orleans architect James Dakin, who began work on it in the summer or fall of 1835. Shryock took over as supervising architect after Dakin returned to New Orleans to supervise construction of the Merchants Exchange. Shryock likely began his supervision of the construction in early 1836, and the work was completed in 1837 (Scully 1973:26–31). Late that same year, serving in his position as city architect, Shryock designed the Louisville Medical Academy for the city and began supervision of its construction. Work on the Medical Academy proceeded fairly smoothly, aside from a minor disagreement over Shryock's fee, and the building was completed in 1839 (Flynn 1971:59; Haggard 1971:86, 89).

During the same period as his work on the Medical Academy, Shryock finally began work on the Jefferson County Courthouse. The courthouse project was a joint venture of the county and city that was intended to serve as the next state capitol—a big idea for Louisville that never came to fruition. Shryock probably got caught up in the unrealistic and bold plans. As Elisabeth Louise Flynn observes:

> It is amusing to note that Shryock's reputation was based partly on his capitol at Frankfort, and now Louisville was asking him to outdo himself in another enterprise that would persuade the legislature to move to another Shryock capitol. (Flynn 1971:53)

Despite the city council's enthusiasm for the project, nothing went right with it. Problems included a financial crisis in 1837, the inadvertent omission of the rotunda in the contract, and alterations of the plans to fit a different and smaller site. In addition, the masonry contractor incorrectly estimated the quantity of the stone needed, and the stone itself was found to be porous and began to disintegrate. Progress was so slow on the building it became known derisively as "Gutherie's Folly" after city council member James Gutherie who had promoted it (Andrews 1944:74–75; Flynn 1971:51–58, 146–147; Haggard 1971:105; Newcomb 1953:116–117).

Shryock's original plans for the courthouse called for a six-column Doric portico on the front, four-column porticos on the side wings, and a clock tower with lantern. As it was built, the courthouse entry was reduced to a four-column portico, and the side porticos and clock tower were eliminated (Collins 1877:plate opposite page 372; Newcomb 1940a:plate 113 and 1953:116–117). In 1842 with the work still not finished, Shryock was called before the city council to make a report and was shortly after removed as city architect (Flynn 1971:53). The city then left the building in an unfinished condition for 16 years before hiring Albert Fink to serve as architect for the courthouse in 1858. The building was finally completed—after nearly a quarter of a century—in 1859 (Andrews 1944:74–75).

Shryock's career as an architect was severely damaged. After the fiasco with the Jefferson County Courthouse, Shryock's work slipped into virtual anonymity. As John C. Haggard so aptly summed up:

> When Gideon Shryock presented his (report) . . . to the City Council on October 17, 1842, he abandoned, so far as is known, his career as an architect of significant buildings. Five years before, accepting the commission must have seemed another important step in a sparkling career. Yet, he would practice architecture for almost another forty years only to die poverty-strickened and forgotten. He was so well forgotten that his subsequent career seems to neither have interested historians nor afforded much information. (Haggard 1971:102)

After losing his position with the city in 1842, it is surprising that Shryock remained in Louisville. It does appear that a couple years later in 1844 he was planning a move to St.

MEDICAL COLLEGE, LOUISVILLE, KY.

Fig. 2.7: Louisville Medical Academy, Kentucky. *Courtesy of Kentucky Historical Society.*

Louis when he received a request from officials in Nashville, Tennessee, to visit the city and discuss designing a new capitol for the neighboring state. Shryock made the visit, drew a set of plans, and returned to present them to the commissioners overseeing the project. The commissioners also contacted James Dakin of New Orleans and Adolphus Heiman of Nashville about submitting plans, but apparently Shryock thought his chances good to win the Tennessee commission and canceled his move to St. Louis. When the commissioners discovered that the renowned William

Fig. 2.8: Jefferson County Courthouse, Louisville, Kentucky. *Courtesy of Historic American Buildings Survey, U.S. Library of Congress.*

Strickland was available, they quickly hired the premier architect, putting an end to Shryock's ambition. Two years later Shryock wrote to the commissioners requesting reimbursement for his trips to Nashville and his time for preparing the plans. The commissioners allowed him $148.52 (Dekle 1966:218–219; Mahoney 1945:104–106; Shryock 1846a, 1846b).

What Shryock worked on after this date is unknown. He remained in Louisville for the rest of his life and, according to city directories, continued to work as an architect. Perhaps he designed some commercial buildings whose attributions are no longer known, but many of the major commissions were going to other architects. Among such works were the Gault House Hotel (1865), the City Hospital (1870), the Louisville Exposition Building (1872), and the Louisville City Hall (1873). In addition several of Shryock's buildings were altered by other architects while Shryock was still in practice. These were the Louisville Medical Academy (rebuilt 1857), the Kentucky State Capitol (extension designed 1869), and the Jefferson County Courthouse (completion begun 1858) (Haggard 1971:16, IV.1–IV.2).

Sometime after 1845 Shryock may have drawn a plan for a Masonic Temple that was never built (Flynn 1971:71–72). Aside from that he probably turned his business toward the design and construction of Louisville residences, including a number of houses for James Gutherie in the 1850s (Haggard 1971:15). He may even have attempted houses in the Victorian style after Greek Revival lost favor (Andrews 1944:76). In 1851 Shryock was appointed city measurer by the Louisville Board of Aldermen to measure carpentry, but it is not until 1878 that he is listed as such in a city directory (Flynn 1971:9).

For all of Shryock's talents as an architect, it appears from the problems discussed above and records of numerous court proceedings in Louisville that he may not have been a very good businessman. Between 1836 and 1878 he was called to defend himself in court many times due to owing money to myriad craftsmen and merchants. On three occasions his property was auctioned to pay debts (Flynn 1971:9–10, 215–217; Haggard 1971:VI.1–VI.4). In 1878 close to the end of his life when years of accumulated business acumen should have allowed him some comfort, Shryock stated in a court case about his personal property:

> I have no money, or other property, chases in action legal or equitable in my possession, or in the possession of others belonging to me, or in which I have a beneficial interest—I am indeed a ruined man; everything gone; nothing to shew for the trouble, labors, and weary of 60 years . . . neither houses lands or money. . . . All I owned was sold except what was exempted by law. (Haggard 1971:VI.7–VI.8)

At the end of his life, Shryock was in financial ruin. As his lawyer explained:

> [J]udgments have recently been rendered against this defendant . . . ; to satisfy which judgments this defendant's household and kitchen furniture have been sold under executions, his homestead has been encumbered, mortgaged and sold and all of his other means for the time being consumed to the same end and purpose, and for all which this defendant has . . . been unsuccessful in obtaining reimbursement or compensation for his services, expenses, attorneys and cash of extravagant litigation and numerous suits against him. (Haggard 1971:17)

On June 19, 1880, at the age of 77, Gideon Shryock died at his home in Louisville. Aside from his architectural legacy, he had nothing to leave to his children, not even a will. He is buried in Cave Hill Cemetery in Louisville (Flynn 1971:13). Despite the problems Shryock faced as an architect and his beginner's luck with the Kentucky capitol, it is important to realize the impact his buildings made in Kentucky and throughout the middle West. His practical interpretation of Greek architecture met the needs of his clients while addressing the ideals of a young nation and, ultimately, created historical symbols that are still viable today. The use of Arkansas's Old State House as election night headquarters in 1992 and 1996 by President Bill Clinton leaves no doubt as to this fact.

Let us conclude with one biographer's summation, providing us with an appreciation of Shryock's life and architectural accomplishments:

> Shryock's greatest professional success came to him early in life, and we prefer to avoid considering what disappointments his later architectural career may have held for him. However bitter these may have been, it is to be hoped that the beauty of the Greek Revival form which he had brought over the mountains into Kentucky, and sent on into the Middle West, offered him some consolation. Latrobe, Strickland, Mills, Shryock, and Walter, and the countless architects influenced by this mighty group, were responsible for the introduction and maintenance of Greek Revival into what amounted to a national architecture for over six decades. It is as a pioneer and guide that Shryock showed true greatness. (Andrews 1944:77)

Other Reputed Arkansas Works by Shryock

Because the Old State House was a prominent building on the Little Rock landscape from the very beginning, it is understandable that residents attributed other early buildings to Shryock, either by a desire to associate with the notable architect of the Old State House or by confusing Shryock with builders who worked on both buildings. Several earlier accounts note that at least three residences in the Little Rock area—the Brownlee House, the McHenry House, and Trapnall Hall—were rumored to have been designed by Shryock, but as will be explained, this attribution is unlikely (Andrews 1944:75; Calloway 1981:26–27; Flynn 1971:72; Hudson 1944:313–315; Quapaw Quarter 1976:A-2).

The Brownlee House, built about 1846, is part of the architectural holdings of the Historic Arkansas Museum. It was built by Robert Brownlee and Sam McMorrin, Scottish stonemasons who worked on the Old State House, for Brownlee's brother and sister-in-law (Roy and Witsell 1984:68–69). The McHenry House was built in the mid-1830s and is located at what was then about ten miles from Little Rock on the old Hot Springs highway. The McHenry family, who moved to Arkansas from Tennessee, were acquainted with craftsmen working on the Old State House, and tradition has it that several of them worked on the house (Roy and Witsell 1984:34–35). The McHenry House also has been known as the Stage Coach House (Hudson 1944:315) and is currently called the Ten Mile House (Flynn 1971:72). Trapnall Hall was built about 1843 in the Greek Revival style, and its details are similar to examples found in builder's handbooks of the day (Calloway 1981:26).

Regarding the Brownlee and McHenry houses, there is no reason to believe that Shryock provided plans for either house, since he never came to Arkansas and neither of the owners was from Kentucky. George Weigart, Shryock's supervising architect, however, did reside in Arkansas for over a year and it would

Fig. 2.9: Brownlee House, Little Rock, Arkansas. *Courtesy of Historic Arkansas Museum.*

Fig. 2.10: McHenry House, Little Rock, Arkansas. *Courtesy of Historic American Buildings Survey, U.S. Library of Congress, John T. Murray, Photographer.*

not be unreasonable to suppose that he may have made some income on the side by drawing plans for residences when so requested. Was Weigart, then, responsible for the design of either the Brownlee or McHenry houses?

The Brownlee House can safely be ruled out as Weigart's design, since it wasn't begun until about twelve years after Weigart's death. The McHenry House, however, appears to have been built during the time when Weigart was working on the Old State House, although there is nothing about it that suggests the need for an architect. As F. Hampton Roy and Charles Witsell (1984:36) state, the residence "exemplifies the sort of vernacular house built on many large Southern farms before the Civil War," and there is no reason to assume that its design and construction couldn't have been handled by the competent builders of the day.

Regarding Trapnall Hall, Jan Calloway (1981:87) interviewed Wilson Styles, an architectural historian who studied both the works of Gideon Shryock and early Little Rock architecture. He felt that Trapnall Hall did not resemble residences Shryock was known to have designed. Further, Styles noted:

> There has been some speculation that Shryock designed some residences in the Little Rock area, though no conclusive evidence has been found. . . . It is known that Shryock had an affinity for 18th century architecture which is evident in the few documented residences he designed in Kentucky. Perhaps he felt the Greek forms were too severe for domestic building. At any rate we have no architectural documentation on Little Rock Greek Revival residences. (Calloway 1981:26)

Therefore, based on all the above, it is reasonable to conclude that the Old State House stands as the only known example in Arkansas of the architectural style of either Gideon Shryock or George Weigart.

Fig. 2.11: Trapnall Hall, Little Rock, Arkansas.
Courtesy of Arkansas Historic Preservation Program.

Research on Gideon Shryock

Although Gideon Shryock is not as well known as architects Benjamin Henry Latrobe or William Strickland through whom his training descends, Shyrock did make a significant contribution to American architecture. Because of this several research projects examining his life and work have been undertaken.

Shryock is best known in his native state of Kentucky where virtually all of his work was done. Trained in Philadelphia during the efflorescence of the Greek Revival movement in American architecture, Shryock brought the ideals of Greek Revival to what was considered at that time America's West. He is credited with designing the first Greek Revival building—the Kentucky state capitol—west of the Alleghenies (Andrews 1944:70) and has been called the "pioneer Greek Revivalist of the middlewest" (Newcomb 1928a, b).

Research into Shryock's life, resulting in published articles, was most active during the period of the late 1920s to early 1950s. His most noted biographer of that period was Rexford Newcomb, a professor of architectural history at the University of Illinois. His articles on Shryock and his buildings include "Gideon Shryock: Pioneer Greek Revivalist of the Middlewest" and "Gideon Shryock—Pioneer Greek Revivalist of the West" (both published in 1928); "Transylvania College and Her Century-Old Greek Revival Building" (1930); as well as treatments on Shryock in his two books on Kentucky architecture: *Old Kentucky Architecture* (1940), which mostly contains photos and plan drawings, and *Architecture in Old Kentucky* (1953), which provides more textual interpretation.

Newcomb connected with a niece of the architect, Elizabeth Shryock Field, and corresponded with her for many years. Among her family possessions, Field had several letters written by Shryock, a portrait of the architect, and inherited oral traditions. She was also interested in seeing that knowledge of Shryock in connection with his important Kentucky buildings was not lost, resulting in research and a paper that she read before the Woman's Club of Central Kentucky on October 30, 1920, which was later published in four sections in the *Lexington Herald* in 1921 (Field 1923, 1952:111; Haggard 1971:82). She also provided information to the Kentucky State Historical Society upon their move to Kentucky's old capitol (Anon 1920:5–6). Because of her willingness to share her knowledge and family papers with Newcomb and other researchers, Field was instrumental in keeping alive Shryock's memory. Much later, her papers were recombined and published in slightly different form as "Gideon Shryock: His Life and His Work" (Field 1952).

Other articles dealing with Shryock or his buildings that were published during the same period include "Two Early Mississippi Valley State Capitols" (Laist 1926); "The Capitols of Kentucky" (Hardin 1945); "The A.I.A. Meets in Kentucky" (Hamlin 1940); "Gideon Shryock and John McMurtry: Architect and Builder of Kentucky" (Lancaster 1943); "The City of Three Capitols" (Tintner 1946); and two articles by Alfred Andrews, "Gideon Shryock, Kentucky Architect, and Greek Revival Architecture in Kentucky" (1944) and "Gideon Shryock: Kentucky Architect" (1945). Probably the earliest article on Shryock was George Bush's "Gideon Shryock: An Appreciation" published in *The Transylvanian* (1911), which provides a brief biography. Shryock's buildings were noted in early works, such as Lewis Collins and Richard H. Collins's *History of Kentucky* (1877). Shryock is also mentioned, in greater or lesser degree, in various works of a more general nature, such as Talbot Hamlin's *Greek Revival Architecture in America* (1944).

Interest in Shryock waned until 1971 when two important research projects were completed, although neither was published. Elisabeth Flynn's Ph.D. dissertation, *Gideon Shryock, 1802–1880: Greek Revival Architect in Kentucky* (1971), is very thorough, but exhibits a number of weaknesses. Written in the field of art history, the thrust of the work is a largely subjective analysis of Shryock's skills as a Greek Revival architect. The section on Arkansas's Old State House contains several errors of fact and interpretation, casting doubt on the accuracy of the remainder of the work. The most glaring error pertaining to the Old State House was Flynn's mistaking the 1885 additions for Shryock's original design, although she was not the first to do this, as Andrews (1944, 1945) makes the same error.

The work's strengths include Flynn's analysis of Shryock's known buildings as well as those of questionable attribution, offering her reasoning for accepting or rejecting them as Shryock's. Her most valuable contribution, however, may be the appendices in which she transcribed a number of original documents pertaining to Shryock. These include letters from Shryock to his family, court and real estate records, genealogical material, Shryock's obituary, numerous documents pertaining to Shryock's buildings, and an unpublished article on Shryock's architect brother, Cincinnatus, by his daughter Elizabeth Shryock Field.

The second work is John C. Haggard's master's thesis, *The Architecture of Gideon Shryock* (1971), which is a straightforward historical study of the architect and his work. Haggard's research uncovered several items that Flynn either missed or chose to ignore, and his interpretation of Shryock's life and problems is insightful. He also included appendices of letters, city directories, and legal proceedings. Unfortunately, in regard to the Old State House he relied almost exclusively on John L. Ferguson's (1968) brief work on the building, so offers nothing new to its interpretation.

CHAPTER 3

Seeking Shryock's Vision

IT IS TANTALIZING to try to surmise what Shryock's original design for the Arkansas State House might have been. We know only, from Governor John Pope's statement (*Arkansas Gazette,* November 20, 1833), that it was "a splendid plan . . . but on too large and expensive a scale," and that Pope and George Weigart abridged the plans to fit the funds available. Pope briefly described the abridged plans stating that the Legislative house would be two stories high and have two fronts, one facing the town and the other the river, with four columns on each front. The courthouse would be forty feet to the east of the center building, and the office wing forty feet to the west, with the two wings connected to the center building by dwarf colonnades. Finding Shryock's original plans or Weigart's changes would add much to our understanding of the architecture of the Old State House, but both sets of plans seem to be lost to posterity. The loss of building plans is not unusual for very old structures; in fact, none of Shryock's original plans exist for any of his documented buildings (Flynn 1971:20). Unfortunately, neither do we know the nature of the requirements Pope outlined to Shryock, for a copy of Pope's letter to Shryock has not been found either.

In the early stages of conducting research for this publication, it was thought that Pope might have taken the plans with him when he left Arkansas or that a copy might exist among Shryock's papers. Letters sent to various libraries and archives in Kentucky, as well as the National Archives, inquiring as to the existence of Arkansas State House plans among the papers of Shryock or Pope proved unsuccessful.

Studying Elijah More's account of his visit to Pope and Shryock in Kentucky indicates that the plans were already missing by 1837, just three years after Weigart's death (More 1837:203). Pope readily turned over to More all the papers pertaining to the building of the State House, so it can be assumed that if Pope had the plans he would have given them to More. In addition, if More had received the plans from Pope, there would have been less reason for him to visit Shryock to obtain information relating to the original plan. In fact, More states in his 1837 report on the construction that the plans were already lost, which was creating problems in completing the work:

> The architects, who for Gov. Pope, changed the original design, as furnished by Mr. Shryock, subsequently, and leaving no writing or sketch by which to indicate the alterations. The principal building being erected on the altered plan, and it being lost, much difficulty is encountered in making contracts to complete them after the manner indicated by the legislature. (More 1837:203)

Contractor Thomas Thorn, who took over supervision of the construction of the State House after Weigart's death, apparently didn't have the plans either as he also turned over to More "all his vouchers and papers of every description relating" to the State House (More 1838:333). Considering all of the above evidence, it is most likely that the plans were in the possession of George Weigart and were lost among his things after his death.

As an architect, Shryock was certainly aware that original plans were often changed by the clients and building committees for whom they were drawn. Both his Jefferson County Courthouse and Morrison College underwent major changes from their original designs, and undoubtedly a number of his other buildings suffered at least minor changes, even if there are no records that indicate it. Costs of construction would have been just as much a concern in Shryock's day as today, so it is not surprising that in outlining costs for the building of Morrison College, Shryock offered suggestions on how to reduce construction costs, one being to construct only the center building and eliminate the wings (Flynn 1971:105). Since Shryock knew the plans he sent to Arkansas were likely to be changed, it is not unreasonable to suppose that Shryock may have discussed with Weigart how his design could be effectively reduced. If that was the case, the end result may still largely represent Shryock's vision as an architect.

In trying to reconstruct Shryock's original plans for the Old State House, we can examine his other buildings for personal style in his work, as well as look at the work of other architects designing Greek Revival buildings in the same period (e.g., Hamlin 1944). Doing so provides us with three possible options for Shryock's arrangement of the main building and wings:

1. the wings were intended to be part of the main building, set as side projections;
2. the wings were intended to be connected to the main building with hyphens, much the way the building looks today; or
3. the wings and main building were intended to be three separate buildings.

The first option—that the wings were intended to be side projections to the main building—is a fairly common treatment in Greek Revival buildings. Shryock used it himself in designing the Jefferson County Courthouse and Morrison College. It is also seen in other public buildings, some examples being the Vermont Statehouse by A. Young (Sutton 1992:fig. 2.17); the Missouri Statehouse by S. Hills (Sutton 1992:fig. 2.19); the North Carolina State Capitol by Town, Davis, and Paton (Hamlin 1944:plate LI); and the Old Iowa Capitol by J. Rague (Hamlin 1944:plate LXXII).

The problem with this option is that it seems unlikely that constructing three buildings instead of one would have saved any money, although they may have been easier to build for local craftsmen. At best, if the main building was constructed first and the wings built as money became available, there could have been a stepped delay in expenses. This doesn't appear to have been done, however, since in July 1833, just four months after the start of work, the foundations for both the main building and the courthouse wing had been laid (*Arkansas Gazette,* July 10, 1833). Thus, we can eliminate the first option as reflecting Shryock's original design.

The second option—that wings with hyphens much like the current building were originally designed—also seems unlikely. Although eliminating the hyphens would certainly have reduced costs, eliminating the office space the hyphens encompassed would have immediately created space problems in the remaining buildings, but there is no indication that such problems existed initially.

Considering Shryock's other work, nothing else he designed in any way resembled the Old State House with wings and hyphens. All his other extant buildings are singular, rectangular structures with, at most, attached wings perpendicular to the front of the building. Such a design is not commonly seen in Greek Revival architecture by any of Shryock's contemporaries either. The Burnet House in Cincinnati by I. Rogers (Hamlin 1944:plate XXVII) and the New York City Hall by J. Mangin and J. McComb (Hamlin 1944:plate XXVIII) exhibit a wing-and-hyphen design, but both appear to be much larger buildings than the Old State House.

The Old Courthouse in St. Louis, designed by H. Singleton, who won the commission in 1839, bears a striking resemblance to the Arkansas State House, especially if one ignores the dome added in the early 1860s. The main building has a six-column Doric portico, and the wings are three-bayed structures with Doric entablatures that mimic the main building. It turns out, however, that Singleton's original design was cruciform in shape (the main building with the projecting hyphens); the wings were added in the 1850s (City of St. Louis 1996:3; Hamlin 1944:253, plate LXXI).

Fig. 3.1: Historic St. Louis Courthouse, designed by architect H. Singleton. *Courtesy of National Park Service, Jefferson National Expansion Memorial.*

Considering the rarity of the wing-and-hyphen design and the lack of any indicated need for such a large building in the Arkansas Territory, it is unlikely that the building we know today, with attached wings and two-story hyphens, resembles Shryock's original design.

By eliminating the first two proposed options, we are left with the possibility that Shryock actually did provide a plan that featured not one building, but three separate buildings joined as a complex by colonnades and a related architectural design. This possibility, however, is troubling when considering both Shryock's work and that of other contemporary architects, for designs of Greek Revival complexes are virtually nonexistent. Among Shryock's completed buildings, there is nothing else like it. One of the rare exceptions is the private residence called Berry Hill in Virginia, built between 1835 and 1840. The main building has an eight-column Doric portico and the two smaller buildings have four columns each, but the layout is not as unified as that of Arkansas's State House (Hamlin 1944:191, plate L).

A clue to solving this problem can be found in the architectural style that precedes Greek Revival. In fact, at the turn of the nineteenth century, several state capitols were designed as capitol complexes with separate buildings. The Georgia capitol at Milledgeville was of this type, with the main building holding the Senate and House chambers and the flanking buildings serving the executive and treasury departments. Another example is Stephen Hills's Pennsylvania capitol at Harrisburg, designed in 1810. The main building was flanked by two fireproof buildings that served as state offices and were connected to the main building by colonnades (Cummings 1953:417–420; Hitchcock and Seale 1976:58–61).

Even more pertinent to the issue is that Kentucky's second permanent capitol (built 1814–1816), the one that was destroyed by fire and replaced by Shryock's capitol, was also a *capitol complex*. The main building was two stories high and contained courts and committee rooms on the first floor and the houses of the state legislature on the second floor. The brick state offices were detached and faced the main building; the west building held the offices of the auditor and treasurer, while the east building held the land office and secretary of state's office. When the main building

Fig. 3.2: Stephen Hills's Pennsylvania State Capitol. *Courtesy of Historic American Buildings Survey, U.S. Library of Congress.*

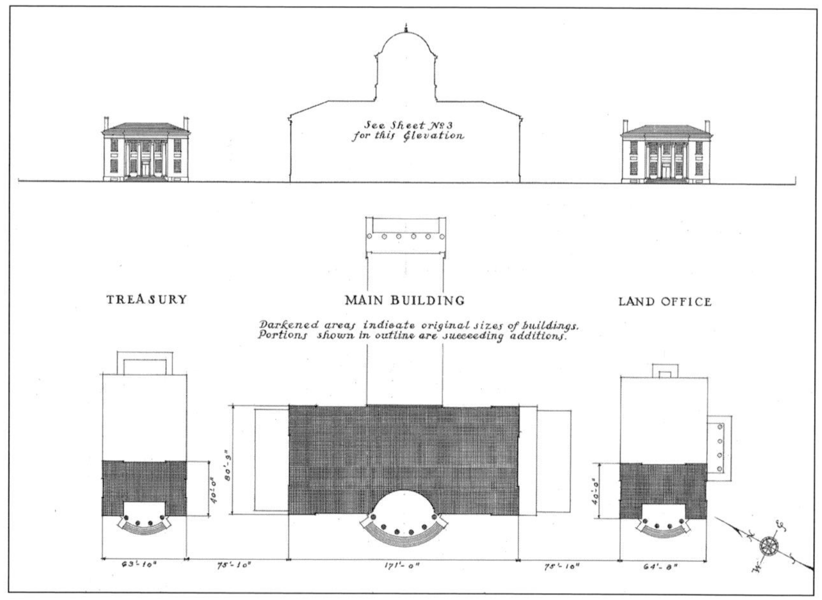

Fig. 3.3: Plan drawing of Hills's Pennsylvania Capitol shows the flanking office buildings that comprise the capitol complex. *Courtesy of Historic American Buildings Survey, U.S. Library of Congress.*

burned in 1824, the brick offices survived (Collins and Collins 1877:246–248).

The solution to discovering Shryock's original design must be sought in the specifications Governor Pope would have outlined to Shryock. As an architect, Shryock was designing buildings not for himself, but for the needs of his clients. A bank building, for example, would have required a specified number of offices, one or more vaults, and a public area for the transaction of banking business. Likewise, a state house would have required both Senate and House chambers, courtrooms, meeting rooms, libraries, and any number of other offices, *as specified by the client*—in Arkansas's case, by Governor Pope.

One can gain an understanding of Pope's specifications despite the loss of his letter to Shryock by considering the manner in which the money to fund the project was acquired and handled. The ten sections of land granted by Congress were intended for a State House, while an additional 1,000 acres granted by them were to be used for a courthouse and jail. Pope expected that the ten sections would fund the construction not only of the main building (the State House proper), but of an office wing as well. As he explained, "From twenty to twenty-five thousand dollars, I think a fair estimate of the whole expense of the centre building; leaving from six to eight thousand dollars of the Ten Section fund applicable to the erection of the west, or Office wing." And in regard to the courthouse, "The funds applicable to the Court-house and Jail, will be very ample for those objects" (*Arkansas Gazette*, November 20, 1833). The jail was not intended to be physically part of the courthouse, but instead a separate building. Pope had already turned over a large portion of the funds to Thomas Thorn to build a jail, but when Fulton was appointed territorial governor instead of Pope, the project languished. In 1838 More was trying to get the project back on track and indicated that a site for the jail had not yet been selected (More 1838:334). Although we have no way of knowing what Pope intended for the jail, it appears unlikely that he envisioned it as part of the capitol complex.

It is important to remember that Pope had served as a state senator in Kentucky from 1825 to 1829 before accepting the Arkansas appointment. He certainly would have been familiar with Kentucky's capitol complex of a state house and office wings. He may have perceived it as a nicely workable design. Thus it is probable that the Greek Revival complex that became Arkansas's State House was not Shryock's idea; instead it was most likely Governor Pope who specified a three-building design.

Where then were reductions made? Since the central building—the State House itself—was of greater importance than either the office or courthouse wings, it is most likely this was the building splendidly designed and therefore the one most in need of restraint. Bringing the cost of the building within funds available could have been achieved not only by reducing the overall size, but also by eliminating perceived decorative elements and substituting less costly materials. We can again consider Shryock's other buildings for clues to the reductions.

Let us consider size first. It is very likely that the main building was intended to be larger than what was eventually built, so that the portico would have been supported by six or as many as eight columns, instead of the four it has. Shryock did design some of his buildings with four-column porticos, specifically the Franklin County Courthouse and the original plan for Morrison College, but his more important buildings—the Kentucky capitol and the Jefferson County Courthouse, which was intended to become the new Kentucky capitol—were planned with six-column porticos. When a larger building was desired for Morrison College, Shryock enlarged the portico to six columns, while a required reduction in the Jefferson County Courthouse reduced its portico to four columns. None of his known buildings was designed with an eight-column portico. Erring on the side of caution, we can surmise that the Arkansas State House was probably designed by Shryock with at least a six-column portico.

Looking more closely at the Greek design elements, we can also discover some clues as to the building's original size. The Old State House is designed in the Greek Doric order, which is patterned after the Parthenon (Sutton 1992:fig. 2.1) and which has some very specific associated design elements. A traditional Doric column is fluted and has a very plain, rectangular capital. Above the columns, the frieze of the Doric entablature traditionally consists of alternating triglyphs (the projecting group of three rectangular blocks) and metopes (the recessed blank areas). Columns are supposed to be positioned beneath *every other* triglyph. The Old State House, however, has *two* triglyphs between each column.

Shryock, as was true with other Greek Revival architects, was not simply copying

ancient buildings, but was using them as inspiration for his designs. He could freely interpret Greek forms and use them as it was necessary (Hamlin 1940:286; Lancaster 1943:265), so the spacing of the columns on the State House could have been his design. His two other Doric Order buildings—Morrison College and the Jefferson County Courthouse—however, do have the columns properly placed under alternating triglyphs.

Therefore, it is more likely that the placement of columns relative to triglyphs on the Arkansas State House was a result of Weigart's reduction. If the width of a six-column building had been reduced by an amount equivalent to two columns, it might have made the building too small. A reduction only equivalent to one column might have been sufficient in size, but would have left an unbalanced five columns to work with. By reducing the number of columns to four and spreading them out, the visual balance of the building was retained. This also would have been the case if the original building was designed with eight columns, so that the reduction would have been less than half but still balanced visually. In either case the reduction in size, even by only a small amount, would have translated into monetary savings.

Another way in which to save money was by the substitution of less costly materials for more costly ones. The Kentucky State House was faced with "Kentucky marble," a type of native limestone, and was roofed with copper

Fig. 3.4: Close-up view of the Doric columns and entablature on the Old State House. *Courtesy of Historic American Buildings Survey, U.S. Library of Congress.*

(Flynn 1971:29, 92–93). The Arkansas State House was faced with a stucco finish intended to look like stone and was roofed with tin (*Arkansas Gazette*, November 20, 1833; Kennan 1950:34–35; More 1838:332; Smyer 1976:6). This suggests that Shryock's original plans may have called for a stone facing and copper roof for the Arkansas State House as well, materials that would have been more expensive than those used.

Finally, one other way to reduce expenses in building the State House was by eliminating what may have been perceived as purely decorative or superfluous elements. Interior decorative detail was an important aspect of Greek Revival style, and Shryock made much use of it in the Kentucky capitol:

> The interior decoration is white stucco and there are patterns on the baseboards and friezes while the walls are flat. The decorations found on the second floor are more elaborate than those on the first. The principle of unity is maintained throughout the program by variation of the motifs. One of the finest of the decorations is that of the pendentives with the pattern of the relief of cornucopia and acanthus leaves filling the triangular area with its own three-point formation. (Flynn 1971:29)

Fig. 3.5: Acanthus leaf decoration inside Shryock's Kentucky State House. *Courtesy of Historic American Buildings Survey, U.S. Library of Congress.*

One would expect that Shryock provided detailed drawings of the decorative elements he envisioned for the Arkansas State House, but eliminating these would have saved money. As Pope explained in regard to the cost for construction of the State House and office wing:

> Much must, however, depend upon the manner in which the interior of the building is finished.
>
> The carpenter's work of the lower rooms of the State-house, and the interior of the Office wing, will be done in the plainest and most economical manner, and, indeed, the interior of the whole buildings, except the Court and Legislative rooms, which ought to be finished with a reasonable regard to taste and elegance. (*Arkansas Gazette*, November 20, 1833)

Thus, it appears that savings were made by eliminating decorative elements of the building's interior. This then brings us to the exterior of the building and the matter of whether or not a dome was intended for the roof of the State House.

It was common for architects designing in the Greek Revival style to incorporate a dome (which was actually a Roman element) into their buildings, especially into many kinds of public buildings (Hamlin 1944:345). Shryock used "lanterns" (roof structures with glazed or open sides to light interior spaces in buildings) as part of both domes or towers in almost all of the public buildings he designed. In fact, only Morrison College does not have either. The Kentucky capitol and the Bank of Louisville have domes; the Jefferson County Courthouse and the Franklin County Courthouse have clock towers; and the Louisville Medical Academy has an elongated domed lantern. It is interesting to note that in reducing the size of the Jefferson County Courthouse, the tower was eliminated. Architect Ithiel Town, working during the same period as Shryock, argued that cupolas, lanterns, and wings were expensive and costs could be cut by omitting them (Hitchcock and Seale 1976:84).

An intriguing decision about the roof of the Old State House was made in 1839 as the work neared completion. The builders left a space in the roof for what they thought would be a dome, but Commissioner of Public Buildings W. W. Stevenson, who was overseeing the work at the time, was not sure about it. As he explained in his report:

> I found a space left in the main building for a dome finish. Upon a close examination of the building, and the space for such a finish I found that the proportion would be so imperfect that I could not believe that such a finish was intended at first. The space between the partition walls which would form the base of the dome, is only fifteen feet. Before taking any decisive steps I addressed a note to Mr. Pendleton, asking such questions as would illicit such information as was needed. He fully concurred with me, and accordingly I closed the roof. (Stevenson 1840:554)

Henry Pendleton was serving at that time as carpenter for the construction of the building. In a letter to him, Stevenson asked whether he thought the original plan had intended a dome, whether the dome could be extended beyond the partition walls, and if not, what height of dome could be attained. Pendleton answered that the dome could not be extended without damaging the roof and that within the partitions it could only be 18 feet high. He also stated that he was "very certain that in the original plan a dome was not intended" (Stevenson 1840:555–556).

It is unlikely that Pendleton ever saw Weigart's plan, much less Shryock's original, as the first we have found of him is no earlier than 1837 when he was repairing the problem with the roof (*Arkansas Gazette,* January 2, 1838), and at which time, as we have noted above, the plans were already missing. When Elijah More was attempting to settle the accounts in 1837, he noted that David Eller and Stephen Cotter "did all the carpenter's work which has been done on the public buildings" (More 1837:202). In the phrasing of Stevenson's question, he asks for Pendleton's "opinion," and based on his experience as a carpenter, that is probably what Pendleton gave (Stevenson 1840:555).

Therefore, Stevenson's decision was probably a misinterpretation of Weigart's changes. Shryock most likely intended the State House to have a dome similar to the one on the Kentucky capitol. Weigart may have eliminated a prominent dome not only to save money, but also because in reducing the size of the building, there no longer may have been adequate space for one. Weigart still may have intended to use a small lantern or skylight on the roof over the stairs, however, and this was probably why a hole had been left in the roof.

To summarize, Weigart probably used reduction in size, substitution of materials, and elimination of elements to bring the costs of the Arkansas State House within the means available. Based on Shryock's other buildings and the Greek Revival style by other architects, we can deduce what Shryock's original vision for the State House *may* have been:

1. The State House complex was to consist of three buildings; the center building was the largest and served as the State House proper, while the two smaller buildings that flanked it served as an office wing and a courthouse. The three buildings were to be connected by dwarf colonnades.
2. The center building was intended to be larger that it is today, with a six-column Doric portico facing both the river and the town.
3. The building was meant to be faced with stone and roofed with copper. A dome with lantern was to be visible on the roof.
4. The interior spaces were to be richly ornamented with Greek decorative details.

Shortly after coming to these conclusions, an unidentified painting that may represent one of Shryock's designs was brought to our attention. The painting, held in a private collection, was first illustrated in a 1972 issue of *The Magazine Antiques* (Garrett 1972:598, 602). It appears to be a project presentation and depicts a complex of Greek Revival buildings connected by colonnades. The large central building exhibits a six-column portico and a small dome on the roof. The smaller side buildings have four-column porticos. The 1972 article suggested that the painting was an early design for Shryock's Kentucky capitol. The accompanying text is a reprint of Shryock's description of that building, which was published in the periodical *Atkinson's Casket* in 1833. Shryock mentions "flanks" in his 1833 description, which are interpreted in the 1972 article as the side buildings, noting that they were never built.

Fig. 3.6: This painting, originally from Kentucky, appears to be a presentation piece for an architectural design, most likely one by Gideon Shryock. It may represent Shryock's original design for Arkansas's Old State House. *Private collection.*

The painting appears again in a 1974 article in *The Magazine Antiques* (Ellesin 1974:602). William Seale, who provided the information, suggested that, instead of the Kentucky capitol, the design represented Shryock's 1844 plans for the Tennessee capitol. As noted in a previous chapter, Shryock's design was not built when the commissioners changed course and hired William Strickland. Seale argued that the design appeared to be of a later date than the Kentucky capitol and that its placement on a steep rise was more in keeping with the Tennessee site.

Additional information on the painting was received from the present owner and the gallery that sold it to him. The owner described the painting as an oil on canvas, 10 x 12 inches, with no initials or dates. The building depicted has an Ionic portico (Banks 1997). The gallery that sold the painting—at that time titled *The First Capitol Building at Frankfort, Kentucky*—to the current owner, provided the following provenance:

> This painting belonged to Henry Clay. It was given by him to the Hon. John Janney of Leesburg, Virginia, who was Clay's campaign chairman in Virginia when Clay ran for the presidency. The painting descended to a niece of Janney from whom it was acquired. (Feld 1997)

The fact that the painting once belonged to Kentucky's Henry Clay strongly suggests that it originated in Kentucky and therefore is very likely to represent a work of Shryock's. Henry Clay ran three times for the presidency; he was defeated by John Quincy Adams in 1824, Andrew Jackson in 1832, and James K. Polk in 1844. Clay died in 1852. The time during which Clay was politically active and could have given the painting to John Janney certainly fits within the time that Shryock would have designed the Kentucky capitol (1827), the Arkansas State House (1833), or the Tennessee capitol (1844).

The main building in the painting does resemble the finished Kentucky capitol with its six-column Ionic portico, and the similarity would have been evident to contemporary Kentuckians. It also exhibits major differences of additional windows and roof treatment, not to mention the wings and colonnades. The painting is unlikely to have been Shryock's original design for that structure, however, which replaced an earlier capitol destroyed by fire in 1824. Because the separate brick office wings survived the fire and continued to be used, there would have been no reason to present a design that replaced them. In fact, the building commissioners were very specific in requesting a structure to fit the available space; it was not to exceed 120 x 70 feet. Shryock's capitol, by his own description, measured 132 feet in length, including the portico, by 70 feet in width, obviously meeting the specifications (Flynn 1971:92, 94). In addition, Shryock's description of the building that appeared in *Atkinson's Casket* in 1833 was written after the building was complete. The "flanks" he describes are not unbuilt elements, but rather the *sides* of the completed building (Flynn 1971:94). There is, therefore, no reason to presume the painting represents the Kentucky capitol.

It is more difficult to determine whether the painting represents Shryock's original design for the Arkansas State House or his later design for the Tennessee capitol. As noted above, William Seale suggests that the painting may represent this later project for a couple reasons. Seale notes that the Tennessee capitol was built on a steep eminence and that the painting illustrates a raised site. Tennessee's site, however, is considerably steeper than that indicated in the painting. Arkansas's site, also on a rise, is more in keeping with that illustrated, especially prior to grading of the land. Seale also points out: "The confident detailing of its colonnades and openings indicates a later date, well into the 1840s" (Ellesin 1974:602). Yet, Shryock's design for Morrison College, which he was building at the time he drew the Arkansas plans, exhibits window treatments and a raised foundation similar to that which is seen in the painting.

More important than these arguments, however, is that no other three-building Greek Revival complex designed by Shryock was ever built, nor is the design seen among the work of other Greek Revival architects. As argued above, we suggest the reason for this was that the design was requested by Governor Pope, based on his concept of an earlier Kentucky capitol. That being the case, Arkansas's Greek Revival complex was essentially an *outdated* design. By 1844 in order to remain competitive, it seems unlikely that Shryock would have presented a design to the Tennessee commissioners that was some 30 years out of date.

Conversely, there are two elements of the painting that raise doubt about an Arkansas attribution. The first is the Ionic order of the design, as it is not clear what purpose would have been served for Weigart to change from Ionic to Doric. The second is that the painting appears to represent a project presentation. Since Shryock was asked by Governor Pope to provide plans for a new building, not to compete with others to win a design competition, a project presentation probably wasn't needed. Shryock may have provided only elevation and plan drawings in ink. For Tennessee, however, Shryock would have needed to sell his design to the building committee who was considering Shryock's design as one of several. Creating a project presentation for Tennessee would be expected, and Shryock visited Nashville and would have known what the site looked like.

Nothing has been found to indicate specifically what kind of design Shryock presented to the Tennessee capitol commissioners. Certainly architects reused designs; architect Ithiel Town, a contemporary of Shryock, marketed his capitols all over the United States (Hitchcock and Seale 1976:86–89). There is no reason to think that Shryock may not have done the same during this period of major capitol construction. Even if his Tennessee design was outdated, his successes with the Kentucky and Arkansas capitols may well have encouraged him to present a similar design to Tennessee.

Whether the painting represents Arkansas or Tennessee, the importance of the painting to our understanding of Shryock's design of the Arkansas State House must not be underestimated. It is important to realize that no other completed building designed by Shryock or any other Greek Revival architect comes closer to that seen in the painting than does the Arkansas State House. Therefore, we must consider the painting in that light and what it can tell us about Shryock's original design relative to Weigart's and Pope's reduction.

As fitting our suggestions of Shryock's Arkansas design based on his other works, the main building does have a six-column portico and a small dome on the roof. The painting is not precise enough to see fine details nor, obviously, the interior of the building. Elements of the architecture we did not suggest based on Shryock's work but which seem fitting to the design include four-column porticos on the wings, front-facing windows, raised foundations, and more substantial colonnades. The loss of those elements in an abridged plan would be expected to provide a monetary savings to bring the design within the budget available to Pope. It also is interesting to note that the three buildings as constructed were originally connected by "dwarf colonnades" (*Arkansas Gazette*, November 20, 1833) that in 1861 were roofed and paved with bricks (Ferguson 1968:15), thus coming to more closely resemble the treatment in the painting.

Although Arkansas's Old State House may not have been built in as grand a manner as its architect intended, it is nonetheless an elegant and refined example of Greek Revival architecture. Shryock must be given credit for creating a classic and enduring structure. It has survived 175 years of the state's progress, yet still stands as an important symbol for Arkansans today.

SECTION 2

History of the Old State House

CHAPTER 4

The Construction Years: 1833–1842

THE YEARS DURING WHICH the State House was under construction were turbulent ones in Arkansas as two major political factions squared off against each other and waged their battles through the newspapers. On one side was territorial secretary Robert Crittenden and his supporters, who would eventually become linked with the Whig Party. On the other side were the Conway brothers (Henry, James, and Elias), along with Benjamin Johnson and Ambrose Sevier, who made up what became the politically powerful Arkansas Dynasty or Family. The political factions had their media supporters, and *Arkansas Gazette* founder and editor William Woodruff aligned with the Dynasty. Into this maelstrom came John Pope (Whayne et al. 2002:102–103).

By the time Pope arrived in Arkansas at the age of 56, he had many years of political experience in Kentucky, serving in the Kentucky General Assembly and the United States Senate. He was serving a term as Kentucky state senator when he was appointed Arkansas territorial governor by President Andrew Jackson to succeed the recently deceased George Izard. At about the same time, President Jackson replaced Robert Crittenden with William Fulton as secretary of the territory. Pope received the Arkansas appointment for his support of Jackson's 1828 presidential campaign, although

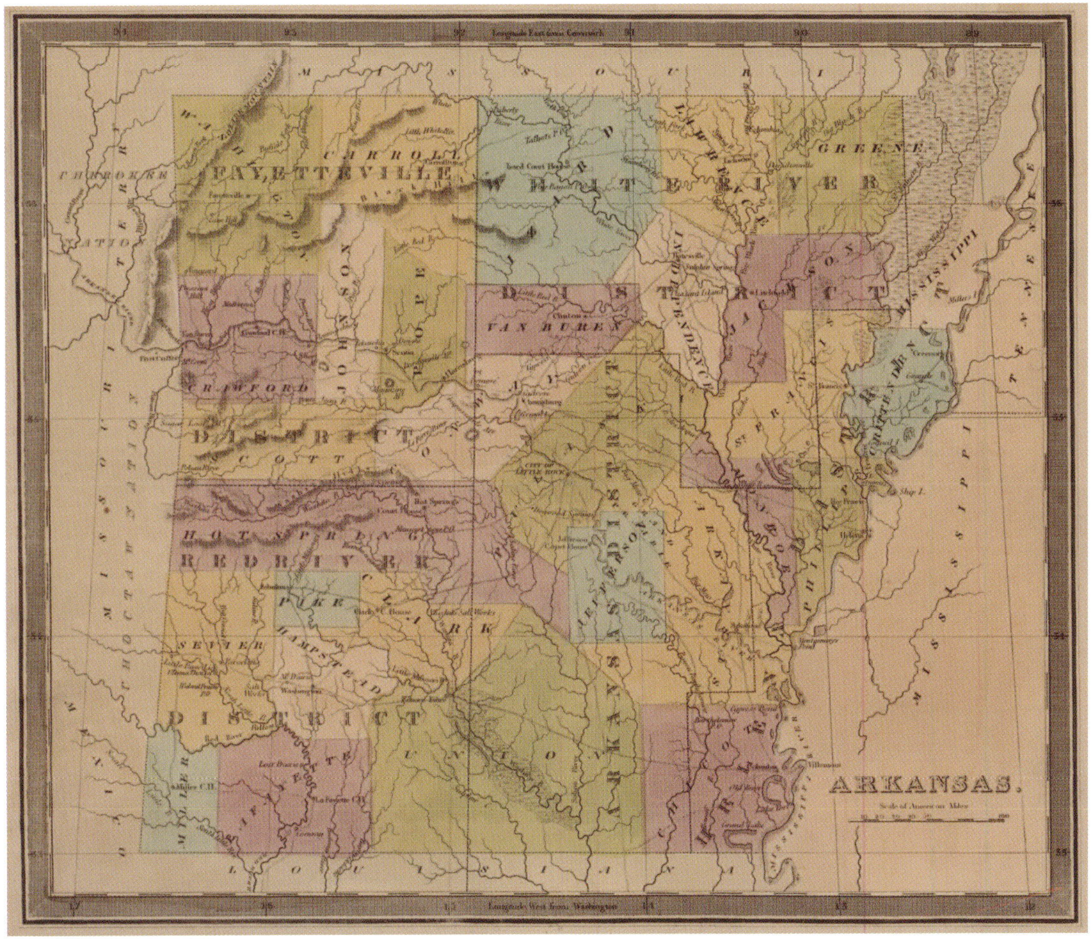

Fig. 4.1: In 1836 Arkansas had a few large counties and a sprinkling of towns. *Old State House Museum Collection.*

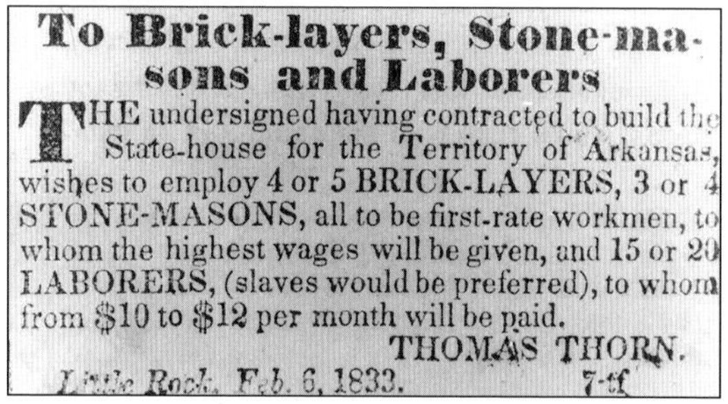

To Brick-layers, Stone-masons and Laborers

THE undersigned having contracted to build the State-house for the Territory of Arkansas, wishes to employ 4 or 5 BRICK-LAYERS, 3 or 4 STONE-MASONS, all to be first-rate workmen, to whom the highest wages will be given, and 15 or 20 LABORERS, (slaves would be preferred), to whom from $10 to $12 per month will be paid.

THOMAS THORN.

Little Rock, Feb. 6, 1833. 7-tf

Fig. 4.2: Stone- and brick-contractor Thomas Thorn advertised for workmen in the *Arkansas Gazette. Courtesy of* Arkansas Gazette.

Fig. 4.3: Supervising architect George Weigart and Governor John Pope discuss progress on the construction of the State House. *Drawing by John Deering, cartoonist for the* Arkansas Democrat-Gazette, *1994, Old State House Museum Collection.*

he had hoped to be given the position of United States attorney general. Despite his disappointment, Pope brought a vision of positive improvements to the state, gaining the support of Sevier and the *Gazette* (Rose 1917:290–291; Whayne et al. 2002:102–103; Williams and Whayne 2000:226–227).

In the meantime, Crittenden continued to influence Arkansas politics from behind the scenes, with his supporters gaining control in the Arkansas Legislature in 1831. When Congress granted the ten sections of land for the construction of a capitol building, it was up to the Legislature to sell the land to the best advantage. Several offers were made, including ones from Chester Ashley and Robert Crittenden to trade their homes for the ten sections of land. Crittenden especially desired the trade to free himself from large debts, so was delighted when the Legislature accepted his offer. Crittenden's house was greatly over-appraised, however, and Pope vetoed the sale, cementing their animosity. With battle lines drawn, the Crittenden faction fought bitterly to discredit and embarrass the governor. Thus began the extended battle over the construction of the State House and the use of the funds (Ross 1969:98; Whayne et al. 2002:103; Williams and Whayne 2000:226–227).

Amid a continuing debate in the Little Rock papers over Governor Pope's handling of the sale of lands, the work commenced by March 1833. George Weigart, who had brought the architectural plans from Gideon Shryock and revised them with Governor Pope, remained to take over as architect and superintendent for the construction. Thomas Thorn and William Cook, in partnership as Thorn & Cook, were hired as contractors for the brick and stone work. Little Rock attorney and land speculator Chester Ashley was appointed by Pope to manage the ten-section grant and the building construction, which led to growing opposition by Secretary Fulton (Ross 1969:110).

Only three months later, the *Arkansas Advocate* charged that work on the building had been stopped due to lack of funds and that materials were being misappropriated by Chester Ashley, the agent handling the sale of the land, which ignited another battle. The *Arkansas Gazette* jumped into the fray, defending the construction progress. On July 10, 1833, the *Gazette* reported that since March from 30 to 60 hands had been employed on the work, which entailed "quarrying rock for the foundation, cutting and hauling wood to burn the brick, digging out and laying the foundation, digging clay, making mortar, moulding, setting and burning brick, quarrying and burning limestone, hauling lime, sand, &c, &c, &c." The paper admitted that some construction delays had been encountered due to spring floods, which had inundated the sandbars where the masons procured sand for their mortar and delayed delivery of lumber, but nonetheless, by that time, the foundation of the main building and one of the wings was already completed.

Going directly to the source, *Gazette* owner and editor William Woodruff addressed letters to the principals involved in the construction and printed their replies in the paper. Supervising architect George Weigart personally responded to the charges:

> I received yours of the 6th July, which I will endeavor to answer as briefly as possible; but I assure you it gives me no pleasure to find it necessary to do so, as I have always been averse to political controversy. The progress of the building alluded to has not stopped for want of funds, as all demands have been paid, so far as have come under my knowledge; and I do not believe a single brick made on the State-house square, has been removed by Col. Ashley, for his own private use, or any other purpose. I can farthermore state, that there are no brick to be paid for by the Public, except such as may be counted in the wall &c, about the construction of said building. As to the progress of said building, it has not gone on with that mushroom growth, that some individuals might expect it should have done; but that the work is going on, any may see by viewing the premises. The foundation for the main building is laid, except that on which the columns for the porticoes are to stand; also, the foundation for the court-house. The brick work would have been in progress ere now, but for the late high waters, and other causes beyond the control of man; but, as materials can now be obtained, I will endeavor to have the work progress as speedily as circumstances will permit. This brief reply, I hope, will be amply sufficient to satisfy the minds of an unbiased public. (*Arkansas Gazette,* July 10, 1833)

Brick contractors Thorn & Cook also replied in the same issue, reporting:

> work on the State-house has been, and is still progressing as rapidly as the force under our control would justify. We have entirely completed the foundation of the main building and one of the wings, and have made more than six hundred thousand brick, more than three hundred thousand of which are burnt and ready for use. There has been some delay in erecting the building, in consequence of the extreme high waters preventing the arrival of the necessary lumber for the frames to be worked in the walls; and we have employed the whole force in making brick, and shall continue to do so until the frames can be supplied. We are now, and have been for some time past, making from twelve to sixteen thousand brick per day. (*Arkansas Gazette,* July 10, 1833)

Accusations and arguments continued to wage in the local papers throughout the year as work continued on the building. In late November the *Arkansas Gazette* printed a long report from Governor Pope himself detailing and accounting for the sale of the land, the design of the building, and the current state of progress. The report included an itemized list of expenses from Chester Ashley. Pope reported:

> The stone work and brick work of the first story of the State-house are done, and well done, firm, and lasting. One million of brick or more are made. The carpenters are preparing and will put up a tier of timbers on the wall in a few days, and, in a few weeks, the brick work of the building will be finished, with the exception of the pavements and columns. (*Arkansas Gazette,* November 20, 1833)

While Pope's report may have satisfied some readers, it couldn't stop new problems from arising, the worst of which, one can imagine, was the illness and subsequent death of supervising architect George Weigart on July 25, 1834, just a little over a year into the project. Weigart left a widow, America Weigart, and two young sons, Horace Anthony and Oliver Perry (*Arkansas Advocate,* August 29, 1834; *Arkansas Gazette,* July 29, 1834; Hinkle 1974). His widow sold Weigart's estate at public auction; the items included a clock, a watch, a dining table, a bedstead, a feather bed, brass andirons, a set of china, glass ware, chairs, a cow, a set of architectural books, a chest of carpenter's tools, and a set of drawing instruments (*Arkansas Advocate,* August 29, 1834). After Weigart's death, brick contractor Thomas Thorn, who by

Fig. 4.4: Territorial governor William Fulton. *Courtesy of Arkansas History Commission.*

Fig. 4.5: James Conway, first governor of the state of Arkansas. *Old State House Museum Collection.*

then had dissolved his partnership with William Cook, took over superintendence of the building (*Arkansas Gazette,* September 17, 1967; Smyer 1976:2).

In the meantime Pope's political alliances began to weaken, even losing support of *Gazette* editor William Woodruff. Finally in March 1835 Pope's political convictions ran up against the policies of Andrew Jackson's administration, and he was not appointed to a third term. Pope received the information only three weeks before the end of his term, and before he could get his business and papers in order, he left in a rush trying to reach his only daughter as she lay on her deathbed in Kentucky. Unfortunately, the loss of a third term prevented Pope from seeing the completion of the building he had worked so hard to bring about and prevented him from serving as governor in its halls. Secretary William S. Fulton was appointed the new territorial governor. Even after Pope left Arkansas, the political controversy surrounding the State House never completely died down, and Fulton, who believed that Pope had exceeded his authority in the use of the funds to plan and build the State House, refused to push the project to completion (*Arkansas Gazette,* September 17, 1967; Ferguson 1968:6; More 1838a:334; Ross 1969:110, 120–122; Williams and Whayne 2000:226).

About this time Albert Pike, who had arrived in Little Rock in late 1833 and soon became publisher of the *Arkansas Advocate,* described the State House in his "Letters from Arkansas," published in two eastern periodicals. His description was not complimentary:

> There are no public buildings . . . except the State house—to erect which, congress gave the territory ten sections of land, which sold for thirty-two thousand dollars. It is a great, awkward, clumsy, heavy edifice, of brick, with a smaller building on each side—one a court house, and the other for secretary's office, &c. The main building is partly covered with *tin;* and is commonly called "Pope's folly"—after the Hon. John Pope, Ex-governor of the territory, its projector. (Pike 1973:221–222)

Pike's comments probably reflect not only the unfinished and confused condition of the State House, but also the controversy still brewing over Pope's handling of the business and Fulton's refusal to finish the project.

Fortunately, Fulton's tenure was short-lived, for in 1836 Arkansas was admitted to the Union. Despite Fulton's opposition to the building, enough work continued so that by the fall the main building was nearing completion and the west wing was ready to be roofed. Things were far enough along that on September 12, 1836, the first session of the first General Assembly of the State of Arkansas met in the main building, and on the following day James S. Conway, a member of the Dynasty, was inaugurated the first state governor in the Representatives' Chamber. Immediately after his inauguration Governor Conway made a plea to the state Legislature to complete the construction of the State House buildings, and the Legislature responded by passing an act allowing him to sell the five additional sections of land that had been granted by Congress to raise funds (Ferguson 1968:7; Flynn 1971:133; Smyer 1976:3).

Many in the new state thought that Arkansas was not ready for statehood, but many more desired the benefits and advantages that statehood brought. Even so, Arkansas was still a wild and woolly frontier on the western edge of settlement. Legislators and businessmen went armed with large hunting knives. Political opinions were easily whipped to passionate extremes, and tempers were volatile. Disagreements might be settled by formal duels or less formal bursts of violence.

One such act of violence occurred not long after the infant state passed its first birthday. The smell of fresh paint had barely dispersed in the new State House when the most infamous event in the history of the Arkansas Legislature occurred. During a special session of the Legislature on December 4, 1837, House Speaker John Wilson and state representative Joseph J. Anthony got into a heated argument that quickly escalated to a knife fight. The legislators watched in horror as Wilson fatally stabbed Anthony on the floor of the House of Representatives. Wilson was charged with first-degree murder, but acquitted on the grounds of self-defense, although he was expelled from the Legislature as an act of censure (Ferguson 1968:8–9; Whayne et al. 2002:113). Residents of the new state condemned such uncivilized and lawless actions, but the story quickly spread and influenced Arkansas's reputation for years to come.

Fig. 4.6: House Speaker John Wilson delivers the fatal wound to Representative Joseph J. Anthony in the Representatives' hall on December 4, 1837. *Drawing by Bill Reames, 2009, Old State House Museum Collection.*

The First Commissioner of Public Buildings

Money for the completion of the State House and pugnatious legislators were not the only problems facing Conway. Between Weigart's unexpected death, Pope's loss of the governorship and quick departure from Arkansas, and Fulton's obstructionism, the building accounts were now in a state of confusion. By the time Conway took over and intended to see the State House completed, it was unclear who had been paid, who was owed money, and how much remained in the building fund. To solve this problem, Conway appointed Elijah A. More* as commissioner of public buildings in the fall of 1836 to superintend the construction and get the finances straightened out (*Arkansas Gazette,* September 20, 1836, May 23, 1837, September 17, 1967; Eno 1945:243; More 1837:201–203;).

At 37 Elijah More had sufficient experience to be a likely choice for commissioner. He had served as the mayor of Little Rock and the director of the Bank of Arkansas, and later, as a lawyer, would be elected as a county probate judge (*Arkansas Gazette,* May 13, 1834, November 8, 1836, January 16, 1839). But his tenure as commissioner of public buildings was rocky. While he attacked the problems at hand with a swift diligence, he may have lacked needed diplomacy in dealing with the established workmen. Not long on the job in August 1837, he angered local craftsmen when he advertised for laborers in the papers of Kentucky and Ohio (*Arkansas Gazette,* August 15, 1837, August 29, 1837). He was critical of the work that had been done, reporting to the

* Because of the similarities of their names, E. A. More is frequently confused with E. B. Moore in writings on the Old State House. E. A. More served as commissioner of public buildings from 1836 to 1838; E. B. Moore served as secretary of state from 1885 to 1889 and was involved with concerns of the building when the 1885 addition was built.

governor that the courthouse, "is completed, with exception of plastering and painting, though on a wretched bad plan" (More 1837:202). More may have had good reason to be skeptical of the ability of the workmen when it was discovered that the roof over the State House was sagging (*Arkansas Gazette,* January 2, 1838).

In trying to unravel what had been done, what remained to be done, what was paid and what was owed, More went directly to the source. In the latter half of 1837, More took a trip to Kentucky to meet with John Pope. The two of them examined all the accounts, vouchers, and papers pertaining to the State House

Fig. 4.7: Carpenter John Wassell. *Courtesy of Arkansas History Commission.*

fund, and then Pope turned them over to More to bring back to Arkansas (More 1837:201). While in Kentucky, More also visited Gideon Shryock to discuss the original plan of the State House and discovered that Shryock had not yet been paid for his work (More 1837:203). More encouraged the Legislature to settle the account with the architect and on March 3, 1838, an act was approved by the General Assembly authorizing the governor to pay Shryock $100 out of the State House fund for the plans of the public buildings he had provided to Pope (Acts of Arkansas 1838:86).

Also while in Kentucky, More conducted interviews at his hometown of Danville with workmen and contractors desiring employment on the State House. He specifically advertised for good workmen of good character who were sober and reliable, and preferred married men who would emigrate to Arkansas with their families (*Arkansas Gazette,* August 15, 1837). He instructed them to be prepared to leave by the first of October and to accompany him back to Little Rock. More hired Henry Pendleton, probably out of Kentucky, to do the carpentry and take over as superintending architect. Pendleton hired carpenter John Wassell as his foreman. Once in Little Rock, Wassell and his wife set up housekeeping in the west wing, along with plasterer Stephen Fagan and his family. Although their unusual residency arrangement originally may have been intended to reduce vandalism to the buildings, later More appeared to be dismayed by the situation (*Arkansas Gazette,* January 2, 1838; More 1838a:356; Ross 1967:6e).

Even with the new workmen problems continued to arise. Commissioner More disagreed with the stonework contractors over differences in the way of measuring to determine payment —differences that amounted to some $2,000 (More 1838a:336). Hoping to solve the problem, More wrote to Shryock on August 26, 1838, with specific questions:

> I must again trouble you, in relation to the mode of measuring cut-stone work, after the same is set, where the contract is to pay for it by the *foot superficial.*
>
> In making the contract referred to, I designed to make it so plain that no difficulty could grow up in settling with the workmen under its provisions; yet it seems we have different views in relation to its intent and bearing.
>
> That you may have the subject matter fully before you, I will set forth the contract as it is: "We have agreed with E. A. More, Commissioner of Public Buildings, to do all the stone-cutting work in and about said buildings, steps, flagging, door-sills, window-sills, and also the capping for the iron railing inclosure, *furnishing* every thing, and putting up. We are to have one dollar and fifty cents per foot, superficial measure; or we will do any part of said stone-work on said terms."
>
> With reference to the foregoing contract, please answer the following interrogatories:
>
> In getting the length of window-sills, do you carry the line around each end to the wall, by which to give, *in the length,* the projection at each end?
>
> When you speak of the whole width of the top, do you mean that portion which is hid under the window-frame? In this instance they run under the window frame five and six inches.
>
> In measuring steps where the ends are worked, and project over an ashler, are they added to the length by running the line around the side of the step, or is a separate calculation made to get the exact superfice of the end?
>
> In measuring buttresses is there an allowance of one or more inches in every joint or bed at the side of the buttress, or elsewhere, or is it only the

actual superfice which is taken? I would also ask, how do you measure the capping of said buttress?

How would you measure a base or block on which to set a wooden column? It is two feet square, worked eight inches on every side; the line around it is eight feet.

In measuring flagging, where there are columns, is the space occupied by the column taken into the estimate? If not, what allowance, if any, is made for inserting the flagging under the exterior of said column? Those columns are of brick, *and fluted,* and with the whole of the exterior of the building are to be marbleized, to receive which at their base, a belt of stone six inches wide with flutes corresponding with the columns, are inserted. This belt is composed of divers pieces, put in at the time of flagging, and on top of the flagging. How are those belts measured under this contract?

How are *water tables* measured?

And, lastly: how are chimney-caps measured? Does the *line* go inside of the chimney? or does the outside, or part worked, measure more than a girt?

It is with the full consent of all parties, that this letter is addressed to you. Hence your kind attention to it will be thankfully acknowledged by all. (More 1838a:336–337)

Fig. 4.8: A workman applies plaster over the bricks that fit together to shape the columns. *Drawing by John Deering, 1994, Old State House Museum Collection.*

More had not heard from Shryock by November 3, 1838, when he made his report to the governor, but Shryock eventually did answer. The copy of his letter, postmarked "Jan. 4, Louisville, Ky.," is missing its year date (presumably 1839) and first page, but is the only document available from Shryock in regard to the State House:

measuring buttresses I would make no allowance for the joints or beds; but would take only the actual superfices; and I would measure capping of a buttress by taking the exact superficial contents of every part that shows after the cap is set, and I would measure a Base or block on which to set a wooden column of the dimension you mention (viz. 2 feet square and worked 5 inches on every side) as nine feet four inches superficial. In measuring flagging I would only measure that part under the columns which was actually flagged and no more.

The belts of stone at the base of the column which are fluted to correspond with the flutes of the column would be so difficult to estimate by the superficial foot; that I am at a loss what to say in relation to the measurement of them; but am of opinion that according to the contract the actual superfices of the top and face, would be a fair measurement, and charge two prices for the fluted part. I would measure water table the same as window sills for the width; by the actual length.

In measuring chimney tops, if the stone is worked all round I would measure the front and back or inside and the top bed for the width, and give the top in the largest part for the length.

In making the above statements I have been

> concerned by what I should think correct more than by a strict construction of the contract as stated in your letter. (Shryock ca. 1839)

Despite More's diligence in going to a neutral authority to solve differences with the workmen, More continued to have problems with everything and everyone. He was dissatisfied with the quality of the work, the monetary costs, and the laborers. He faced delays in receiving supplies due to miscalculation of needed materials and especially transportation problems. The sinking of the cargo boat *Ozark* resulted in the loss of lime and plastering materials, while the delivery of locks, hinges, glass, and carpentry supplies ordered from Cincinnati were delayed due to low water (More 1838a:331–332). Critical of the quality of the work and distrustful of workmen he didn't know, More was reluctant to provide monetary advancements, withholding a quarter or a half of the contracted amount against satisfactory completion, which only angered the workmen.

The craftsmen finally had their fill of More's management, and in late 1838 they presented their own reports to the Legislature. Henry Pendleton and John Wassell (1838:356, 360), contractors for the carpentry, S. Fagan (1838:358–360), contractor for the plaster work, and James McVicar (1838:360–361), contractor for the stonework, accused More of misrepresentation, misstatements, and inattention to his duties. More (1838b:356–358) was surprised by the charges and believed they had been timed to coincide with the Legislature's vote on his appointment in order to remove him from office. A joint committee on public buildings (Thornton 1838:94–97) investigated

Fig. 4.9: The Arkansas River provided a critical transportation corridor to Little Rock. Recognizing this importance, the Old State House was designed with two fronts, one to the river and the other to the town. *Drawing by John Deering, 1994, Old State House Museum Collection.*

the charges, and their December report tactfully concluded that most of the problems seemed to be caused by miscommunication. They praised the work of the craftsmen, noting they had followed "a course of vigilance, attention, and correctness, rarely to be met with under circumstances so embarrassing," yet felt that More's report had not been intended to impugn the workmen. The committee also confirmed that they believed More had performed his duties "faithfully and diligently" as he understood them, but that the law of 1836 authorizing a commissioner had intended more hands-on superintendence than More was giving. Despite the diplomacy of the committee's report, it is clear that More had lost the confidence and trust of his workmen, creating a rift that perhaps could not be bridged. Ultimately, whether by mutual agreement or otherwise, Elijah More's appointment was not renewed (*Arkansas Gazette,* September 17, 1967; Stevenson 1840:557).

Despite the manner in which More handled problems, many of his concerns appear to have been legitimate. An examination of the Old State House by two engineers in 1922 noted problems with the roof that they believed were caused by a lack of technical knowledge (Flynn 1971:134–140). It is difficult to know who may have been responsible for this, but it is likely that Weigart's death and the subsequent and frequent changes in construction superintendents were a major factor. It is evident that More did make sincere efforts to straighten out the accounts and determine the methods to properly and fairly assess charges. His was not an easy job. Perhaps his replacement as commissioner was as much a relief to him as it was to the construction crew.

Moving on from More

The General Assembly selected a new commissioner of public buildings on December 11, 1838, electing Little Rock resident Richard C. Hawkins to the position. The Legislature then adjourned six days later and were not scheduled to meet again for two years. But Governor Conway never followed through to commission Hawkins, and instead selected his own man, Samuel H. Hempstead, to be the new commissioner. Hempstead held the position for only half a year before resigning and seems to have left no reports to detail what he did during his time in charge. Conway then appointed W. W. Stevenson on July 31, 1839, to complete the two-year term. In the meantime, the absurd situation of competing commissioners became apparent, and instead of settling it in an expeditious manner in order to get on with the business of overseeing the construction of the State House, the state brought suit against Stevenson in the Arkansas Supreme Court (Arkansas Reports 1841:260–281). The Court decided that although the General Assembly had enacted a law that reserved the right of the General Assembly to elect a commissioner of public buildings, the law hadn't yet gone into effect, so the governor was within his rights to appoint the commissioner.

So, the Reverend William W. Stevenson, a Little Rock Presbyterian minister, retained the position of the next commissioner of public buildings for the two-year term of 1839–1841. After More's contentiousness, Governor Conway may have selected Stevenson, believing that his religious demeanor would bring a calming influence to the situation. Nothing in Stevenson's 1840 report suggests otherwise. By the time Stevenson took over, the State House was nearing completion. Work by the carpenter and joiner was completed, and the plastering had progressed well. Before it could be finished contractor S. Fagan had died, but his partner, Robert Frail, completed the job. The stonework on the north portico and the steps to the passageways connecting the wings had not yet been finished due to a rash of illness that affected the workmen. Stevenson found a space left in the roof of the main building for what he thought was meant to be a dome, but after conferring with contracting carpenter Henry Pendleton, he decided that one was never intended and had the roof closed (Stevenson 1840:553–559).

One of the more serious problems Stevenson faced appeared to be one that occurred with the west wing. Alterations to the wing removed two partition walls from the lower level, which caused the floor and roof to settle and pressed out the west side of the main wall, causing the wall to give way in several places. Stevenson quickly had the partition walls replaced (Stevenson 1840:554).

Stevenson allowed the sheriff of Pulaski County to put a wooden floor in the east wing to create a circuit court room, but as Stevenson was uncertain what legal right Pulaski County had to the space, his permission was given only at the risk of the county. Sufficiently concerned about the legal status of the east wing, Stevenson recommended that the Legislature designate the specific uses of each part of the public buildings to avoid future confusion and inconvenience (Stevenson 1840:554, 557). Had the Legislature followed up on Stevenson's suggestions, the battle with Pulaski County over the east wing in the 1880s might never have occurred.

Stevenson also began trying to secure and beautify the grounds. He erected a fence to keep

Fig. 4.10: The Reverend William W. Stevenson served as one of several commissioners of public buildings during the construction of the Old State House. *From* Arkansas Pioneers, *Volume 1, No. 2, January 1913, courtesy of Arkansas History Commission.*

Fig. 4.11: Governor Archibald Yell officially declared that work on the State House was complete on November 8, 1842. *Old State House Museum Collection.*

Fig. 4.12: Artist's conception of how the Old State House looked when it was completed in 1842, view from the Arkansas River. *Drawing by Ken Oberste, 1994, Old State House Museum Collection.*

the wagon drivers going to and from nearby sawmills from stabling animals inside the buildings. He also planted trees and worked toward finishing the grading that was necessary to support the foundations. Money was running short, however, and after Stevenson made a plea for the funds to complete the work, the Legislature appropriated a final $37,000 (Hawkins 1843:42; Stevenson 1840: 553–559).

By the time Stevenson's term came to an end, the law the General Assembly had enacted back in 1838 was finally in force, and they did not reappoint Stevenson. Richard C. Hawkins, who had been the General Assembly's choice for commissioner after Elijah More and who had lost the court decision when the state found itself with two concurrent commissioners, was elected as the new commissioner for the term of 1841–1843. Little remained to be done on the State House complex. Hawkins reported in late 1842 that the north portico had been completed, as had the outside paving and stone steps. Grading of the land surrounding the State House had been done, and grass and trees were added to the grounds. In fact, most of Hawkins's report focused on settling the

Fig. 4.13: Artist's conception of how the Old State House looked when it was completed in 1842, view from town. *Drawing by Ken Oberste, 1994, Old State House Museum Collection.*

accounts with the workmen, including bringing suit against former governor Pope for $750 and describing the construction of a penitentiary (Hawkins 1843:40–48).

With work on the State House largely wrapped up, Governor Archibald Yell made it official on November 8, 1842, when he announced to the General Assembly that the State House was now completed (Ferguson 1968:7). Despite taking nearly a decade to construct, the State House became the building and the symbol territorial governor John Pope had originally envisioned. An early visitor to Little Rock was duly impressed by it, and his assessment of the building and Governor Pope has come down to us today:

> It was my good fortune to become acquainted with a few respectable and agreeable individuals here. Governor Pope, the governor of the territory, is an unaffected, worthy person: he was once a conspicuous politician in Kentucky. . . . This gentleman has been of great service here in various ways, especially in the judicious use he has made of the funds entrusted to him by the general government for the erection of a legislative hall, which is a very handsome building, placed in an advantageous situation, on the brink of the river, and one of the neatest public buildings I have seen in North America. The Governor showed it to me with great exultation, and I complimented him sincerely on the taste he had shown. (Featherstonhaugh 1844:52)

Pope was again in Little Rock in 1844, in part to defend himself against the lawsuit. The trip gave him the opportunity, shortly before his death, to see the culmination of his vision. John Pope must have viewed with pride and pleasure the handsome and inspiring State House he helped to create (Baylor 1943:474)

CHAPTER 5

The Early Years: 1842–1885

FROM 1842, when Governor Archibald Yell announced that the State House was completed, until 1885, when a major renovation to the building substantially increased its size and gave it the appearance it has today, the Arkansas State House stood as the focus of both government and current events. What happened to Little Rock and to Arkansas as a whole affected the State House. During this period in the state's history, the State House was witness to the work of state government, the struggles of the General Assembly, and the troubles of the state exemplified by both the Civil War and the Brooks-Baxter War.

Information on the condition and changes to the State House during this period comes largely from the reports of the secretaries of state. These reports may be more or less informative depending on the length of time the secretary was in office, his interest in the upkeep of the building, and how pressing the need for repairs might be. In the first years of the new building, upkeep should have been minimal, but as the building aged during the 43 years of this period, repairs became critical. At the same time, many secretaries served only one 2-year term, limiting their involvement with the building and motivation to fight for needed funds. The reports also tend to focus on problems, which creates a more negative view of the condition of the State House than might actually have been the case.

As government officials settled into the new State House, the three buildings of the complex were delegated to specific functions. According to reminiscences of William F. Pope (1895:150–151), a relative and personal secretary of territorial governor John Pope (Hempstead 1911a:116), the use of the State House buildings originally were allocated in the following manner:

- *The Main Building:* The first floor held offices of the auditor and the treasurer. The second floor held the Senate and House chambers.
- *The East Wing:* The south end was occupied by Pulaski County, the space including a courthouse and office of the clerk of the circuit court. Originally there was no second floor in the south end, the space being open all the way to the roof. Later, the second floor was finished and the space used as a county courtroom. The north end was used by the U.S. Superior Court, and included a law library and judges' chamber on the second floor.
- *The West Wing:* The north end of the first floor held the U.S. District courtroom, the office of the U.S. court clerk, and a jury room. The south end of the first floor held the U.S. marshall's office and another jury room. The state governor had two rooms in the south end of the second floor, and the secretary of state's office, along with his library of state records, occupied the north end of the second floor.

Oversight of the buildings and grounds of the State House initially was assigned to the commissioners of public buildings working directly under the governors. James Conway began his term as the first governor of Arkansas in 1836, and in the fall of that year the General Assembly authorized him to appoint a commissioner of public buildings (Acts 1838:84–86). As noted in the previous chapter, Conway appointed Elijah A. More as the first such commissioner. Two years later, perhaps because of the problems surrounding More, the General Assembly repealed the 1836 Act and instead placed the appointment of the commissioner into their own hands, appointing him for two years at an annual salary of $1,000. The commissioner, however, was still expected to answer to the governor, who could fire him. The duties of the commissioner were outlined in sixteen sections in the 1838 Act, which included superintending the construction and repair of the public buildings, making contracts for work, keeping accounts of expenditures, and safe-guarding the furniture and stationery when the Legislature was adjourned (Acts 1838:84–86). Despite the specified requirements for accounting of expenditures, subsequent commissioners of public buildings continued to find inadequate records of accounts left by their predecessors.

Elijah More was followed as commissioner of public buildings by Samuel H. Hempstead for half a year in 1839, William W. Stevenson continuing 1839, Richard C. Hawkins in 1841, and Henry F. Pendleton in 1844. In 1846 the position was abolished, and care of the buildings and grounds came under the responsibilities of the secretaries of state. D. B. Greer, in his 1858 report, identifies himself as both secretary of state and ex-officio commissioner of public buildings, indicating the transition of the roles. The responsibilities of the secretaries of state continued to grow over the years, so that by 1879, when Jacob Frolich won the position, the duties included management of the use of the halls when the Legislature was not in session, allotment of space for public officials, purchase of furnishings, care of the legislative records in the State Library, and procurement of portraits of distinguished Arkansans. Based on the reports of the secretaries of state, or lack thereof, some took a much more active interest in the care of the State House than did others (Ferguson 1968:7; Frolich 1880; Greer 1858).

Fig. 5.1: A river view of Little Rock, with the Old State House pictured on the far right, was used as the masthead of the *Arkansas Gazette* in 1850. *From the collection of the* Arkansas Democrat-Gazette.

Fig. 5.2: The Old State House is also seen on the far right in this sketch of Little Rock by John Barber made before 1861. *Courtesy of I. N. Phelps Stokes Collection, Miriam and Ira D. Wallach Division of Art, Prints and Photographs, The New York Public Library; Astor, Lenox and Tilden Foundations.*

Settling In

In 1844, just two years after the building had been officially declared complete, additional work continued, which probably represented some of the last minor details as well as corrections to unanticipated design problems. Henry F. Pendleton, the longtime contractor for carpentry who had faced off against More, was appointed commissioner of public buildings following Richard Hawkins.

Pendleton reported the need for removing the plaster on the framework of the north and south porticos of the State House and replacing it with wood. There was also a contract let to insert cast-iron jambs and backs into the fireplaces (Pendleton 1845:135–137). At the same time, the Legislature continued to wrangle over former governor Pope's tangled accounts, until Pope made a trip to Little Rock late in the year to personally present his case (Select Committee 1845:141–146). It was then that he finally had the opportunity to see the completed State House complex.

With construction essentially complete, the State House began to serve in its normal function as legislative halls, courtrooms, and state offices, but the buildings also served the Little Rock community as public facilities. Events of all sorts were held in its rooms, including lectures, parties, social meetings, sermons, funerals, shows, and balls. The doors were kept unlocked, and people wandered in and out as they pleased (Ferguson 1968:10, 21). When collections of the Antiquarian and Natural History Society were placed in the State House in 1849, the unguarded public access led to the pilfering of the collections (Ross 1966a; Sherwood 1952). All of these activities contributed to the wear and tear on the building. While the first decade of use should have been relatively problem-free, by the early 1850s expenses for upkeep were beginning to accumulate. A new roof was one of the most pressing needs, followed by a boiler vault for the secretary of state's office (Smyer 1976:10–11).

Traveler Gilbert Hathaway visited Little Rock probably in November 1856 and sent letters of his experiences to the *Magazine of Travel*, which published them in 1857. His description of the State House confirms that the building was due for a renovation. Hathaway observed:

> The capitol, when new, was rather an imposing building, but being in an advanced state of dilapidation, it produces an unpleasant effect on the mind of a stranger. It is built in the Grecian style of architecture, with colonade front and rear; on the bank of the river; or, more properly speaking, where the river used to run, for the water is now so low that it would be really a misnomer to dignify it by that appellation.
>
> The lower part of the main building is devoted to offices, and the second story to the Hall of the House of Representatives and Senate Chamber, with a large two story building on each side, affording rooms for legislative committees, but in a like state of decay. After the State consents to pay the interest on her bonds, I suppose she will repair her capitol, but when that is done will be when a different set of men from those now in office, preside over her destinies. (Hathaway 1973:449)

The following year, perhaps spurred by Hathaway's account, Secretary of State David B. Greer did not mince words in his report on the condition of the State House:

> As ex-officio commissioner of public buildings, I consider it my duty to call your attention to the condition of the state-house. A bare inspection of the building, will make it manifest to every one that it is rapidly going to decay; and that it needs thorough, substantial, and permanent repairs, to preserve it from total ruin—something more than the mere patch-work that has, heretofore, been done upon it. (Greer 1858:29)

Sufficient action must not have been taken by the Legislature, however, for just two years later, Secretary of State Samuel M. Weaver reported the State House was in a "dilapidated and decaying condition" and advised:

> It is evident that some immediate action should be taken of the matter by the legislature to have thoroughly repaired the main building and the west wing of the capitol to preserve them from further injury. The system of patch work that has been pursued in regard to it by every legislature that has assembled here since 1840; whenever an appropriation was made, it was wholly inadequate to have the repairs necessary done in a style and finish to correspond with the work done on the building in the first place. Nothing short of a thorough and complete repairing of the center building and the west wing will be of any permanent service to the house or value to the state. (Weaver 1860:1)

He also reported that the State Library had outgrown its space and was exerting so much weight on the second floor of the west wing that he feared a collapse:

> The number of books now in the library is considerable, and rapidly increasing; and their weight on the second story is too great for security, without very thorough repairs on the west wing of the building. There are a number of books now on hand, that cannot be put in the library for the want of more room and thorough repairs. A number of volumes of the reports of the decisions of the supreme court of this state, for the want of room for them in the library, have been stored away in one of the committee rooms until recently, when they were removed from it to the room containing the geological specimens of the state, as the only place they could be put about the building to be preserved. These reports are in a very damaged state, and the binding will have to be made new in many instances, to put them in a condition to be preserved and kept from ruin and total loss. The library rooms should be repaired, or a building should be erected for its use. (Weaver 1860:2)

In addition, the furniture used by the Senate and House of Representatives was 22 years old and "much worn and so defaced that it cannot be patched up any longer" (Weaver 1860:2). Thus began the biennial complaints of the secretaries of state, who repeatedly reported the deterioration of the building to the Legislature and begged for adequate funds to make repairs. With money in the young state in short supply, complete repairs were continually deferred.

The Colonnades

Weaver also reported on the condition of the colonnades and the effect they were having on the main buildings. There are only meager descriptions and a few sketchy illustrations pertaining to what was built in the open spaces between the main building and the wings before they were enclosed in 1885 to form the hyphens as we know them today. Changes to the design also were made during that period, most of them not well documented. The original design, as described by Governor Pope, was that each wing would be "connected to the centre building by dwarf colonnades" (*Arkansas Gazette*, November 20, 1833), a feature that would have matched the Greek Revival architecture of the buildings. A colonnade is a series or row of columns that are connected by an entablature. They may consist of a single row, often

Fig. 5.3: The open walkway of the south-facing east colonnade between the main building and east wing is clearly seen in this ca. 1874 photograph. It shows the colonnade had four columns connected by a lintel. The west colonnade is hidden by a tree, but the well house can be seen in front of the west wing. *From the D. L. Phillips Collection, courtesy of Butler Center for Arkansas Studies, Central Arkansas Library System.*

Fig. 5.4: This Scribner's engraving, ca. 1874, probably used the above photograph as a model. Notice the similarity in the placement and size of trees and location of people along the fence. The engraving enhances details of the colonnade and buildings. *Old State House Museum Collection.*

seen as a portico on a building, or paired rows forming a passage or walkway. At the State House they were part of a walkway raised a few feet above ground level, as indicated in an early report describing "stone steps to the connections" (Hawkins 1843:45).

A photograph from the Civil War and another from 1874 both clearly show the east colonnade as an open passageway bounded by four columns supporting a horizontal element above head height. What cannot be seen, however, is whether the colonnades consisted only of single rows along the outside of the walkway or paired rows on both sides of the walkway. If the colonnades were in pairs, it also is not known whether the passages were unroofed, partially roofed, or completely roofed, and surviving descriptions do not clarify the situation. A colonnade built in the late nineteenth century in Louisville, Kentucky's Central Park shows a slightly raised walkway with alternating roof timbers and open spaces that would provide some shade but not protect the area from the elements. The State House colonnades may well have looked the same.

Fig. 5.5: Photograph, ca. 1908, of the colonnade walk in Central Park, Louisville, Kentucky. The colonnade was built in the late nineteenth century. It was roofed with alternating beams and open spaces. *Old State House Museum Collection.*

The colonnades were built on both the north and south sides between the east and west wings and the center building. Their position near the outer edge of the buildings created open, unroofed courtyards between the buildings. Unfortunately no bird's-eye illustration exists that shows all four colonnades or the courtyards between them. At some point, the open courts may have been partially walled up, or this effect might have been created by the colonnades themselves. William F. Pope provided a description of this area in his 1895 reminiscences:

> The east and west wings were separated from the main building by open courts, on the north and south sides of which ran paved porticos, with brick columns supporting the roofs. These open courts were walled up several feet high, but had no roof. They stood exposed to the weather for several years and peach bearing trees grew up within them. (Pope 1895:150)

By 1860 the colonnades were contributing to damage of the buildings, but Secretary of State Weaver's description of what he called "wood houses" is confusing. Weaver reported:

> I would suggest the propriety of removing the walls of the wood houses, between the main building and the wings, and have the roofs closed, and supported by columns; the space paved with brick to correspond with the pavements on each side of these wood houses. This improvement would add considerably to the appearance of the buildings, while it would also afford more light to the rooms in the wings, and those in the main building at the north end of the house. It would also keep the walls dry and prevent the dampness that is now injuring the

walls, particularly, of the main building. These wood houses are of no practicable use or value to the premises. (Weaver 1860:1–2)

What are the "wood houses," and why would additional columns be needed when the Civil War photograph clearly shows that the outside of the east colonnade had columns? The answer may be that Weaver mainly was describing the open courtyards. Perhaps, following William Pope's description, the unseen inside of the colonnades had been walled up at some point, which would have blocked light and contributed to dampness. What Weaver called "wood houses" are probably the colonnades, and his recommendation was to remove them in order to open up the outside edges of the buildings to more light. What he wanted to roof and pave were the courtyards.

An 1871 bird's-eye view perspective map of the city of Little Rock includes two drawings of the Old State House that show the 1867 changes to the west colonnade after it was enclosed to form the west hyphen. *Drawn and published by A. Ruger. Courtesy of Geography and Map Division, U. S. Library of Congress.*

Fig. 5.6: View from the river shows the peaked roof of the west hyphen, although the east structure, still a colonnade at this date, is incorrectly shown as a two-story building.

Fig. 5.7: View from town, with the enclosed west hyphen sporting a peaked roof. The east colonnade is not clearly shown, but does have a different roofline. The well-house can also be seen to the left of the walkway.

Fig. 5.8: This 1870 image from a stereoview card is the only known photograph of the west hyphen enclosed as a one-story structure. The peaked roofline can be seen. *Courtesy of Arkansas History Commission.*

The legislators did not follow through on Weaver's recommendations, as the start of the Civil War the following year diverted their attention. It was not until 1867 that renovations to the State House were undertaken. In that year the open courtyard between the main building and the west wing was enclosed to provide quarters for the United States district court, creating what came to be called the west "hyphen." Few images exist of the one-story structure, as the west hyphen is hidden behind a well house and foliage in most pictures. An 1870 photograph taken from the southwest, as well as an 1871 bird's-eye illustration of Little Rock, however, show the peaked roofline of the newly enclosed space.

Damage from Two Wars

Leading up to the Civil War, the legislators were duly concerned about the condition of the buildings and recognized Secretary Weaver's warnings. A joint committee on public buildings was organized to study the condition of the west wing in 1861 and concurred with Weaver's assessment. The committee recommended "the removal of said west wing, and the erection of a fire proof building of the same dimensions" and further recommended "that two rooms be added to the eastern wing of said capital, for the purpose of preserving the library of the supreme court" (House Journal 1861:660).

The bill to construct a new library building was tabled, and before any further action could be taken, the concerns of the General Assembly became focused on the war. After the state seceded on May 6, 1861, the State House served as the seat of the Confederate state government. A year later Little Rock was threatened with the approach of the Union army, and Governor Henry Rector reacted by packing up the state archives and moving them to Hot Springs, although the move proved premature. In the fall of the following year, however, 14,000 Federal troops surged into Little Rock, capturing the city on September 10, 1863. Government officials abandoned the State House and moved operations and papers to the Hempstead County Courthouse in the town of Washington, leaving the buildings to be occupied by Union soldiers. Between the fighting and the occupation, the State House suffered additional damage. In 1864 when a Unionist government was organized with Isaac Murphy as governor, the new legislators reconvened once again in the State House. They discovered damage needing repairs and the loss of most of the furniture (DeBlack 2010; Ferguson 1968:12; Smyer 1976:14).

The earliest known photograph of the State House is from this period. It pictures the Third

Fig. 5.9: In this earliest known photograph of the Old State House, taken during the Civil War in 1863 or 1864, the east colonnade can be seen, as well as damage to the pediment of the main building. With Little Rock under Union occupation, the Third Minnesota Infantry occupies the grounds. *Courtesy of Ohio Historical Society.*

Minnesota Infantry on dress parade in front of the building, probably in 1864. Some damage can be seen in the pediment of the main building, and the colonnades between the buildings are visible (Ferguson 1968:12). Archeological work conducted around the State House in 1996–1997 recovered two brass buttons lost off the uniforms of soldiers in the U.S. Infantry. The military buttons have a motif of a spread eagle and shield.

Secretary of State Robert J. T. White procured an order from Major General F. Steele in the winter of 1864 to begin repairs of the State House. White rounded up forty workmen, and repairs commenced until the Union troops returned from the failed expedition to Camden and the workmen were withdrawn. Major General J. J. Reynolds also assisted in protecting the grounds by erecting a new fence (White 1866:15–16). The building further deteriorated once it was returned to the control of state government, however, as financial losses from the war left no money available for repairs. As Secretary White explained:

Fig. 5.10: A corner of the Old State House is seen in this 1910 painting, *Third Minnesota Infantry Entering Little Rock*, by Stanley M. Arthurs. *Courtesy Minnesota Historical Society.*

> It is unnecessary, indeed difficult, to describe the wrecked condition of the destructible portions of the capitol buildings. . . . With the spouting stopped up, or broken, and the glass and sash of the windows shattered to pieces, and the rain turned in upon the legislative halls, and the offices beneath, there was no alternative but to proceed to the work of preservation. (White 1866:16)

That work did begin in earnest. With reserved encouragement, White reported on the advances made in improving conditions:

> The windows have been entirely renewed, and painted in a neat and most substantial manner; and . . . the gas fixtures have been replaced with some improvement in arrangement; making the whole of the passages, and rooms and halls, of the principal building as convenient as daylight for the transaction of ordinary business.
>
> During the war, and for some time after its termination, the dark passages, and unoccupied rooms of the capitol, had become a nightly haunt and resort for vagabonds and desperadoes. But, after the withdrawal of the military guard, the introduction of light led to their immediate and permanent expulsion. On the whole, I am satisfied that these improvements have conduced to the preservation of the public interest, and are appropriate to the dignity of the capitol of the State. (White 1866:16–17)

It was not until 1867, however, that the Legislature was won over to the need for major improvements and passed an act authorizing changes. The work was concentrated on the west wing, which had already been in serious decline prior to the war. Its walls were rebuilt from the ground up, a stairway was constructed on the outside of the building, and the open courtyard between the main building and the west wing was enclosed to provide one-story quarters for the United States district court, thus creating the first "hyphen." This change also freed up space to improve the library (Ferguson 1968:10; Smyer 1976:15). Kirkwood & Behen were awarded the contract for the work (*Arkansas Gazette*, July 9, 1867). The *Evening Republican* described the renovations:

> A greater portion of the walls of the west wing are new entire from the ground up, and the portion connecting that wing to the main building is re-built and instead of being an open space of little or no practical use, it is fashioned into a light, airy, spacious room, and neatly fitted up for the use of the United States Court. Secretary R. J. White effected a change of this court room from the main wing, in order to economize space and make room for the State library. The room set apart for that purpose is on the second floor of the north half of the wing, and with the exception of a small office, comprised that entire space. The book cases around the room and through the centre are very neat, and in workmanship, especially painting and graining, excel anything we have seen. In this room upward of 10,000 volumes hitherto almost useless for want of convenient arrangement are so classified and arranged as to enable the librarian to put his hand on any one of them at pleasure. (*Evening Republican*, Little Rock, Arkansas, December 16, 1867)

Despite the 1867 renovations, space was still at a premium in the buildings, so much so that the Legislature began to eye the east wing, portions of which were occupied by the offices of Pulaski County. Representative R. W. Wishard from the Sixth District (Newton, Johnson, and Yell counties) submitted a resolution requesting Secretary of State Robert White to report "by what authority the sheriff of Pulaski county appropriates a part of the Capitol building for the use of an office" and "by what authority the county clerk's office and circuit courts are held in the Capitol buildings" (Wishard 1870:101–102). Although Pulaski County had been authorized to use the east wing since the very beginning, after some 25 years the history of that authorization had been forgotten.

Secretary White reported back to the House that the money appropriated for the construction of the buildings had been combined to serve both the state and county, but that space provided for the United States District Court was through the courtesy of Arkansas, although "present inconvenience might not justify a violation of etiquette, even by suggestion, on the part of the State, towards so generous a benefactor as the United States Government" (White 1870:130–131). In other words, it might not be politically wise to kick the United States Government out of the State House just three years after the end of the Civil War.

A committee on public buildings also looked into the matter of Pulaski County's use of the east wing, describing in their report, the "arduous task" of searching through the state's records:

> After examining all the records that could be found in the archives of the State respecting public buildings, as thoroughly as it was possible to do in the present condition of the State library, in which the various public accounts lie in confused heaps, or crowded in double rows upon the shelves, for want of sufficient space to distribute them properly, and arrange them in order. (Ramsaur 1870:132–136)

The committee also concluded that the money for both state and county buildings had been commingled and that the plan of the buildings had been united, but that "the legal title to the entire public buildings . . . is vested in the State of Arkansas" and the rooms occupied by Pulaski County were done so "by courtesy" (Ramsaur 1870:134–135).

At that point, however, no move to evict Pulaski County was undertaken and when White made another report at the end of his term in 1872, neither the issue of Pulaski County nor the repair of the State House had been settled. White reported:

> The question as to how much longer the present dilapidated capitol building can be made habitable, recurring as it does every two years, again arises for consideration, and is of course for the legislature and Executive to determine. . . .
>
> The entire building is now used and [occupied] by the State officers, with the exception of a portion of the east wing, which is still in the possession of the clerk and sheriff of Pulaski county, and the Pulaski criminal court. Little or no change has been made in any of the rooms or offices since the adjournment of the last general assembly, and the question as to the propriety of causing the Pulaski county officials to vacate the building remains as it was then left. . . .
>
> The entire state house, if much longer used, will require repairs to a considerable extent. The roof being of tin, and in many portions almost destitute of paint, is eaten and corroded by rust and the weather. The water conduits and the under drains for the outlet of water as collected, are in great disorder, while the falling plaster and crumbling bricks and stones, admonish the observer that the old capitol has nearly served its time. (White 1873:8–9)

Before anything could be accomplished by the new Legislature, however, state government again came to a halt as the Brooks-Baxter War broke out. Southern Unionists and former Democrats supported Joseph Brooks in the

Fig. 5.11: Leslie's 1874 illustration depicts reinforcements crossing the Arkansas River to the Old State House during the Brooks-Baxter War. *Courtesy of University of Arkansas at Little Rock.*

Fig. 5.12: Famed illustrator Howard Pyle (1853–1911) depicted an incident in the Brooks-Baxter War, but mistakenly shows the Old State House as it appeared after the 1885 expansion. *Courtesy of Bettmann Collection, CORBIS.*

1872 election, while the Republican party, under the leadership of former governor Powell Clayton, backed Elisha Baxter. Baxter won the election, but Brooks claimed fraud. When Baxter began to pursue a course independent of the Republican power structure, the courts declared that Brooks was the rightful winner of the election, and swore Brooks into office. On April 15, 1874, with an armed force of about twenty supporters, Brooks forcibly ousted Baxter from the State House. Brooks's forces proceeded to fortify the State House, and armed men filled the building. Cannons were placed on the lawn, including the siege cannon "Lady Baxter." A 200-foot-long barricade was erected, and an ammunition magazine was constructed behind the building. The stand-off lasted a month until President Ulysses S. Grant ordered the Legislature to vote on the disputed claim. Baxter won and he regained the governorship (Barnes 2000:50–54; Dougan 1994:259–263; Smyer 1976:20–21).

Secretary of State James M. Johnson, along with a contingent of generals, colonels, and staff officers, took possession of the State House and assessed the damage. The *Arkansas Gazette* reported on what they found:

> Earthworks on the southeast and the east corner of the building of rather a formidable character were to be seen, together with plank barricades scattered throughout the grounds and in the building. The facing of the front doors, which lead into the main hall, as also the rear doors, were cut down so as to admit of the easy egress and ingress of the artillery. Everything was topsy turvy. Guns were piled pell mell about the building; plank barricades were met with at every turn, and throughout there was a scene of desecration which can hardly be described.

> The building was in a fearfully filthy condition, a mixed perfume of sour bacon and human beings pervading the entire edifice which was positively nauseating. (*Arkansas Gazette*, May 20, 1874)

In addition to the damage to the buildings, the records in the library had been badly abused: "The shelves had been turned into extempore tables, with sheets of the geological survey doing duty as table-cloths, while the books were trodden under foot and soiled, many of them utterly ruined" (*Arkansas Gazette*, May 20, 1874).

Johnson had his work cut out for him. To return the State House to its former condition, he had to level earthworks, clean up barricades, dispose of gunpowder and firearms, and repair the physical damage. The inside of the buildings had to be thoroughly cleaned and disinfected, and the library had to be reorganized and the records restored. Whatever claim Brooks might have had on the governorship, his disregard for the State House was a strong indictment against him.

Once the cleaning and repair was completed, the concerns of the State House returned to normal, as the Legislature remained tight with funds and the secretaries of state tried to keep a jump ahead of the continual deterioration. As Secretary of State Benton Beavers reported in 1878, the money allotted for repairs in the previous year was not even sufficient to cover expenses (Beavers 1878:3). The state debt was so severe by this time that the Legislature's reticence in spending money on the State House is understandable. By the time Augustus Garland was inaugurated as governor in 1874, the state debt had risen to over $17 million, much of it acquired during Reconstruction (Donovan et al. 1995:65–66).

Fig. 5.13: The only known photograph of the columns of the north portico that faced the Arkansas River, probably taken during the exceptionally cold winter of 1875. Visible are the barracks built during the Brooks-Baxter War of 1874. *Old State House Museum Collection.*

Fig. 5.14: Secretary of State James M. Johnson. *Courtesy of Arkansas History Commission.*

A Hospital and a Fair

In the late 1870s, two events outside the regular concerns of the secretaries of state impacted the appearance of the State House and grounds. The first was an epidemic and the second was a celebration.

In the summer of 1875, an epidemic of malaria spread throughout Arkansas. A fever-ridden family with five children was brought by wagon from outside the town, and as there was at that time no hospital in Little Rock, they were left in the yard of the State House. Various townspeople rose to their cause. In back of the State House were two rows of buildings;

Fig. 5.15: Secretary of State Benton B. Beavers. *Courtesy of Arkansas History Commission.*

Lewellyn (1947:146) attributes them to barracks erected following the Brooks-Baxter War, although they might have been the cook and mess house erected for the governor's guard in 1874 (*Arkansas Gazette,* May 30, 1874). Regardless, they were essentially unused and quickly procured to serve as a hospital for the sick family. As word got out that Little Rock had a charity hospital, the "Poor House" began attracting more of the sick (Lewellyn 1947:146–147).

The Ladies Benevolent Association, which had been organized shortly before 1875 to aid women in Little Rock unable to find employment, was soon called to take responsibility for the hospital. The fledgling hospital struggled along, but eventually began to obtain both city and county aid. By 1878 Dr. James Lenow was appointed county physician (Lewellyn 1947:145–147). The hospital continued to operate in the barracks for several years, until 1881 when the Ladies Benevolent Association was granted two acres south of the state penitentiary on the condition that the association remove the buildings on the State House grounds (Frolich 1882:11–12). This was done, and the new charity hospital eventually evolved into the Pulaski County Hospital (Lewellyn 1947:145). Once the buildings were removed, Secretary of State Jacob Frolich wasted no time in reclaiming the land:

> All the buildings which, used as they were, greatly endangered the capitol, have been removed, the grounds leveled, sodded in grass, shade and ornamental trees planted, and enclosed so as to extend the capitol grounds to the railroad; all of which adds greatly to the safety, comfort and appearance of the capitol. (Frolich 1882:12)

In 1876, a year after the formation of the hospital, the United States celebrated its centennial with an exposition in Philadelphia. Governor Augustus Garland had focused his efforts on improving the state's image as part of a plan to increase the population through immigration, and thus increase prosperity. He made an impact with the octagon-shaped Arkansas Building at the exhibition, which won acclaim (Donovan et al. 1995:66). Items displayed in the building were brought back to Little Rock after the exposition ended and were added to the State House. One was the great seal of the State of Arkansas, which was placed in the center of the pediment in 1877. Another

Fig. 5.16: Image of the Arkansas Building at the 1876 Centennial Exposition in Philadelphia. *Courtesy of the Philadelphia Print Shop, Ltd., Philadelphia, Pennsylvania.*

Fig. 5.17: A view from ca. 1890 shows the fountain, state seal, and figures of Law, Mercy, and Justice that were brought back from the Centennial Exposition and added to the Old State House. *Old State House Museum Collection.*

was a three-tiered water fountain, purchased by the ladies of the Centennial Club of Arkansas, which was installed in 1878 and began operating the following year when the city water system was turned on. The final item was a statuary group, representing Law, Mercy, and Justice, which was first placed in the fountain and later on the roof of the main building (Ferguson 1968:14–15).

Jacob Frohlich Takes Over

In 1879 Jacob Frohlich was elected secretary of state for the first of what would become three terms. If his reports are any indication, he was a conscientious public servant who took pride in caring for the State House as well as in promoting Arkansas to the world. He recommended adding walkways and benches on the State House grounds, as well as improving the sidewalk in front of the buildings, to enhance appearances. As he pointed out:

> [The] public buildings are generally the first places visited by persons who come to this State, seeking new homes—and the number is very large. Such improvements are calculated to produce favorable impressions, and the number of those thereby influenced to settle in the State is largely increased. (Frolich 1880:4–5)

Frolich also encouraged the Legislature to approve repairs needed on both the exterior and interior of the buildings because "visitors from other States sometimes indulge in severe criticisms upon their appearance" (Frolich 1880:5). Since requests by his predecessors to repair a deteriorating State House had fallen on deaf ears, Frolich presented the same plea in a new package—the reputation of Arkansas and

Fig. 5.18: Secretary of State Jacob Frolich. *Courtesy of Arkansas History Commission.*

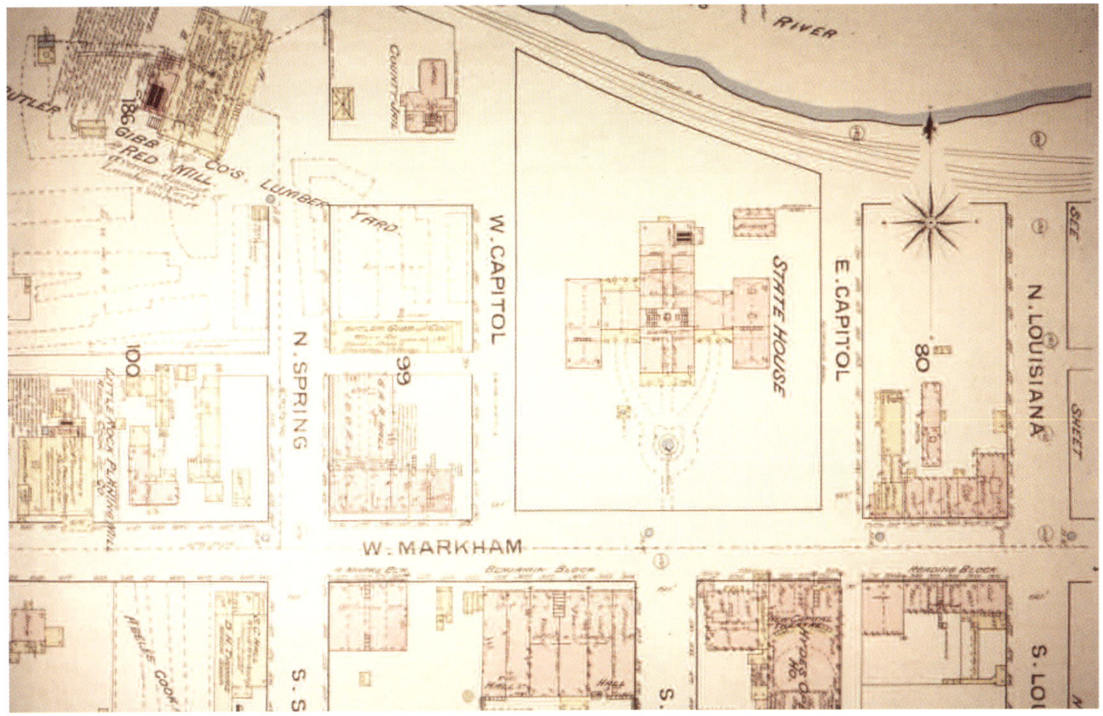

Fig. 5.19: The Butler, Gibbs, & Company Planing Mill is shown just to the northwest of the Old State House on the 1886 Sanborn Insurance Map. *Photograph courtesy of Arkansas Archeological Survey.*

its ability to attract new settlers and new tax dollars. If reason and observable facts had not swayed the Legislature in previous years, perhaps shame and the hope for prosperity would.

Fitting into his goals of state promotion, Frolich ordered a new gate for the entrance to the State House grounds:

> The new iron gate, at the main entrance to the grounds, is home-made, in every respect—even to the self-shutting device, which was patented by Mr. J. R. Booth, of Prairie county—the iron work of the gate and posts was executed at the foundry of McGuire & Bro., and the bronze eagles at the works of Wing & Co., both firms of Little Rock. The work might have been executed for a few cents less in another State, but, as ours is a growing and prosperous State, the opportunity seemed good to demonstrate to visitors that Arkansas can invent and manufacture things useful as well as ornamental. Therefore preference was given to home talent and mechanical skill, in the construction of the gate, from designs executed by Maj. G. P. C. Rumbough, of Little Rock. (Frolich 1880:4)

Despite the state's desire for economic growth, the effects of that growth in Little Rock were beginning to negatively impact the State House. Frolich recommended fireproof vaults for all the offices in order to protect the public records, because of "flimsy and tinder-like" structures surrounding the State House. He pointed out that steam locomotives would soon be running hourly just fifty yards to the north, greatly increasing the risk of fires, and went so far as to suggest that the Legislature should enact building codes for private development in the surrounding area (Frolich 1880:8–9). Frolich's warning was proven valid in late 1880 when the Butler, Gibbs & Company Planing Mill exploded. It was located in the block just west of the State House grounds and can be seen on the 1886 Sanborn insurance map. The blast was strong enough to damage the plaster on the walls and ceilings of the Senate, the House, and the central corridors. Repairs and a thorough cleaning followed (Smyer 1976:26).

We can be thankful, however, that the Legislature did not follow up on at least one of Frolich's suggestions. He wanted to erect a new front on the building, "fifty feet deep, covering the present State House front from wing to wing, hiding the old structure, and affording suitable accommodations for every department for years to come, at a cost below that of an entire new structure, and yet enjoy the appearance of a new building" (Frolich 1880:6). Such a plan would have essentially destroyed the historic building.

The issue with the use of the east wing by Pulaski County had not yet been resolved by 1880, resulting in the ludicrous situation of the state paying to rent rooms off-site for state officers. As Frolich bluntly pointed out, "The rent paid by the State for public offices and legislative committee rooms during the last seven years would have purchased the interest of Pulaski county in the east building, and made the State the owner of the entire property, and stopped the annual outlay" (Frolich 1880:6).

In 1881 the issue with Pulaski County came to a head, and the General Assembly "passed an Act requiring the Secretary of State to take possession of all the rooms in the Capitol buildings occupied by the county of Pulaski, so that the entire State house buildings and grounds be hereafter used exclusively for State purposes" (Frolich 1882:11). Pulaski County refused to leave, however, forcing the attorney general to begin legal proceedings. The suit was filed in the Pulaski Circuit Court, and then transferred to the Pulaski Chancery Court, where the papers were conveniently lost until June 1882. The suit dragged on for several years presenting, as Frolich (1882:12) quipped, "the strange and anomalous spectacle of a State suing her own officers, in her own court, for possession of her own property." By 1884, the case was settled in favor of the state (Frolich 1884:7).

Unexpected expenses for repair of the State House arose in 1881–1882 after the building was inspected by Major George P. C. Rumbough, a civil engineer for the city of Little Rock and also the designer of the new State House gate. Rumbough found problems with a number of the chimneys and reported that the sandstone capping the flues "is now cracked and ready to fall with any high wind" (Frolich 1882:13). Even worse was the condition of the roof over the hall of the House of Representatives. Rumbough reported:

> The roof over the hall of the House of Representatives is supported by a queen post, most primitively hewn and formed; the ridge of the roof, contrary to custom and all rules of proper construction, runs parallel with the queen post-truss frame. By this method the said queen post-trusses have a clear span of fifty feet, and as the posts of the lowest trusses have an altitude of only two feet, the flattened brace has more the tendency to break down the ceiling, by its absolute weight, than to support the weight of the superincumbent roof; the result of this is the breaking down of the ceiling, as is now apparent, and unless immediately repaired, will result in a fall of the roof through the ceiling into the hall of the House of Representatives. (Frolich 1882:13)

As if that wasn't bad enough, repairs also had to be made to the tin roof on the main building, which was ripped off in a storm (Frolich 1882:14). Frolich paid for the repairs as required, but the cost ate into the funds that

Fig. 5.20: Civil engineer George P. C. Rumbough. *Courtesy of Virginia Military Institute Archives, Lexington, Virginia.*

originally had been allocated by the General Assembly for other improvements—even so, Frolich had received only half of the money he had requested to handle those. As he reported, "These unexpected and costly repairs have prevented the making of such improvements as were intended" (Frolich 1882:14).

Fig. 5.21: A remnant of the 1883 cistern was uncovered during archeological excavations at the Old State House during 1996–1997. *Photograph by Randall Guendling, Arkansas Archeological Survey.*

The Mystery of the Cistern

On the front lawn near the walkway leading to the west wing was located a well, which had been there for many years (Ferguson 1968:13–14). It was covered with an open-sided, roofed structure, which can be seen in early photographs and drawings going back to the Civil War. By 1883, however, the well had gone bad and could no longer be used to supply drinking water, so Frolich hired Nick Murphy to build a 75,000-gallon cistern (*Arkansas Gazette,* July 4, 1883). Frolich described the cistern in his 1884 report: "In 1883, I had built a large cistern just in rear of the State House 12x40 cylindrical, with filter attached. This cistern now affords abundant supply of good, pure water" (Frolich 1884:7).

Unfortunately, the cistern only served for a few additional years. When the main building was extended to the north during the 1885 renovations, a wall of the extension covered the cistern (Ferguson 1968:15). Apparently, the cistern's short life and hidden location allowed it to be quickly forgotten, leading to an Old State House legend that thrives today. Over 50 years later, on May 13, 1936, George Crosson, the caretaker for the Old State House (then known as the War Memorial) accidentally discovered an underground cavern (Brown et al. 1978:161). Nobody knew what it was, and the excitement of its discovery generated a substantial report in the *Arkansas Gazette,* which is worth repeating in its entirety:

> A large underground chamber at the rear of the War Memorial building, older possibly than the building was discovered yesterday morning.
>
> It is about 40 feet long by 12 feet high, and shaped like a capsule. Floor, sides and roof comprise an oval, and the ends are circular. The walls are of brick covered with plaster. Apparently, entrance was through two manholes, one of which had been cemented over at some time or other. The other manhole was opened yesterday to disclose the old chamber beneath.
>
> The discovery was made when caretakers removed the manhole cover planning to use it at another place on the grounds. When they saw the cavern beneath they obtained a ladder and investigated.
>
> Mrs. Bernie Babcock, director of the Federal Writers Project for Arkansas, was the first to explore the excavation. She said it appeared that the chamber might have been intended either as a powder magazine or dungeon.

The chamber is partially filled with debris emptied into it through one of the manholes. Caretakers said that the grounds are criss-crossed with dead sewer lines, and that it has been the practice at times to empty debris into these lines through manholes.

The roof of the chamber is about four feet under ground. It extends from a point several feet under the west wall of the rear of the War Memorial building to a point about 35 feet west. The manhole by which it was entered is almost flush against the wall of the building. The one which has been closed is several feet distant.

The chamber is virtually water-tight. No water stands on the floor of the cavern and its walls are dry. The air is fresh, although those who entered it were unable to determine how circulation was obtained. The pile of debris consisted mostly of dirt, cinders, bricks, tin cans, bottles and jugs. However, the skull of a horse or mule found on the floor directly under the entrance afforded a thrill to several young women who explored the chamber. (*Arkansas Gazette,* May 14, 1936)

The story of the discovery of this "cavern" soon became one of the legends of the Old State House. Today the story has evolved to that of a mysterious tunnel, possibly used to travel from the State House to other buildings that once sat west of it. It is obvious by comparing accounts, however, that the 1883 cistern and the 1936 cavern are one and the same. The 1883 cistern was covered by the extension of the main building; the 1936 cavern was discovered extending from the west wall of the rear of the main building. The description of the 1883 cistern is of a cylindrical structure 12 x 40 feet; the description of the 1936 cavern is of an oval, capsule-shaped structure *12 x 40 feet!*

One more confirmation to the identity of the cistern was also provided by archeological work conducted in 1996–1997 as part of the restoration of the Old State House. Uncovered during the excavation was a remnant of the cistern partially covered by the west wall of the northern extension of the main building, just as would be expected from the documentary evidence. The size of the remnant matched that of the cistern. The legend of the mysterious tunnel can now be layed to rest.

As Jacob Frolich's term as secretary of state came to an end, it was obvious that the 50-year-old building was in need of more than just patchwork repairs and maintenance. Beyond structural issues, the business of state government had grown beyond the vision of territorial governor John Pope—more space was needed. The conscientious efforts of Secretary of State Frolich to care for, improve, and promote the State House laid the groundwork for the expansion that was to begin in 1885.

CHAPTER 6

The Expansion: 1885–1886

BY 1885 THE CONSTANT deterioration of the State House and the need for additional space could no longer be ignored. Early that year the Legislature approved $5,000 for repair, remodeling, and furnishing rooms in the east wing to be used by the Supreme Court. Shortly following that, and after years of pleading by the secretaries of state, the Legislature appropriated $30,000 for a major renovation to the entire building (Smyer 1976:29; Acts of Arkansas 1885:33–34,161–162). The renovation was under the supervision of Frolich's successor, Secretary of State Elias B. Moore.

Contractors Harding & Bailey won the bid for the renovation (*Arkansas Gazette*, July 28, 1885), and submitted detailed specifications of the work to be done (Harding & Bailey 1885). Among many minor details, the most important changes entailed removing the north portico of the main building, extending the building fifty feet to the north, and constructing permanent two-story buildings between the central building and the wings. These two-story additions are now known as the "hyphens." A description of the changes appeared in the *Arkansas Gazette:*

> The present senate chamber will be extended toward the river, and be converted into the hall of the house of representatives, while the house of representatives will become the senate chamber. The one-story rooms sandwiched in between the . . . main building and the wings will be run up another story, and a hall secured from the governor's office to the supreme judge's chamber.
>
> Four committee rooms will be secured by this improvement, and while the general arrangement of the rooms on the first floor will not be changed, still by the enlargement of the senate chamber two additional rooms will be secured below, which will be occupied by the land office. The first floor will be tiled, and it is believed by this plan the old state house will look much more respectable. (*Arkansas Gazette*, June 30, 1885)

A sketch of the floorplan was included in the article and showed the Senate Chamber in the south of the central building and the House Chamber in the north. The west wing would be occupied by the governor and secretary of state, with the library in the west hyphen. The Supreme Court library and judge's chambers would occupy the east wing, with committee rooms in the east hyphen.

Fig. 6.1: Secretary of State Elias B. Moore. *Courtesy of Shiloh Museum of Ozark History, Springdale, Arkansas.*

Fig. 6.2: Advertisement for architects Harding and Bailey. *Public domain.*

Construction details for the hyphens, or "connecting wings" as they were called by the contractors, were included in the contractors' specifications, as follows:

> The east wing showing in red lines will be taken down, and all the dirt removed. The ground will be excavated under that portion enclosed on the first floor plan, this excavation will be three feet deep below the bottom of the floor joist.
>
> The foundation will be rubble stone work 22 inches thick to the bottom of the joist, and will have a footing course three feet wide by 6" thick, the footing stones will all be the full width of the trench, this trench will be 18" below the general excavation.
>
> The superstructure walls will be brick, laid up as specified for the center building, the first story walls will be 18 inches and the second story 12 inches thick, arches will be turned as showing on plans, and a groove will be cut in the old walls where the new ones connect, a brick bearing wall will run through the center of the room on the first story, flues will be put in as shown on plan and will be well plastered. There will be a marbleized iron mantel, and a grate of the torrid patent put in the room in the first story, all flues will be furnished with 6" thimbles where required. (Harding & Bailey 1885:15–16)

Other improvements to the State House also were made. The central stairs in the main building were redesigned, blocking the side windows, and skylights were added to bring in more light (*Arkansas Gazette*, April 1, 1885 and January 6, 1886; Harding & Bailey 1885:13). Octagon skylights were placed in the Senate and House chambers as well (Harding & Bailey 1885:12). A vault was constructed (Harding & Bailey 1885:5–6), and boilers were installed to provide heat to the building (*Arkansas Gazette*, January 27 and 29, 1886).

Surprises and Mysteries

As work began surprises were encountered. Workmen discovered that the floor of the east wing was originally laid on brick over sand, a foundation they considered very odd (*Arkansas Gazette*, April 8, 1885). Other workmen found an 1826 justice-of-the-peace bill hidden behind a baseboard (*Arkansas Gazette*, April 10, 1885). When the north portico was being removed, the workmen were surprised to discover the columns were solid brick only halfway up and were hollow the remainder of their height (*Arkansas Gazette*, August 7, 1885).

The most unnerving discovery, however, was finding human burials at the rear of the State House on August 14, 1885:

> A discovery yesterday in the excavation at the rear of the state-house brought back the past in a vivid manner. As the workmen were shoveling away the dirt, some seven feet from the surface, the outline of a coffin was plainly discovered, pointing east and west. Not long afterwards another coffin outline was unearthed by its side, and still another, making three in all. The outlines were distinct, but all that was left of the coffins themselves was a few pieces of wood. As the excavation proceeded, in one grave was found a tooth, and a porous bone, evidently part of the pelvis of a human being; in another grave were found several pieces of bones, and half a dozen teeth in various stages of preservation. In the third grave, nearest the river, nothing was found. The contents of the coffin had returned to earth. The bones were carefully collected and taken into the state land office, where they are at present. (*Arkansas Gazette* August 15, 1885)

The find generated considerable interest among Little Rock's residents and "a good many persons called at the state-house . . . to see the surviving remnants" and to conjecture about the burials:

> The state-house was built over forty years ago, and among some of the old citizens there is a tradition handed down by their grandsires that about sixty or seventy years ago a family was camped at the spring, and there were deaths in it. It is said that they were quite a prominent family, in those early days, and had come to the spring for health, but that a man, his wife and their child died and were buried where the coffins were found. Tradition also says that other graves may be found in the state-house yard. (*Arkansas Gazette*, August 15, 1885)

A week later the paper carried a story provided by former Perry County treasurer W. G. Rankin, who identified the graves as those of his maternal grandparents, Edmond and Frances Jane Hogan, and their 15-year-old son. Rankin stated that his grandmother died in 1828 and his grandfather, credited with being the first settler in Pulaski County, died in 1831. He continued:

> In my younger days while growing up and after the state-house was built my mother frequently referred to the fact of her father and mother's early settlement in Arkansas and frequently told me that right where the state-house stood they and her brother were buried, and it has always been the impression with me that they were buried to themselves, that it did not become a common burying place. (*Arkansas Gazette*, August 22, 1885)

That potential solution to the mystery was soon questioned, for two other letters shortly followed suggesting that Rankin's memory was faulty. Instead, the writers noted, the Hogan family had moved from the vicinity of Little Rock to Crystal Hill in 1820 and that Edmond

Fig. 6.3: Artist's conception of the Old State House after the 1885 expansion, view from the river. The north portico was removed and the central building extended to the north, while the space between the buildings was enclosed as two-story additions. *Drawing by Ken Oberste, 1994, Old State House Museum Collection.*

Hogan had actually died in 1828 not 1831 (*Arkansas Gazette*, June 4, 1828, August 26, 1885, September 6, 1885, and January 19, 1959). Although this information did not conclusively contradict that the Hogan burials were where Rankin said they were, neither did it verify the identities of the deceased.

The Cornerstone

Although the question of the identities of the burials was never settled, it was decided that the remains would receive a fitting disposition by placing them in the new cornerstone of the addition. The fragments were placed in a small box, and the box was then "neatly tied with narrow black ribbon" (MacDuff 1949). Just a month later, the cornerstone was ready to be sealed and a ceremony was set for the afternoon of September 24. The northeast corner of the addition was chosen for the site of the ceremony, and the following items were placed in the cornerstone:

> There was a copy of the resolutions offered by Hon. W. M. Fishback in the legislature, stating his reasons for the adoption of the Fishback amendment; the bones and teeth found in the graves which were unearthed nearly beneath the cornerstone; three pieces of confederate money; an old war treasury warrant; an estimate of the cost of the additions by Messrs. Harding & Bailey, $13,377.15; the original plates from which the state treasury warrants were printed during the war; a large number of clippings from the state press of births, deaths, fires, proceedings of meetings of the agricultural wheel, etc.; autographs of the state officers on their official letter heads; a copy of *The Gazette,* containing the trade edition recently published; a copy of the Evening Democrat; a copy of the acts of the last general assembly; a copy of the last report of the secretary of state; a copy of the rules of the house of representatives; a roster of the state and county officers; a copy of the Arkansas Evangel . . . the names of Treasurer Woodruff and all the employees in his office on a treasury office letter head. And . . . a street car ticket, a nickel and a dime. (*Arkansas Gazette,* September 25, 1885)

Several statements expressing hope for the future also were placed in the cornerstone. The chancellor's office proffered: "To future generations—Let equity and good conscience be your guiding star in all transactions between man and man." The auditor's office suggested: "For the stability, purity and perpetuity of our state government, let us lean upon and trust in God, our strongest pillar and greatest support."

One individual, signed only R. B. W., offered the following pointed verse:

> When I am brought to light again,
> Oh, may this be the glad refrain,
> "The hall above is cleansed of roguery,
> Of buncombe, wind and demagoguery."

At 3:00 P.M. Governor Simon Hughes placed the cap on the cornerstone, sealing it, and "handled the trowel with the ease of an experienced mason." He followed with a speech praising the state's progress, after which Judge S. W. Williams spoke on the same theme. The *Arkansas Gazette* subtitled its article "What Was Put in the Stone for Future Generations to Puzzle Their Brains About," which might have been the case if the paper had not published an itemized list of the contents, although as it turned out, future generations were puzzled. The reporter ended with a sobering comment about the articles placed in the cornerstone: "Future generations will no doubt discover them some day unless the world comes to an end, as has been predicted."

The contents of the cornerstone indeed were rediscovered—during the 1949 restoration project—when they were removed. An article in the *Arkansas Gazette* by reporter Inez Hale MacDuff, who apparently was unaware of the 1885 article, misinterpreted the intent of the human remains and was flippantly critical of the efforts of the earlier state officials (MacDuff 1949). She began her article: "Any Arkansan who hankers to endear himself to posterity by depositing contemporary documents in the cornerstone of a public building may well heed the mistake made by State officials in 1885." She then provided a thirteen-point list of items found in the cornerstone. Most of the objects were identifiable although deteriorated, but MacDuff was puzzled by the human remains: "A small box, originally containing penpoints, in which several assorted teeth and bones and perhaps some ashes have been preserved. The box, neatly tied with narrow black ribbon, apparently was the 1885 idea of a practical joke." At the end of the article, MacDuff concluded:

> And that's all. Not a photograph. Not an official document. Not a smidgen of information about the historic and beautiful building which they had gathered to honor.
>
> Worst of all, the articles were not enclosed in a metal box, as is customary in such instances, but were placed loosely in a hollow in the stone. Since limestone is porous and admits moisture, most of the paper has deteriorated until it cannot be unfolded or touched. The footprints on the sands of time not only are meaningless after 64 years, but they're scarcely legible.
>
> The moral is plain: if you want posterity to gape when your handiwork comes to light in the

> distant future, take pains to preserve it in an air-tight container. Otherwise posterity may merely sneeze among the mouldering ruins of your memoirs. (MacDuff 1949)

Perhaps if MacDuff had done her research, she would have been a bit more respectful of the efforts of the 1885 officials.

Wrapping Up the Work

Work continued on the State House through the rest of 1885 and into the first months of 1886. A short note in the *Arkansas Gazette* (February 16, 1886) announced that the front of the building would be updated with galvanized iron, and that the three figures of Law, Justice, and Mercy that had been brought back from the 1876 Centennial Exposition would be the finishing touch. Prior to placement the statues were stored in a first-floor room, and one afternoon gave four girls a severe fright. The girls were wandering through the building, looking at the improvements, when they accidentally got locked into the room with the statues. As the story continued:

> The girls discovered the lay figures in the dim light, and one of them shrieked. They rushed for the door, and when they could not get out, became frantic. There was no way to escape from the horrible ghosts except through the window and the four girls went pell-mell through the window crashing through glass and frame, getting quite severe cuts. (*Arkansas Gazette*, February 28, 1886)

In April a contract was awarded to James Abbott to build an armory on the grounds at a cost of $1,185.00 (*Arkansas Gazette*, April 25, 1886). Sanborn insurance maps from the period show the armory in the northeast corner of the State House grounds directly behind the east wing. By July contracts for new carpets and furniture also had been awarded (*Arkansas Gazette*, July 15, 1886).

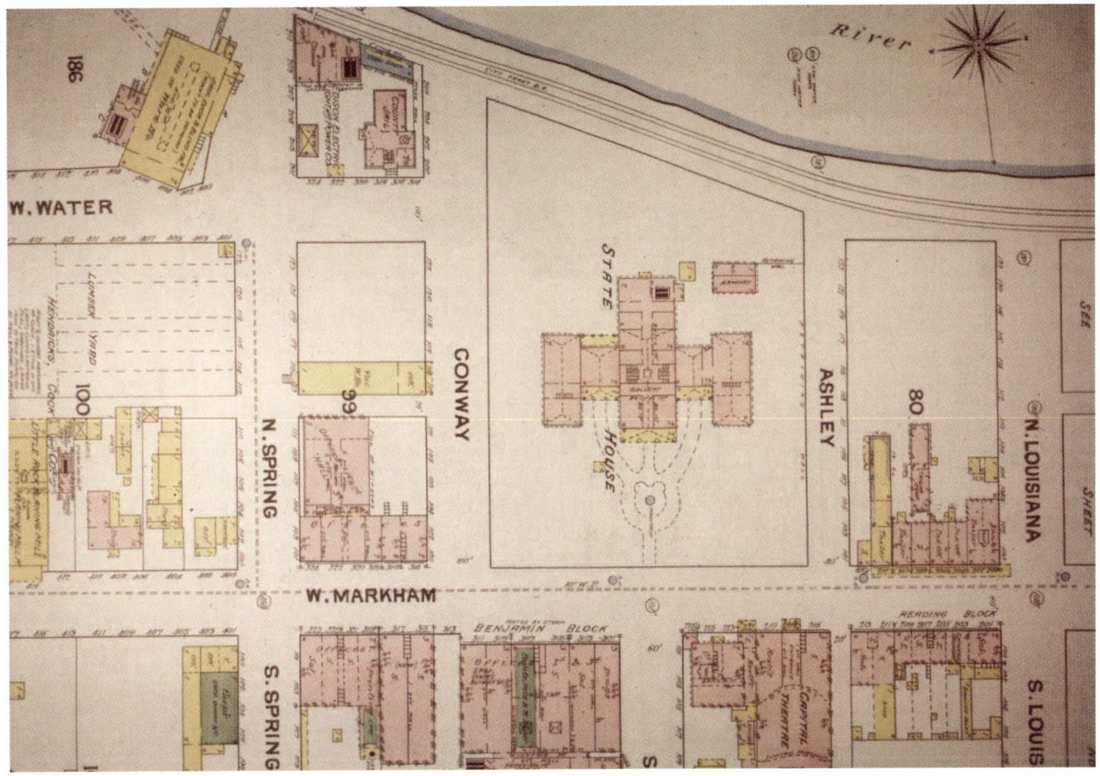

Fig. 6.4: The post-1885 configuration of the Old State House and the new armory to the northeast can be seen on this 1889 Sanborn Insurance Map. *Photograph courtesy of Arkansas Archeological Survey.*

The expanded State House was now ready to begin its second period of use. Secretary of State Elias Moore praised the Legislature for the work that had been accomplished:

> Through the generosity of the last Legislature an appropriation was made for the repairs of the State House, which not only provided for office room within the State House for each State official, but which gave me much additional valuable space for the Library. (Moore 1886:10)

Moore also noted the beauty of the State House grounds, planted several additional shade trees, and praised the work of the gardener. He added:

> I believe that the grounds around the State House are used as a place of rest and enjoyment by more people from all parts of the State than

Fig. 6.5: The 1887 perspective map of Little Rock shows the Old State House in the expanded configuration we know today. The grounds on the north side are landscaped, and the building overlooks both the Arkansas River and railroad tracks. *Courtesy of Geography and Map Division, U.S. Library of Congress.*

> any Park in the city. During the summer months there is hardly a day passes that all the seats are not filled by sun-burned men and ruddy women from various localities. The reflex influence of well kept and tastily arranged grounds here cannot but be of untold value upon the arrangement of private grounds throughout the State. (Moore 1886:13)

Two years later a drawing in the *Arkansas Gazette* (December 23, 1888) illustrated the State House after renovations. The center section can be seen with the three statues perched on the roof and a flag proudly flying behind them. The wings and hyphens are largely hidden by the shade trees, and the Lady Baxter cannon, nestled next to two benches, points toward the town. The grounds are surrounded by a neat iron fence, and visitors stroll nearby.

The expansion of the State House should have inspired pride among the state's legislators and residents, but no sooner was the work completed than the rumblings for a new capitol began. As slowly as the wheels of legislative worked turned, however, the State House would serve state government for another 25 years.

Fig. 6.6: This sketch of the Old State House appeared in the *Arkansas Gazette* on December 23, 1888. The figures on the roof, the state seal, and the Lady Baxter cannon can be seen in the illustration. Trees hide the 1885 improvements. *Old State House Museum Collection.*

CHAPTER 7

The Middle Years: 1886–1911

Fig. 7.1: Even in the early twentieth century, the Old State House was an attraction for visitors and a place of pride, as this postcard mailed in 1907 attests. *Courtesy of Gail Moore Stephens.*

ALTHOUGH THE RENOVATIONS of 1885–1886 solved many of the space problems for state officials, the expansion still was not quite enough. In his 1886 report Secretary of State Elias B. Moore, while praising the Legislature for the appropriation that had financed the expansion, pointed out the still cramped condition of the state library. With 20,000 books in the library, volumes were stacked two deep on some shelves, and the Journal Room and Store Room were packed beyond capacity. Moore requested an additional appropriation from the Legislature to physically extend the library room toward the back of the building (Moore 1886:10–11), and when it was not forthcoming he repeated the request in 1888 (Moore 1888:10).

With the State House now over fifty years old and the nineteenth century coming to a close, the wisdom of pouring money into an aging and out-dated building began to be questioned. The idea of building a new capitol was starting to gain ground. As early as December 1888, in the same issue of the *Arkansas Gazette* (December 23, 1888) that had printed the drawing of the State House expansion, the promise of a new capitol sounded like a done deal: "It is an old edifice, but will do very well a few years more. When Arkansas erects her new state-house, it will be one of the best and handsomest in the union." By early 1889 calls were coming from other parts of the state to build a new capitol (*Arkansas Gazette,* January 26, 1889), and into the 1890s the discussion remained of perennial interest.

The problem was, now that the idea of a new capitol building was in the minds of the legislators, they immediately became reluctant to expend funds on the old State House. Despite the fact that it would take another 25 years to actually make the decision and appropriate the money for a new capitol, as long as discussion continued no substantial amount of money would be expended on the old building.

So, as state government outgrew the space contained in the State House, the Legislature failed to appropriate even the minimum needed to meet yearly maintenance and repairs. They must have believed the new capital was soon to be, but a quarter of a century was a long time to wait.

Annoying the Secretaries of State

By 1890, just four years after the building's expansion, Secretary of State Benjamin B. Chism complained to the Legislature that repairs were constantly required. Already he'd had to repair gutters, lay new tile, repaint part of the roof, overhaul the heating apparatus, and make repairs in the auditor's office, where "valuable records, that money could not replace, were being fast destroyed by foul and fetid exhalations from the rotten floor and the damp earth beneath" (Chism 1891:12). Chism had quickly run through most of the $1,600 the General Assembly had appropriated for a two-year period, spending more than a third of it on the repairs and nearly another third for the water bill. And nothing had yet been done about expanding the library (Chism 1891:12–13, 15).

The General Assembly increased the appropriation for the care and repair of the State House to $2,000 for the next two-year period, but repairs were almost a daily occurrence, and the funds were still not sufficient. In addition, the Supreme Court had been increased to five judges in 1899, but there were no vacant offices to accommodate the new judges. As a temporary measure the judges were assigned use of the legislative committee rooms—but only when the General Assembly was not in session. Chism scolded: "This ought not be. The Judges of the Supreme Court should have permanent apartments for their exclusive use. I regret that I have been a second time compelled to call attention to this matter" (Chism 1893:12–14). Only a second time? It appears that Chism still had a lot to learn about the Legislature's traditional glacial pace in matters regarding the State House, but his impatience was certainly justified.

Fig. 7.2: Secretary of State Benjamin B. Chism. *Courtesy of Arkansas History Commission.*

Fig. 7.3: Secretary of State Henry B. Armistead. *Courtesy of Arkansas History Commission.*

When Henry B. Armistead became secretary of state in 1893, the problems remained, but it may have taken him through his first biennium to realize the extent of them, since he made no mention of the State House in his 1895 report. By 1896 things had only gotten worse, and Armistead pleaded with the Legislature:

> The Secretary has been unable for lack of funds to make any permanent improvement in the

Fig. 7.4: Secretary of State Alex Hull. *Courtesy of Arkansas History Commission.*

> State House, or to ornament or adorn the grounds. The entire appropriation has been consumed in patching and repairing the building and as far as possible rendering it habitable and comfortable. The boilers used in generating steam for heating the building are worn out and valueless, and there being no money to buy new ones, it was necessary to put stoves in all the rooms of the State House, which have proven unsatisfactory. It is hoped the next General Assembly will provide for the purchase of new boilers, and the building of a boiler house so that the capitol can be again heated by steam or hot air. (Armistead 1896:4)

The library was in dire straits with the holdings now exceeding 50,000 volumes, making one wonder if the walls had been constructed of rubber, considering the extent to which the room was expected to expand. Armistead may have been hoping to scare the legislators into action when he reported: "The northwest room is crowded to such an extent as to render access to many valuable books and records there stored well nigh impracticable, and the weight on the floor and walls is so enormous that the safety of the Governor and other officials occupying the rooms above is endangered" (Armistead 1896:4).

Lack of space had been a problem for the regular occupants of the building for some time, but it was finally beginning to affect the legislators: "There is but one small room for the use of the committees of the General Assembly, and these committees are often subjected to great inconvenience and serious loss of time in a search of some place in which to hold their meetings" (Armistead 1896:5). Armistead offered a well-reasoned, but desperate, solution:

> At an outlay of a sum not exceeding $5,000 the library building could be extended north fifty feet. The lower story of this extension would afford all the room required for the library for years to come, and the upper story could be divided into three or four convenient and comfortable committee rooms. The labor required for this improvement can be largely done by the State convicts, so that nearly all the actual outlay would be for the material required for the addition. (Armistead 1896:5)

The continual pleas to the General Assembly to provide funds for another expansion of the building seemed to fall on deaf ears, although the legislators were not really ignoring the problem. For the past four years the construction of a new state capitol had been under serious discussion (*Arkansas Gazette,* January 17, 1893; Armistead 1896:291). The Legislature understandably was reluctant to put money into the old building pending the possible decision to build a new one, but as the discussion dragged on, the deterioration of the State House continued to mount.

By 1898 Secretary of State Alex Hull was faced with maintaining the building on a reduced budget of only $1,250. With repairs needed on nearly a weekly basis, he must have had to pinch pennies to make ends meet. Unexpected problems took an even larger bite out of the meager allotment, with repairs needed to a collapsed corner of the brick armory and replacement of the pipes in the restrooms (Hull 1898:5). The roof was an even worse problem:

> Among the largest expenditures that might be enumerated, was the painting of the roof, which became necessary in order to save the roof sufficiently intact to protect the offices from serious damage. But the roof has been patched up and repaired about as long as it will bear, and I think it would be well for the legislature to provide for a new one, as it is a waste of money to make further repairs on it. (Hull 1898:5)

Following the lead of his predecessors, Hull also recommended an extension to the library, which had grown to hold 60,000 volumes. Besides overcrowding, the rooms were damp and the books were being damaged by mildew and insects. Many volumes needed to be rebound. Hull pointed out that even those offered for sale were damaged, and "no one wants to pay full price for such mutilated books." With proper attention to the library, he snapped, "it may become a pride rather than the unseemly mass of rubbish which it now is" (Hull 1898:6–8).

Two years later, when the Legislature still had not come through with the needed funds to alleviate the building's problems, Hull's report indicated a much-annoyed secretary of state:

> The duties devolving upon the custodian of the State House and Grounds are by no means light or pleasant, but in reality are very annoying. Since I have been in charge the Legislature has appropriated only $1,250 for each two years term as a Care and Repair Fund, and I have been unable because of lack of funds to make any permanent improvements on the house, or to make additional ornamentations on the grounds. By judicious and economical use of means at hand, I have managed to do the necessary amount of patching and repairing on the building to keep it reasonably comfortable and habitable for the various departments. But the roof is so old and worn that it is almost impossible to keep the different departments dry. For the preservation and safety of the valuable records and papers of the

Fig. 7.5: In 1903 the State Land Office occupied what is now known as the Riverfront Room on the first floor of the central building. Note the lighting and heating systems. *Old State House Museum Collection.*

Fig. 7.6: Attorney General George W. Murphy, with his daughter Elizabeth Murphy Armistead, in Murphy's office in the Old State House. Murphy served as attorney general from 1901 to 1905. The Victorian-era wallpaper indicates that interior decor changed with the times. *Old State House Museum Collection.*

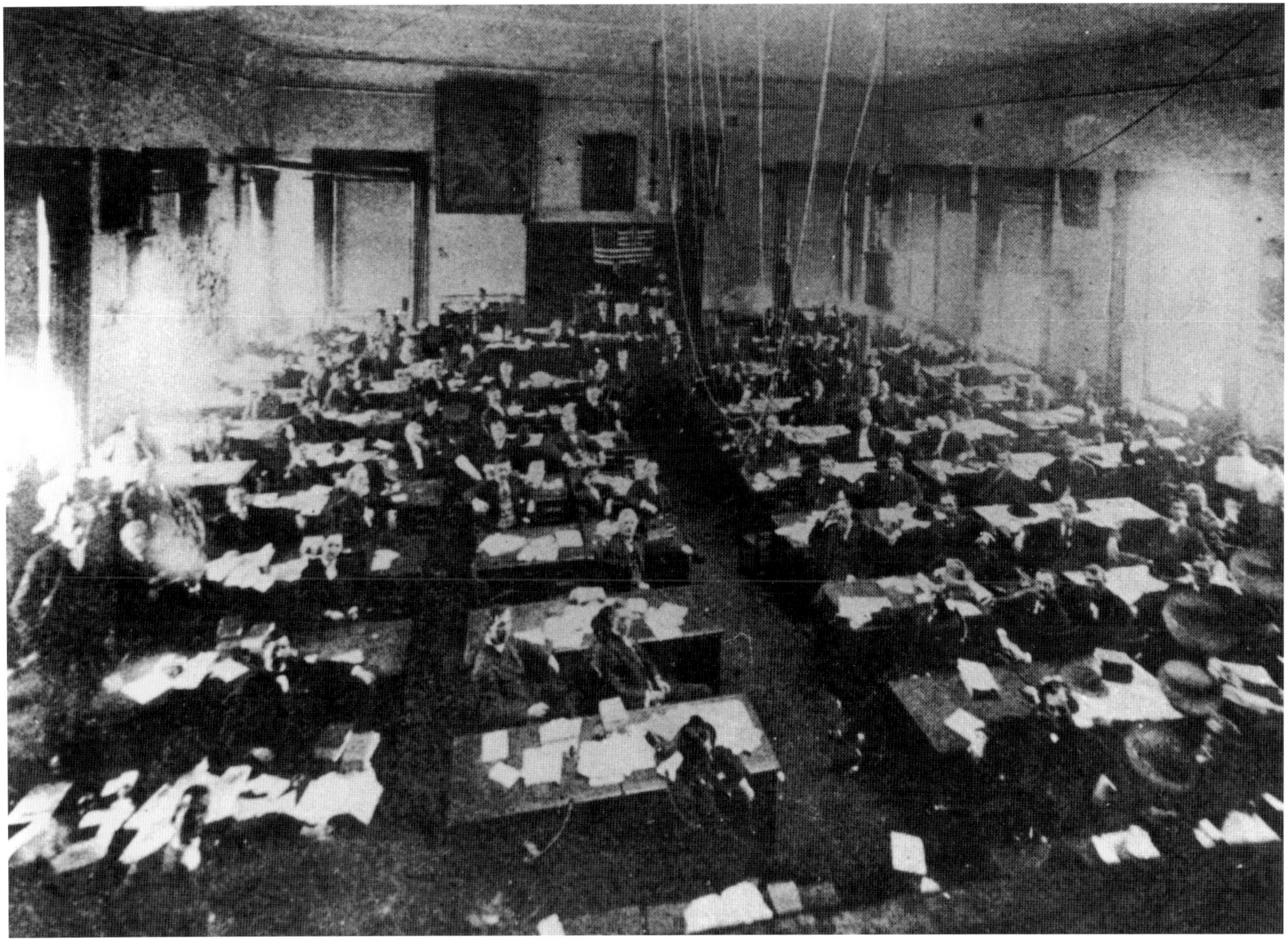

Fig. 7.7: Legislators occupy the Chamber of the House of Representatives in 1909. *Old State House Museum Collection.*

State, I would suggest to the Legislature the necessity of providing for a new roof, even for use during the next five or six years, until, it is hoped, the new Capitol building will be ready for occupancy. It is, and has been for four years, a waste of money to try to keep the old roof repaired. (Hull 1900:4)

Hull's assessment of the condition of the library was no kinder:

> I hardly know what to suggest in the line of enlarging and improving the condition of the library. Unless something is done the State is bound to sustain very great loss by reason of damage to the books, many of which are very valuable. I can only renew my recommendation of two years ago, that more library room should be provided. . . . The enormous weight on the floor and walls very greatly endanger the safety of the west wing of the building. It is absolutely necessary that additional room be provided. . . . If not done the responsibility is with the Legislatures of the past ten years, for my predecessors, as well as myself, have recommended and urged that something be done. (Hull 1900:5)

The Legislature's reluctance to put money into major repairs for the State House continued to be understandable, even if their dreams for a new capitol were overly optimistic. After finally paying off a large portion of the state's debt, the General Assembly could begin serious consideration of how to finance the new capitol building. Opposition to a new capitol continued until January 12, 1899, when the plaster ceiling in the Senate Chamber, waterlogged after several days of rain, collapsed on the senators, injuring several of them. The General Assembly began work on legislation authorizing the construction of a new capitol the very next day, the resolution passed February 13, 1899, and on July 4, 1899, the groundbreaking ceremony for the new capitol was held (Donaghey 1937:8, 25; Treon 1972:99–101).

An Uncertain Future

As the efforts of the legislators turned to the concerns of a new capitol, the Old State House entered a period of uncertainty about its future. Problems arose almost immediately with the new building's construction, and it took 12½ years from the groundbreaking until the legislature moved to the new Capitol. Those years were beset with an almost unending controversy over the new building, which included political obstructionism, charges of fraud and bribery, legal actions, and changes of governors and capitol commissioners. The whole sordid affair is well described in Governor George Donaghey's book, *Building a State Capitol* (1937). With a million dollars initially appropriated to the construction, but over twice that amount ultimately expended, the legislators' reluctance to spend money on the Old State House is understandable. Work on the new building didn't make appreciable headway until Donaghey became governor in 1909, but his discovery that state expenditures were exceeding revenues resulted in a nearly 40 percent budget cut in the first two years of his administration that could only have exacerbated the situation (Williams and Whayne 2000:86).

With funds badly needed for the construction, talk of selling the Old State House began.

Fig. 7.8: Secretary of State John W. Crockett. *Courtesy of Arkansas History Commission.*

Fig. 7.9: Secretary of State Oswald C. Ludwig. *Courtesy of Arkansas History Commission.*

Fig. 7.10: Governor George W. Donaghey. *Old State House Museum Collection.*

Fig. 7.11: Acting governor X. O. Pindall and other officials in an air-cooled Franklin car in front of the Old State House, ca. 1908. Included in the group are Secretary of State Oswald C. Ludwig, Commissioner of Mines, Manufactures, and Agriculture Guy B. Tucker, and U.S. senator James P. Clarke. *Old State House Museum Collection.*

As early as 1901 the General Assembly passed an act relative to the new capitol that included a section authorizing disposal of the old building and division of its grounds into sellable lots (Brown et al. 1978:6). Yet, while construction on the new building was underway, the old building continued to serve state government and thus required a certain amount of care and upkeep. In his 1902 report Secretary of State John W. Crockett reiterated the building's problems:

> Recently the roof of the entire building has been repaired and painted, as the rains in many

> instances penetrated the various rooms; and almost every wall is discolored and mildewed from the perpetual dampness. To renew the building and make it an official home of which the state should feel proud would require, in my opinion, a very large appropriation. (Crockett 1903:14)

Both Crockett and his successor, Oswald C. Ludwig, served as secretaries for the First and Second Capitol Commissions, and so must have been resigned to the fact that with a new capitol under construction nothing more than stop-gap maintenance and repairs of the old building would be funded by the Legislature. Neither made much mention of the State House in their biennial reports (Crockett 1903, 1905; Ludwig 1906, 1909).

Ludwig apparently sided with the opponents to Governor Donaghey's plans, however, and when Donaghey wanted to hold the first session of the 1911 General Assembly in the new but not completely finished Capitol, Ludwig debated him in the papers. Donaghey inspected the House and Senate chambers in the Old State House and reported to the papers that they were in "a deplorably dilapidated condition." He detailed that the carpets "in both are mildewed and moth eaten and most of the plastering has fallen since the adjournment of the Assembly two years ago." Donaghey went on to describe the appearance of the Senate Chamber as "that of an abandoned coal bin" (Donaghey 1937:270).

Ludwig charged that spending money to put light and heat in an unfinished building was bad business, but Donaghey countered his charges with reasonable explanations. So Ludwig dug in his heels, announcing that he would prepare the rooms in the Old State House for the General Assembly, placing the desks and chairs "in position as they have been since 1836, when the territory of Arkansas was admitted to the Union" and that he did not intend "to deviate one jot or tittle from the precedent set by his predecessors in office" (Donaghey 1937:272).

Donaghey responded that as Ludwig was custodian of the State House, "any arrangements that he may make around the old State House are entirely his own affair. As chairman of the State Capitol Commission, it is my duty to have the new Capitol ready for the occupancy of the legislature. This will be done. It will then be up to the members of the legislature to decide where they wish to convene" (Donaghey 1937:273).

On January 8, 1911, both the Senate and the House met in the House Chamber of the Old State House for the last time. After a long debate, they voted 60 to 40 to move to the new building. Donaghey immediately arranged for all furniture and fixtures to be hauled by wagons to the new Capitol, where all was made ready in time for the Thirty-eighth General Assembly to convene at 10:00 A.M. on January 9, 1911 (Donaghey 1937:273–274). This act signaled the official end of the Old State House as the seat of Arkansas government, although it would be four more years until the new Capitol was fully completed.

The Old State House had served nobly through 75 years of the state's birth and growth, and now the state had outgrown it. As it faced the first years of the twentieth century, the fate of the Old State House was still undetermined.

CHAPTER 8

Reuse and Transformation: 1911–1951

AFTER THE GENERAL ASSEMBLY moved to the new Capitol in January 1911, the legislators continued to struggle with the fate of the Old State House and would continue to do so for the next ten years. It was not until 1921 that preservation of the Old State House was ensured by an act of law. From 1901, when the first calls for preservation were made, to 1921 the legislators waffled about preserving the State House or selling it to replenish state funds. Many of those who did want to sell the building, however, also wanted to delay the sale to wait for the value of the property to increase (Brown et al. 1978:6, 28, 32). That delay provided the time necessary to build a preservation movement.

Historic Preservation and Women's Patriotic Associations

The first threat to the building came in 1901 with Act 132, which permitted the sale of the Old State House and the division of the grounds into lots to be sold. A wave of protest erupted from state residents and members of patriotic organizations, but as long as the building was still being used by state government, no action was taken. During the early years of the twentieth century, the building was not necessarily viewed as a historic structure, but rather

Fig. 8.1: The Old State House as it appeared about 1911 after the General Assembly moved to the new Capitol building. *Courtesy of Butler Center for Arkansas Studies, Central Arkansas Library System.*

as a state office building that had outlived its usefulness. Legislators felt that the sale of the building would provide funds to improve the state's financial condition. At the same time, an interest in historic preservation was beginning to grow, spawned by the success of the Mount Vernon Ladies' Association in preserving George Washington's home. Much of the early preservation movement came out of women's patriotic associations, such as the Daughters of the American Revolution and the United Daughters of the Confederacy, who viewed the preservation of historic sites as shrines to encourage patriotism (Brown et al. 1978:1–6).

In 1906 at their annual meeting, the Arkansas Federation of Women's Clubs resolved to back preservation of the Old State House, which coalesced the preservation efforts into a unified force. The Federation's resolution included the first suggestion that the building be used as a historical museum. In 1907 the Colonial Dames, the Arkansas Historical Association, and the Arkansas Historical Society* pushed for a state bill to preserve the State House. In February of the same year, the Arkansas Historical and Memorial Association was formed for the purpose of preserving the State House and beginning a museum. The following year the Arkansas Federation of Women's Clubs elected Sara Van Patten Ellsworth as president, and she led a strong effort on behalf of the building, which included targeting legislators (Brown et al. 1978:8–11; Hanger and Eno 1935:42, 48, 204). After the state elections in 1908, the Federation sent copies of a letter written by Clara B. Eno to each senator and representative urging preservation of the Old State House. As Eno stated:

> It is the desire of the women of Arkansas that the state preserve the Historic Old State House, where for nearly three-quarters of a century the laws and history of the state have been made. We wish it as a valuable heirloom to be handed down to a future generation and where the relics can be kept which are fast disappearing from the state for the want of a proper receptacle. . . . It is said that Wisconsin has more papers and charts of Arkansas than we possess. And why? Because they have proper buildings in which to house them. Arkansas will be able to do it also if we can preserve the old State House. (Hanger and Eno 1935:207)

Various organizations continued to support preservation during these early years. The Daughters of the American Revolution and the United Daughters of the Confederacy continued their activism for preservation of the Old State House and were joined in their efforts by the Arkansas Pioneers Association and the United States Daughters of 1812. Mrs. John Barrow, president of the latter in 1909, stated in the *Arkansas Gazette* that it was up to women to plan for the future as men were too involved in the present to have the vision to do what would benefit their children and grandchildren (Brown et al. 1978:11–16, 24). The Arkansas Federation of Women's Clubs also sent a petition to the General Assembly in 1909 that cited 4,000 members requesting that the legislators "preserve to the State the classic old State House" as a "home for relics, records, and whatever of value may pertain to the history of the state" (Hanger and Eno 1935:205–206; Shank 1977:14, 16–17).

Other women's patriotic associations also went directly to the legislators. For example, Mrs. Josie Cappleman, a member of the United Daughters of the Confederacy, addressed a joint session of the General Assembly in 1911 and spoke for 40 minutes on the preservation of the Old State House and the need for a historical museum. Another key supporter was Elizabeth McConaughey Wassell, a member of the United States Daughters of 1812. Elizabeth was the wife of Samuel S. Wassell, who's father, John Wassell, had done much of the carpentry on the Old State House during its construction (Brown et al. 1978:18–19, 24; Cantrell 1900:40–41).

During this period various bills for the preservation or repair of the building were introduced in the House and Senate, but despite the best efforts of their supporters, none passed. Neither did the bills of those desiring to sell the building, so the Old State House was caught in a stalemate (Brown et al. 1978:13, 14, 28). As the General Assembly moved the seat of state government to the new Capitol in January 1911, the need to save the Old State House became more urgent. In order to better coordinate the efforts of all the associations and individuals working for the building's preservation, the Current Events Club of Little Rock called a meeting on March 23, 1912, the results of which created the State Historical Museum Association. The meeting was held in the Old State House in the office of the commissioner of state lands, now the Riverfront Room, which became the headquarters of the new association. Its main objective was to prevent the sale or destruction of the Old State House and transform the building into a repository for relics, manuscripts, and mementos. The organ-

* There were numerous and short-lived organizations over the years that went by the name "Arkansas Historical Society" (Sherwood 1952).

izers also had a new idea: Rather than continue to ask the legislators to appropriate money for the building, they wanted the legislators to *give* the building to three organizations—the Daughters of the American Revolution, the United Daughters of the Confederacy, and the United States Daughters of 1812—who would serve as custodians and raise funds for its preservation. The Historical Museum Association promoted the formation of local branches and auxiliary boards and was successful in securing support from the Democratic and Republican state conventions, the Arkansas Bar Association, and the Arkansas Press Association. Probably their most effective action, however, was the selection of Secretary of State Earle Hodges as their president (Brown et al. 1978:21–23, 31).

The secretary of state had always been a key figure in the oversight of the State House, and Earl Hodges proved to be a strong ally for the building's preservation. He was outspoken about the preservation of the building and took direct action to keep the State House safe. When Governor George Donaghey vetoed the appropriation by the Legislature for care of the building, Hodges paid for some expenses out of his own pocket and borrowed the salary of the day watchman-groundskeeper from the Southern Trust Company until the Legislature could remedy the situation (Hodges 1913:9). Hodges weighed in on the need to protect the building until some decision was made as to its disposition:

> No insurance is carried on this structure, and as, on account of the lack of an appropriation, no night watchman is employed, the building is in constant danger of being destroyed by fire.

Fig. 8.2: Secretary of State Earle Hodges. *Courtesy of Arkansas History Commission.*

> Whether or not the State is to retain the property, and regardless of what it is to be used for, the building should be insured, and, too, a night watchman employed, and I recommend that the Legislature make such provisions. (Hodges 1913:9–10)

Despite his concession to the uncertain future of the building, Hodges was direct in stating his support for preserving the State House:

> I am heartily in favor of the preservation of this old State House. I believe that it is the one sacred landmark of the State's greatness, and to barter it for a few shekels with which to replenish our depleted coffers is not only to forsake the teachings and traditions of our fathers, but is to "sell our birthright for a mess of pottage." (Hodges 1913:10)

Suggestions for the use of the building came from many quarters. The *Arkansas Democrat* thought the State Historical Society should have use of the building for a museum, while allowing patriotic organizations to each have a room to furnish and maintain. Dallas Herndon of the State History Commission suggested the building be used by women's clubs, while serving as the headquarters for his agency. The State Historical Museum Association added support for an exhibit hall in the building to advertise agricultural and mineral products from each county, and a bill was introduced in the House of Representatives in 1913 to move the Department of Mines, Manufactures and Agriculture to the Old State House to maintain the building and collect exhibits. The Legislature, however, took no action on any of these suggestions (Brown et al. 1978:25–27).

Home for the Medical School

While discussions as to the fate of the Old State House were ongoing, the vacated building was left to the superintendence of Secretary Hodges. Since direct appeals had failed, Hodges slipped through the back door with a solution. As soon as the legislators had abandoned the building in 1911, Hodges wasted no time in locating agencies and organizations wanting space in the building, which he gave them in exchange for maintaining their assigned areas at their own expense. Once the deed was done, the legislators acquiesced, passing House Concurrent

Resolution #8 in March 1913, which officially gave rent-free space to the United States Agriculture Department, the University of Arkansas law and medical departments, the State Historical Museum Association, and the Arkansas Humane Society—agencies that were already occupying the building thanks to Hodges. The resolution also permitted use of the building by the Arkansas Division of the United Daughters of the Confederacy and the United Confederate Veterans and stated that the building and grounds should neither be sold nor disposed of in any way (Brown et al. 1978:30–32).

The 1913 resolution was only a temporary reprieve, but it was enough to keep the Old State House in existence. In his report for 1913–1914, Hodges stated:

> The final disposition of the old State House is now, as it was two years ago, a matter of general interest. My candid opinion is that no effort will ever again be made to dispose of the building "on the auction block," the money received from such a sale to be turned into the State Treasury and paid out immediately; building and grounds gone forever, money gone; although there were several such plans being formulated in 1911. But the good people of the State, led by the ladies, who are always to the front in matters that concern our material welfare, rose up solidly in opposition to such ideas and stated in no uncertain terms that the sacred old landmark must not be sold. The result is that the building still stands, as a heritage of the past, bringing us memories of glories of other days. (Hodges 1915:6)

Hodges then went on to make recommendations for the future:

> The appropriation made for necessary repairs on the old Capitol building was used judiciously, and much good has been done in the way of preserving the building, but other repairs are badly needed at this time. The building should be insured against fire, something which has never been done in the past, and put in a good state of repair, and a night and day watchman should be employed for the grounds. (Hodges 1915:6)

While the legislators continued to allow no money for the maintenance of the building, numerous agencies were willing to maintain their areas at their own expense in exchange for office space. In addition, not all of state government abandoned the building in 1911, since offices in the new Capitol were completed gradually over a number of years. The State Land Commission and State Insurance Commission moved out of the Old State House in 1912, followed the next year by the State Library, State Treasurer, and State Supreme Court. As most state departments left the Old State House, others moved in. The State Tax Commission had an office in the Old State House from 1913 to 1915, and the State Serum Plant arrived in 1918 and remained through the 1920s (Brown et al. 1978:47–48, 59).

The U.S. Department of Agriculture Extension Service had offices in the building from 1911 to 1918, which included their agriculture and geology exhibits. The University of Arkansas Law Department used rooms in the Old State House from 1911 to 1915. In 1912 the Railroad Commission, the Arkansas Humane Society, and the State Historical Museum Association began occupancy. The Railroad Commission stayed until 1915, and the Humane Society remained until the end of the decade (Brown et al. 1978:47–50, 53).

The Old State House also served as a focus of patriotic and historical meetings and activities. The local women's clubs that had been instrumental in the preservation effort held their monthly meetings in the building, and the Arkansas Pioneers Association offered to beautify the grounds. In 1911 the United Confederate Veterans sponsored that year's Confederate Reunion, and the Old State House served as the registration headquarters and site of a concert and parade reviewing stand (Brown et al. 1978:53, 56, 60).

The most important occupant of the Old State House during this period was the Medical Department of the University of Arkansas, which occupied the east wing and central building from 1912 to 1935 for its classrooms, laboratories, store rooms, and offices (Shank 1977:20–41). Had the Medical School not needed the available space of the Old State House—and occupied it for nearly 25 years—the fate of the Old State House might have been different.

The Medical School was founded in 1879 by the State Medical Society. It became an independent department of Arkansas Industrial University (now the University of Arkansas at Fayetteville), but without any financial support from the university. Through the support of eight founders, enough money was raised to purchase a hotel building on west Second Street, which served as the school in its early years. In 1911, following recommendations by the American Medical Association to improve the standards for medical education, the state merged the UA Medical Department with the College of Physicians and Surgeons, a competing school in Little Rock. With new oversight by

Fig. 8.3: The Arkansas Medical School occupied the Old State House from 1912 to 1935. This photograph was taken about 1918. *Courtesy of Historical Research Center, University of Arkansas for Medical Sciences.*

the university, the Medical School began to receive regular, but limited, appropriations. The following year, the school moved into the Old State House (Puryear 2006).

During the quarter century the Medical School made its home in the Old State House, rooms were remodeled to suit the school's needs. Windows and skylights were added and large rooms divided, as various departments moved in and out of the spaces. The Medical School first occupied the east wing. On the first floor were the laboratories for General Chemistry, and Organic and Physiological Chemistry, as well as an office and lecture hall. On the second floor of the east wing, rooms were used by the Department of Anatomy and Histology, and the Department of Physiology, which included offices, research laboratories, a lecture room, a dissecting room, and a museum (Shank 1977:20–27).

Within the first year of occupancy, the Medical School expanded from the east wing into the central building. On the first floor of the central building were laboratories of Physiological Chemistry and Organic Chemistry, two lecture rooms, the bookstore, and the dean's office. On the second floor, there was a general assembly hall, a library, the museum of the Department of Pathology and Bacteriology, as well as additional laboratories, including one for aseptic animal work used by Physiology and Pharmacology. The State Board of Health also maintained a Hygienic Lab in this area. In 1919 the Hygienic Lab moved to the east wing, and in 1923 the lab of the Department of Physiology moved to the west wing. On the third floor of the central building, the balcony of the House of Representatives was used as a labora-

Fig. 8.4: Part of the gallery above the House Chamber was converted into a pathology laboratory for the Medical School. Doctoral students are seen performing small-animal surgery, ca. 1925. *Courtesy of Historical Research Center, University of Arkansas for Medical Sciences.*

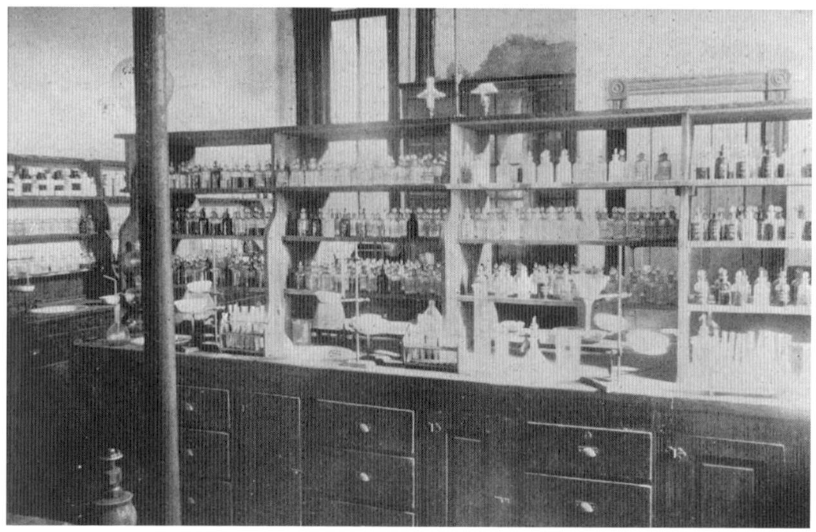

Fig. 8.5: The Chemistry Work Bench held numerous bottles of chemicals and drugs. Fragments of similar bottles were found during archeological excavations of the Old State House grounds. *Courtesy of Historical Research Center, University of Arkansas for Medical Sciences.*

tory for surgical technique beginning in 1915. By 1923 it served as the lab for Pharmacology, and in 1928 it became the incinerator room (Shank 1977:28–38).

The west wing was the least used by the Medical School. On the first floor was a pharmaceutical laboratory, library, classroom, and office, as well as the State Veterinarian's Office. The physiology laboratory moved to the second floor in 1923 and a pharmacology lab was also housed there, but after 1928 the space was occupied by the offices of the American Legion. After educating two generations of Arkansas doctors, the Old State House finally was vacated by the Medical School in 1935 when funds were received from the Works Progress Administration (WPA) to build a new medical facility across from MacArthur Park (Puryear 2006; Shank 1977:39–41).

Because of its long occupancy it would be expected that the Medical School would have left some mark upon the grounds of the Old State House—and, in fact, it did. During the archeological excavations of 1996–1997 prior to the restoration of the Old State House, archeologists found a number of artifacts that most likely represent trash from the Medical School. Most of these artifacts were parts of glass laboratory equipment, such as fragments of test tubes of various sizes, pipettes for removing small amounts of liquid, stirring rods, syringe barrels marked with gradations, and thermometers. Other glass fragments probably came from Petri dishes, beakers, or bottles. The lips from some bottle fragments were designed with a pouring spout or slanted inward to keep medicine from spilling. Unglazed porcelain or ceramic sherds probably were fragments of mortars used to grind medicines. Six metal syringe hubs—one still containing its needle—were also found (Guendling and Kwas 1997:94–95).

One artifact the archeologists found predated the Medical School, but still was related to Little Rock's medical community. This was a portion of a colorless glass medicine bottle, embossed with the company name of McALMONT & GIBSON. John J. McAlmont was a well-respected physician and pharmacist in early Little Rock. He was one of the eight founders of the Medical School and was chosen chair of Materia Medica and Therapeutics. In 1854 he opened a drugstore on the northeast corner of Markham and Main streets. James Edwin Gibson worked in the drugstore, learning pharmacology from McAlmont. In 1872 Gibson purchased an interest in the business, so from 1872 to 1883, when Dr. McAlmont left the business to return to private practice, the drugstore had the name of McAlmont & Gibson. Perhaps someone who worked at the Old State House during those years purchased a bottle of medicine from the drugstore just down the block, and after it was consumed, discarded the empty bottle where it was found over 100 years later (Ewbank 1986:33–34; Guendling and Kwas 1997:86; Williams and Whayne 2000:183–184).

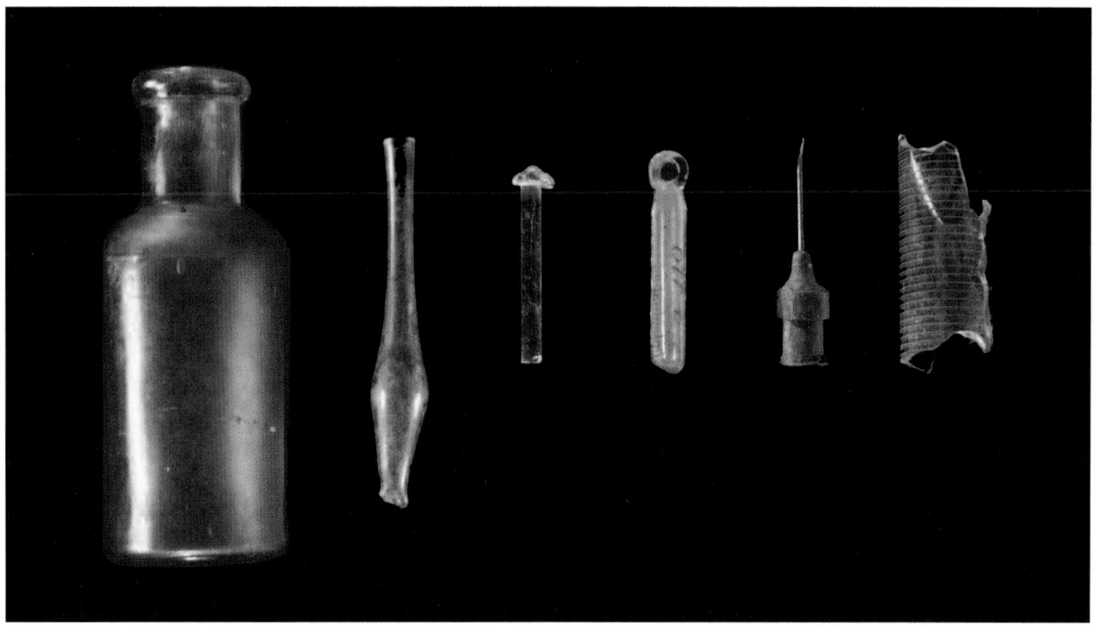

Fig. 8.6: Fragments of bottles, pipettes, stirring rods, thermometers, and syringes were among the Medical School artifacts recovered during archeological excavations. *Photograph by Jane Kellet, Arkansas Archeological Survey.*

The Arkansas War Memorial

While the Medical School's long occupancy kept the Old State House from destruction, sentiments in the aftermath of World War I gave the building a more public focus. When the war ended Arkansans turned their attention back to local issues, including the fate of the Old State House. The women's organizations continued their efforts on behalf of the historic structure, this time led by the Arkansas Pioneers Association, which in 1921 proposed a Senate bill to declare the building a memorial and establish a board of trustees with members from the various patriotic and women's groups (Brown et al. 1978:84). The bill failed in favor of another that gave the Old State House to the Arkansas Department of the American Legion as a war memorial.

The American Legion provided a variety of services to returning veterans, including the publication of a newspaper, the operation of a soup kitchen, and fundraising for services to disabled vets and their children. The Legion saw the Old State House not only as a fitting headquarters for their activities, but also as a memorial to those who had lost their lives in the war. Sentiments favored the veterans, and the Legislature of 1921 passed Act 385 that transformed the Old State House into the Arkansas State War Memorial. A board of trustees was appointed, operating as the War Memorial Commission, and the adjutant general of the American Legion became custodian of the building. Perhaps the most remarkable turn of events was that the General Assembly finally appropriated modest state funds for the upkeep of the building. Despite all these changes in oversight and to the building's public face, little changed on the interior as the Medical School and other smaller agencies continued to occupy most of the interior space (Brown et al. 1978:83–89; Hopper 1924:10).

Fig. 8.7: Mr. and Mrs. Claude A. Brown and their daughter load a truck with Christmas gifts, ca. 1928, as part of the work of the American Legion. *Old State House Museum Collection.*

Besides the American Legion and the Medical School, other groups and agencies using the building during the 1920s included the Arkansas Veterans Service Bureau, the Daughters of the American Revolution, the Arkansas Pioneers Association, the U.S. Daughters of 1812, the United Spanish War Veterans, the Stone Mountain Memorial Association, the United Confederate Veterans, the United Daughters of the Confederacy, and the Boy Scouts and Girl Scouts. Space also was given to the USDA Division of Hog Cholera and Tuberculosis Eradication, the State Veterinarian and Serum Plant, and the Arkansas Humane Society, while the Arkansas State Fair Association operated an information bureau (Brown et al. 1978:85–94).

The women's and patriotic organizations regularly used the Assembly Hall and other rooms for meetings, but conventions, banquets,

Fig. 8.8: The Old State House served as headquarters for the Sons of Confederate Veterans' Thirty-eighth Annual Confederate Reunion in 1928. This commemorative medal was lost on the grounds and recovered during archeological excavations in 1996–1997. *Photograph by Jane Kellet, Arkansas Archeological Survey.*

anniversary celebrations, and other activities were also held in the building and on the grounds. The Sons of Confederate Veterans held their Thirty-eighth Annual Confederate Reunion in Little Rock in 1928, and the Old State House served as general headquarters and the site of two grand balls. From May 8–11 Little Rock was taken over by this important event, as evidenced by the many articles pertaining to the reunion that appeared in the *Arkansas Gazette* during those days. An artifact from the festivities—a brass commemorative medal—was discovered during archeological work in 1996–1997. The medal shows scenes of the Broadway and Main street bridges over the Arkansas River, the outline of the state, the new Capitol building, and crossed flags, with the words: "The Wonder State/Little Rock/May 8–11, 1928/S.C.V." (Brown et al. 1978:90–93; Guendling and Kwas 1997:92).

While the intent of Act 385 was to allow the state's patriotic organizations—meaning largely those women's groups that had worked toward preservation—to use the building, in practice this did not work out quite as intended. Although the organizations held their monthly meetings in the building and used the grounds for special events, none of them was initially able to obtain private rooms or offices as they had hoped. While their ideas had focused on the development of exhibits on Arkansas's history and products, instead exhibits of military equipment and memorabilia were brought in (Brown et al. 1978:86). Despite the fact that Act 385 ultimately did help to preserve the building, there must have been some hard feelings among the women's groups—which had devoted more than a decade of concerted efforts and hard lobbying to the preservation effort—when they were essentially shut out of the use and oversight of the historic structure. Nevertheless, the women persevered, keeping their hands in with regular use of the building and gradually gaining control over at least part of its appearance.

Throughout the 1920s care and upkeep of the building continued to be minimal, although the Legislature now regularly appropriated funds for maintenance and the salary of a caretaker. George Crosson was hired as caretaker in 1925 and he became an established fixture, remaining in the position through the 1930s and into the 1940s. Crosson, his wife, and his children—three girls and two boys—lived in the caretaker's cottage that was located behind the east wing of the Old State House.* The cottage was partitioned into a living room, kitchen, three bedrooms, and a bathroom. The cottage increased the value of Crosson's salary, and the on-site living arrangements provided night protection for the Old State House. Crosson also was able to supplement his salary since most of the agencies occupying rooms in the Old State House hired him to provide janitorial services. The Old State House became home to the Crosson family; the children played on the lawn, helped their father with his duties, and grew to adults there. When Crosson left the position about 1946, it went to his nephew, Austin Metzger, who also moved his family into the caretaker's cottage (Brown et al. 1978:100, 168–169, 186–187, 213–214).

* The caretaker's cottage was demolished in 2009, and a multistory building was constructed on the same location.

Fig. 8.9: George Crosson served as caretaker of the Old State House from the 1920s to the 1940s. *Old State House Museum Collection.*

Agencies occupying rooms in the Old State House were expected to maintain their own areas, but many remembered the interior as being gloomy, with poor lighting, peeling plaster, and in need of a paint job. Funds provided by the Legislature went to keeping up the physical condition of the building and its public face. In the 1920s the exterior was painted periodically, the roof repaired to prevent leaks, and some rewiring undertaken. Repairs also were made to the north and east retaining walls, and the north lawn was sodded and sloped toward the river (Brown et al. 1978:98, 100, 163).

Changes to the public face of the Old State House were also made in the early 1920s, as befitted its new image as the War Memorial Building. These changes moved away from historical accuracy in favor of a military focus. Black letters spelling "War Memorial Building" were placed on the pediment, and the state seal was gold-leafed. The metal, eagle-topped gateposts were removed and replaced with granite posts that were topped with pyramids of cannonballs. The top two tiers of the fountain were taken down, the brick walkway was replaced by concrete, and the well house in front of the west wing was removed. The grounds began to fill up as well, as the Civil War–era siege gun, "Lady Baxter," was joined by a World War I caisson, a Gatling gun, four ammunition wagons, and a howitzer. In addition, so many memorial monuments had been erected that the grounds were beginning to look like a graveyard (Brown et al. 1978:98–104).

A return to historical authenticity eventually was maneuvered by the Little Rock Garden Club under the influence of preservationist Louise Loughborough. Loughborough was a charter member of the Garden Club and her interest in historic preservation began with the club's work on the Old State House grounds. She eventually became the driving force for the preservation of the buildings at the Arkansas Territorial Restoration, now known as the Historic Arkansas Museum, while continuing with support of the preservation and historical accuracy of the Old State House (Williams and Whayne 2000:171–172).

Beginning in the early 1920s, the Little Rock Garden Club became interested in improving the Old State House grounds. Initially they had to work around the desire of patriotic organizations for erecting memorials and the landscaping ideas of the War Memorial Commission. Nonetheless, a great variety of trees, shrubs, and flowers were planted, including junipers, redbuds, magnolias, jasmines, daffodils, irises, tulips, and crape myrtles. Although their work was done under the approval of the War Memorial Commission, over the decade the Garden Club gradually gained authority for the appearance of the grounds. By 1928 the club was determined to return the grounds and exterior portions of the building to historical accuracy, which included replacing the granite gateposts with the original eagle-topped gateposts and relocating the many stone memorials to places with less visual impact (Brown et al. 1978:103–108, 159–160).

In late 1928 the Garden Club orchestrated its most controversial act—the removal from the roof of the Old State House of the three Greek statues that had been brought back from the Philadelphia Centennial Exposition. This heist apparently was orchestrated by Louise Loughborough and done without the knowledge of the War Memorial Commission. Hiring H. C. Halliburton to help remove the statues, the group reached them through a trap door onto the roof and sawed off their supporting cypress poles. Halliburton said that the statues were loaded into a truck and taken to a tinshop, but many people believed they were dumped into the Arkansas River. The commission requested their return, but the statues were never seen again (Brown et al. 1978:105–106).

Fig. 8.10: Dating ca. 1927, the Old State House is seen transformed into the War Memorial Building. Although the refocus honored the service of Arkansans during World War I, the appearance moved away from historical accuracy. *Old State House Museum Collection.*

Help from the WPA

The Great Depression years of the 1930s, although tough on the country, were good to the Old State House. Thanks to Franklin Roosevelt's New Deal programs, money became available to refurbish the building, record its architecture, and provide agencies to occupy its spaces. In the first years of the 1930s, use of the Old State House continued much as it had in the 1920s, although as early as 1931 Louise Loughborough solidified her leadership position regarding the Old State House when the Little Rock Garden Club appointed her chairwoman of the Old State Capitol Restoration Committee (Brown et al. 1978:243).

The following year the War Memorial Board of Trustees instructed architect Frank

Fig. 8.11: Preservationist Louise Loughborough. *Courtesy of Historic Arkansas Museum.*

Ginocchio of the firm Thompson, Sanders, and Ginocchio to inspect the War Memorial Building and estimate the costs of necessary repairs. Ginocchio had first worked with the board in 1928 when he prepared specifications for rewiring the building. After a careful inspection, Ginocchio presented an estimate of $4,550 that included recommendations to repair the roof and skylights, tear out old vaults, tuck point and stucco exterior walls, complete steps, replace rotten wood cornices, replace metal gutters, patch plaster, and repaint (Brown et al. 1978:165, 189; Shank 1977:64–65). In his letter to the board, Ginocchio stated:

> I wish to advise that only such items were noted that I felt were absolutely necessary to preserve the building. If the roof is not taken care of in a very short time you will not only lose the roof, but the damage to the interior will run into big money. The skylights are in very bad shape, but the outside walls need painting and the roof of the building in particular needs painting.
>
> Along this line I would like to state that this particular building is pointed to with pride, as one of Arkansas' finest examples of architecture, and the estimates I have given you above will only serve to save and protect it for our people. (Shank 1977:64–65)

At a board meeting in November 1933, Ginocchio recommended that the board apply to the Civil Works Administration for funding to repair the building, and the board leaped at the opportunity. Within three weeks Ginocchio had prepared and submitted an application. The expanded $23,736 project included, in addition to the above recommended work, new wood floors, termite treatment, plumbing repairs, electric wiring, weatherstripping, restoring the well house, and repairing the custodian's house. The project was approved, the firm of Thompson, Sanders, and Ginocchio were employed as architects to supervise the project, and work was begun in early 1934. During the same year, the Historic American Buildings Survey (HABS) took photographs and prepared 27 measured drawings of the building, which now can be viewed on-line at the HABS Web site (Shank 1977:65, 70, 81).

The following year the Medical School moved to new quarters on McAlmont Street, freeing up a good deal of space in the Old State House. Commission members were concerned the building would rapidly deteriorate without occupants, but did not want the Legislature to take it over as a state office building. Citing the monetary benefits received from Federal Emergency Relief and Civil Works for the repair of the building, the commission solved the problem by making space available to agencies of the Works Progress Administration. From 1936 to 1942 WPA agencies making use of the space included the Assistance Professional and Clerical Workers, the Writers' Project, Education Division Supervisors, Historical Records Survey, National Youth Administration, the Recreation Project, the American Guide Project, the Housekeeping Aide Project, the Commodity

Fig. 8.12: Early-model cars line up in front of the Old State House, 1934. *Courtesy of Historic American Buildings Survey, U.S. Library of Congress.*

Distribution Project, and the Women's Measuring Project (Brown et al. 1978:140–143).

Offices for various state and private organizations were also provided during the years of the 1930s. The Little Rock Garden Club, an obvious choice, received office space in 1935, the same year Louise Loughborough was appointed to the Little Rock Planning Commission. Over the next few years, the American Automobile Club, the Arkansas Library Commission, the Arkansas State Plant Board, the Arkansas State Rangers, and the Arkansas Pioneers Association all received space in the building. The entire east wing went to the Centennial Commission, which was established to implement the state's centennial celebration (Brown et al. 1978:144–152; Williams and Whayne 2000:171).

Through the 1930s the Legislature continued to allocate money for the maintenance of the building. The amount included the salaries of the caretaker and his assistant, as well as insurance on the building. It varied from year to year depending on what repairs or upkeep needed to be done, but averaged about $3,500 per year (Brown et al. 1978:188). It was also during the 1930s that the discovery of Secretary of State Jacob Frolich's short-used cistern brought a little mystery and public attention to the Old State House. In May 1936 caretaker George Crosson stumbled upon the cistern when removing an old manhole cover. No one remembered the cistern, so it was misinterpreted as a mystery cavern. Bernie Babcock,

Fig. 8.13: A view of the west stairs, 1934. *Courtesy of Historic American Buildings Survey, U.S. Library of Congress.*

Fig. 8.14: A first-day cover celebrates Arkansas's centennial. *Old State House Museum Collection.*

director of the Federal Writers Project for Arkansas, was the first to explore the space, suggesting that it might have been used as a powder magazine or dungeon, which only increased its romance. The legend survived for decades, and it wasn't until the 1990s that archeological excavations and archival research pointed to the cavern's true identity as Frolich's cistern (*Arkansas Gazette*, May 14, 1936).

As the 1940s dawned, it brought with it the Second World War. Money and public efforts were channeled to the war effort, and the WPA agencies began to be disbanded. By December 1942 their exodus from the Old State House was complete. Again, this opened up space in the building for new occupants. The Civilian Defense Office and the Rationing Board moved in, while the Veterans Service Bureau, the Arkansas Library Commission and the Plant Board exchanged or expanded their space (Brown et al. 1978:200–206, 225). And, after waiting three decades, the women's patriotic groups responsible for initiating the Old State House preservation effort finally received office space in the building. The Daughters of the American Revolution were given space in 1941 after the Centennial Commission moved out. They were followed by the United Daughters of the Confederacy and the Arkansas Federation of Women's Clubs in 1943. The women immediately renovated and decorated their space, bringing in draperies, fine furniture, and office equipment (Brown et al. 1978:210–212).

The Legislature continued to provide funds for upkeep of the building, averaging about $4,300 per year in the 1940s, which continued to include the caretakers' salaries and insurance on the building. In 1941 the Legislature allotted a more generous $5,000 for needed repairs, and the work was completed the following year. The repairs included painting, plastering, roof repair, and remodeling of the balconies (Brown et al. 1978:218–220, 237).

Preservation or Bust

The Second World War pulled the country out of the Depression, but put on hold any local improvements and projects. As the young veterans returned from the war, their ideas were changed and expanded by the experience, and their interest in Arkansas's heritage was stimulated. The time was right for an all-out effort to preserve and restore the Old State House.

The women's groups had not abandoned their efforts and continued to lobby for preservation throughout the 1930s and into the 1940s. A dramatic increase in lobbying by women began in 1939, as more women gained power and influence through their involvement in the business world and the war effort. Louise Loughborough had continued as a strong advocate for historic preservation, although her efforts shifted to saving what became the Arkansas Territorial Restoration. Her successful work set a precedent for what could be done with the Old State House. Loughborough was joined in her preservation campaign by Agnes Loewer, who was involved with almost every patriotic organization in Arkansas. The two became a fixture in the legislative halls of the new Capitol as they lobbied daily for the Old State House (Brown et al. 1978:143–244, 252–253).

In 1944 Ben T. Laney was elected governor. In his first year in office, he appointed a commission to raise $100,000 for the building's complete restoration, and in the same year a Senate resolution empowered the Arkansas History Commission to study the historic sites in the state. Dallas Herndon, chairman of the History Commission, suggested that a restored

Old State House could provide a new home for the collections and archives of his agency. In 1945 the Arkansas Museum Commission was established. But real changes began in 1947, as a new General Assembly infused with young veterans began their work (Brown et al. 1978:246–247, 272).

The women were well organized by 1947 and were determined to succeed. They enlisted the aid of Representative Bob Riley, a 21-year-old disabled veteran, who not only was interested in the restoration of the Old State House but also in the construction of a governor's mansion and a War Memorial Stadium, which he viewed as a source of pride for the people of the state. His hard work in building support for his cause was sweetened by sympathy for his condition. Additional support came from Speaker of the House Roy Riales, who worked the system to give Riley time to gain votes (Brown et al. 1978:252–257). In March 1947 Riley introduced a House bill to establish the Arkansas Commemorative Commission (which would become the governing body for the Old State House) and another House bill to allocate funds for the restoration of the Old State House. By the end of the legislative session, both bills passed without a single dissenting vote, becoming Acts 255 and 256 (Brown et al. 1978:257–259).

Supporters of the Old State House soon after were appointed to serve on the Commemorative Commission. The members consisted of Dr. D. D. McBrien of Arkadelphia, chairman; Agnes Loewer of Little Rock, secretary; Senator Lawrence Blackwell of Pine Bluff; Tom W. Campbell of Little Rock; Ben I. Mayo of Fort Smith; W. H. Etter of Washington; Mrs. J. L. Taylor of Corning; Grady Holland of Heber Springs; and Ted Larimer of Green Forest (*Arkansas Gazette,* February 13, 1951). Their first order of business was to oversee the restoration of the Old State House, and the commission wisely decided to restore the building to its 1885 configuration, since restoring to an earlier period would have required tearing down the hyphens and the extended back of the building.

The Legislature appropriated $150,000 to begin the work, and architect Bruce Anderson was hired to direct the restoration. The contract for the work was awarded to the Baldwin Company of Little Rock. Once the building was thoroughly examined by Anderson, it was discovered that the Old State House was in much worse condition than previously thought. Poor engineering methods used during the 1830s, damage incurred during earlier renovations, and normal deterioration because of age compounded to create dangerous conditions (Anderson 1950:1). Anderson reported that:

> One of the large beams supporting the central skylight roof in the center of the main hall had rotted as a result of a leaking roof and was near the point of collapse. This would have sent a portion of the center roof crashing through the second floor of the building. The roof of the east wing also was in a condition near failure, with a very bad situation resulting from sagging of wooden trusses which had parted at the joints because of defects in the original design by early builders. . . . The ceiling joists in that wing fell to the floor when the plaster and lathe were removed, and might have fallen through at any time. (*Arkansas Gazette* February 27, 1948)

The architect also discovered the foundation had been built of rubble stone and mortar and had "completely disintegrated to the uppermost part of the roof where the block-tin roof had almost disappeared by rusting" (Anderson 1950:1). The west wing also was found to have serious defects, but as the American Legion did not want to move out and the work couldn't be done safely if the building was occupied, the work began on the central building and east wing, initially leaving the west wing untouched. Apparently, those occupying the building had expected to remain during the renovation, but the work was so extreme that most contractors refused to make a bid for the work if the building remained occupied. Most of the groups were reluctant to move, even going so far as to file a lawsuit to prevent the commission members from proceeding with the restoration. The suit was unsuccessful and only resulted in delaying the start of work. When the women's patriotic organizations finally recognized the need for eviction, they complied for the sake of the building they had worked so hard to save. The women, however, did expect to return (*Arkansas Gazette,* June 4, 1948, August 27, 1950).

Discovering that the building required more extensive restoration than originally planned, the 1947 appropriation was used to restore the structural elements, which included a new metal roof and gutters, exterior wood work, installation of steel floor joists, reinforced concrete foundation walls and footings, subflooring, steel tie rods with wall plates to stabilize exterior walls, and the installation of an automatic sprinkler system for fire protection. Most of the interior was left unfinished, awaiting a second appropriation, so remained "without lighting, heating, plumbing, patching, or repairs, or the restoration of any interior details, or replacement of wood windows, doors and failing stucco" (Anderson 1950:1).

The second phase of the restoration began August 10, 1949, with an additional appropriation of $200,000 to complete the interior work. By October the American Legion finally realized they could no longer occupy the west wing amid construction and moved to new quarters. Work progressed steadily and was essentially completed by July 1, 1950, although replacing the exterior coat of stucco, painting interior plaster walls, replacing temporary light fixtures, and landscaping still remained to be completed (Anderson 1950:2–5, *Arkansas Gazette,* October 4, 1949).

The restoration marked a new era in the building's history. No longer a worn-down workhorse of a government office building, Arkansas's first state capitol had not only been saved through the efforts of many dedicated women and men, but it had been reborn as a shrine and symbol of Arkansas's proudly embraced history. As the restoration work wound down and plans were formulated for the dedication and grand reopening in 1951, the Legislature passed Act 114 authorizing the Arkansas History Commission to use the building for an archives and museum. The act also changed the building's name; Arkansas's first capitol now would be officially known as the Old State House (Brown et al. 1978:272–273).

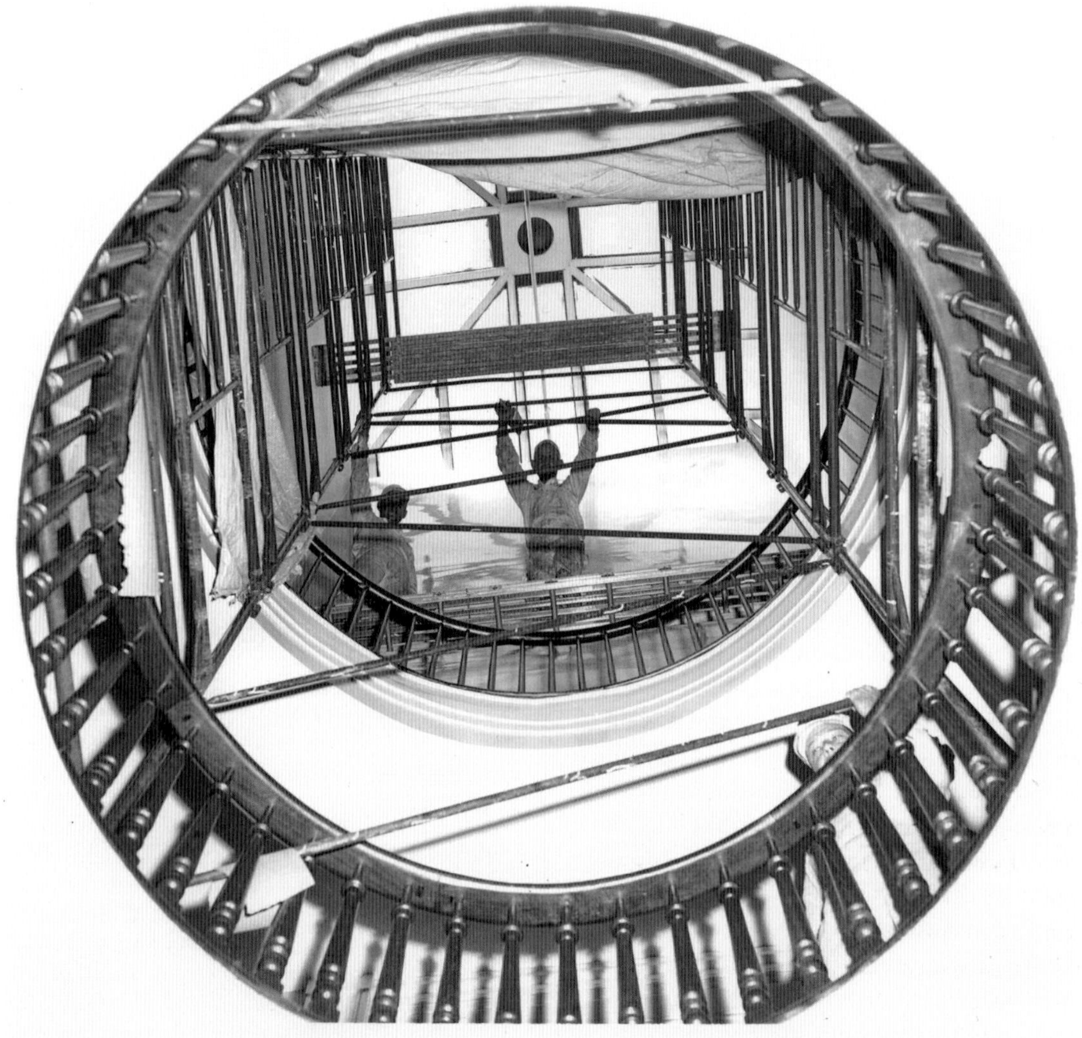

Fig. 8.15: The central stairs during rehabilitation, ca. 1948. *Old State House Museum Collection.*

CHAPTER 9

Rebirth as a Museum: 1950s–1980s

As the restoration of the Old State House progressed toward completion, the building underwent a transformation and rebirth into a symbol of Arkansas's history. That symbol was embodied in the building itself, but also in its new function as a repository for that history. From its reopening to the public in 1951 and continuing to today, the Old State House has served as a museum of Arkansas history. But that does not mean the Old State House is unchanging. The philosophies and methods that guide museum practice—including the ideas for exhibits and programs, and the methods to produce them—have evolved through time as well. The history of the Old State House as a museum illustrates these changes and embraces this evolution.

Before a museum could take shape, however, the Arkansas Commemorative Commission had to guarantee that the refurbished building actually would serve as a museum, not be taken over by space-needy agencies and organizations clamoring for office space. Resisting any pressure, the commission firmly stated their ruling:

> It is the intent and purpose of this Commission that this historic building should be reserved for the benefit of the state as a whole and should not be filled with the offices of various organizations, and that all organizations are requested to refrain from seeking quarters in this historic building and to join with the Commission in making this beautiful structure the shrine it should be in order that the legislative intent as stated in Act 256 of 1947 creating the Commission shall be carried out. (*Arkansas Gazette,* August 15, 1950)

The commission then formed a committee to oversee details for furnishing period rooms and creating displays. Agnes Loewer, Tom Campbell, and W. H. Etter served on the committee. In the meantime, plans were underway for the building's dedication and grand opening on Valentine's Day. On February 14, 1951, the Old State House reopened to the public. It was an appropriate day, considering the affection the building now garnered in the hearts and minds of Arkansans. Members of the patriotic women's organizations in historic costumes greeted visitors, and at least 41 former legislators who had served in the building were invited back for the grand opening (*Arkansas Gazette,* January 28, 1951, February 13, 1951).

The Agnes Loewer Years: 1950s–1960s

It would be a few months until the beginning of the new fiscal year on July 1 before Agnes Loewer was officially appointed the first curator for the Old State House, and along with it the secretary of the Commemorative Commission (which position was later changed to director of the Commemorative Commission). She was an obvious choice for the position. Loewer was both a businesswoman and a member of numerous civic and patriotic organizations, including the Arkansas Federation of Women's Clubs, which had been instrumental in lobbying for the preservation of the Old State House. She had experience in managing finances and directing projects and committees. She belonged to so many organizations and had her hand in so many projects that it is difficult to imagine there were enough hours in the day to accommodate her many responsibilities. Nonetheless, her accomplishments were legion, and her organizational and leadership abilities highly praised (Herndon 1947:1446–1448). Indeed, Loewer already had nearly 40 years of experience when she accepted the position of curator at the age of 58.

Beginning about 1939 Loewer became an active supporter for the preservation of the Old State House, lobbying daily in the halls of the State Capitol with Louise Loughborough. She was appointed a member of the Arkansas Commemorative Commission in 1947, when it was formed to oversee the restoration of the Old State House, and she began work to create

Fig. 9.1: Agnes Loewer, first curator of the Old State House Museum, welcomes visitors at the front gates, ca. 1967. *Courtesy of Arkansas History Commission.*

a museum in the building during the years of the restoration work. She was a good choice for first curator, not only because of her efforts on behalf of preserving the Old State House and her business skills, but also for her role as liaison between the commission and the women's patriotic organizations. As a member of many of those groups, often in a leadership capacity, she well understood their purposes and goals. Essentially, she was the embodiment of the women's organizations inside the Old State House and directed the museum's development in a manner conducive to their ideas and approval.

In addition to the presence of the Arkansas Commemorative Commission in the person of Agnes Loewer, the other state agency that began a long-term residency in 1953 in the Old State House was the Arkansas History Commission. Established in 1905, the History Commission was charged with collecting records of the state's history and activities, and over the years had developed a library, archives, and museum. Since 1915 the History Commission had occupied quarters in the State Capitol building, but after their space had been reduced in 1935, many of their collections were placed in storage and became inaccessible in the basement of the Capitol. The agency was promised new and larger quarters in the Old State House upon completion of the restoration (Baker 2006a).

In May 1951 the History Commission began its move from the State Capitol to the west wing of the Old State House under the direction of longtime director Dallas Herndon. Because the west wing was the last to be restored, the space was still unfinished when the move began. Herndon found his new quarters with no molding to hang pictures, no library shelves, unpainted walls, and missing light fixtures. The aged and infirm director, then 72 years old, undertook some of the work himself to bring the space to usable condition (*Arkansas Democrat,* September 6, 1952, October 1, 1952; *Arkansas Gazette,* May 24, 1951; Baker 2006b).

After Herndon's retirement in 1953, the History Commission's new director, Ted Worley, worked to improve the facilities, which included the construction of a new building to

Fig. 9.2: Dallas Herndon was the director of the Arkansas History Commission at the time the commission moved from the State Capitol to the west wing of the Old State House. *Courtesy of Arkansas History Commission.*

hold the commission's archival collection. Contracts were awarded in October 1953, and the new building—to be known as the Annex—was erected just north of the west wing of the Old State House. In 1962 a third floor was added to the building (*Arkansas Democrat*, October 2, 1953, August 3, 1962).

Besides the construction of the Annex, periodic repairs and upkeep continued on the Old State House. In 1955 a low wall was built to hide floodlights used to illuminate the building. In July 1960 a severe storm rampaged through Little Rock, tearing part of the aluminum roof off the Old State House and damaging the caretaker's cottage. Another storm four years later peeled back more of the roof, blew off ventilators, and destroyed a large elm tree on the grounds. In 1968 a fire started in the attic over the west wing; skillful firefighters managed to remove the furnishings without damage and extinguish the blaze but had to chop a hole in the west wall of the central building to reach the fire (*Arkansas Democrat*, July 28, 1960, July 10, 1964; *Arkansas Gazette*, November 24, 1955, January 11, 1968).

Agnes Loewer began her work as curator in July 1951, but she was not expected to run the museum without assistance. The appropriation to hire a curator also included funds for a support staff to consist of a receptionist, a resident caretaker, a night watchman, two janitors, and a maid. None of those positions, however, included professional museum staff. Instead, Loewer relied on volunteers from the women's groups to serve as guides—positions in museums that later came to be called docents or interpreters. Loewer took a strong hand in instructing her guides, directing details of enunciation, personal appearance, and posture. Guides were required to memorize a script and deliver it without notes, without change, and within a time limit of 35 to 45 minutes (*Arkansas Democrat*, November 4, 1956).

Loewer was a strict and demanding administrator, strong and outspoken, a staunch defender of the Old State House, but at times perceived as tyrannical by her staff. With the air of a drill sergeant about her, Loewer became known to volunteers and visitors alike for the referee's whistle she carried and used to command attention. Her blasts echoed through the building for her guides to form a straight receiving line or to keep a group of schoolchildren fixed to a white line and away from walls. At a time when women were still rare at the executive level, Loewer's administrative style undoubtedly aided her in gaining respect and quashing any underestimation of her abilities (*Arkansas Democrat*, March 31, 1972; Nail 1995:10–11).

While the Old State House itself was the most valuable item in the collection of the Arkansas Commemorative Commission, the idea to build a museum of Arkansas history had always been included in the plans for the restoration and use of the building. As soon as Loewer took over as curator, she announced that gifts and loans of objects would be accepted for display and began work with the various women's patriotic organizations to furnish period rooms. By 1954 six rooms had been furnished to represent different time periods. The groups sponsoring the rooms were the Arkansas Federation of Women's Clubs, the Daughters of the American Revolution, the United Daughters of the Confederacy, the Daughters of 1812, the Auxiliary of the Spanish American War Veterans, and the Arkansas Pioneers Association (*Arkansas Clubwoman* 1954, Vol. 2, No. 5). Work on the rooms continued over the years as pieces were acquired and added to the display. New acquisitions were frequently announced in newspaper stories, such as when the original painting of *The Arkansas Traveler* by Edward Payson Washburn was added in 1960 or when antiques that included a grand piano, pier mirror,

Two period rooms outfitted by the women's patriotic societies, ca. 1955.

Fig. 9.3: Daughters of the American Revolution room. *Courtesy of Arkansas History Commission.*

Fig. 9.4: Arkansas Pioneers room. *Courtesy of Arkansas History Commission.*

piecrust table, and clock were added in 1961 (*Arkansas Gazette,* June 26, 1960, June 11, 1961).

The museum model for the period rooms had arisen from the preservation efforts for Washington's Mount Vernon, a project that involved women's groups in many states including Arkansas. Just as Mount Vernon had become a shrine not only to the first president but also to the country's founding history, it was only natural that Arkansas women's groups wanted the Old State House to be a shrine to Arkansas's early history. And as each of the women's patriotic organizations represented different periods in Arkansas's history, so different rooms in the Old State House would be given a historical focus matching those periods.

While the period rooms as historical exhibits suited the mindset of the times, the execution was rife with problems. The women chose to decorate their rooms to represent a sitting room or parlor as it might have appeared in a well-to-do home of each period. But the Old State House was not a home, it was a government building, and rooms within it had never been outfitted in such a fashion. Nor did the women select a roomful of furnishings from a single Arkansas family, but rather gathered together disparate antiques that simply represented their ideas of a room of the period. This led to a mix of objects acquired through donations, purchases, and even reproductions. The furnishings were not even necessarily pieces that had ever been used in Arkansas homes; in fact, what was considered one of the finest pieces—a mahogany breakfront—had been purchased for the DAR room directly out of an estate in Scotland. The concept of the DAR room was even more problematic than just the choice of a Scottish breakfront, for the land that became Arkansas was not part of the United States during the American Revolution and was not yet home to Euro-American settlers. Although this was recognized by Loewer and others, the DAR was nonetheless allowed to furnish a room (*Arkansas Gazette*, January 3, 1960).

The period rooms were a nostalgic recreation of the past, focused on only a small segment of Arkansas society, ideas that later would be denigrated as "moonlight and magnolias" (*Arkansas Gazette*, August 31, 1979). A more inclusive social history, however, had to wait for the next generation. During the 1950s and 1960s, these exhibits apparently were popular with the visitors who came to tour the Old State House, as numerous articles in the local papers seemed to indicate.

In addition to the period rooms, Loewer also worked to develop other exhibits to showcase Arkansas's history. The first to open, in 1955, was a display of gowns that had belonged to Arkansas's first ladies, an exhibit that had particular appeal to women. In 1960 the Flag Gallery opened, displaying battle flags from units in the Civil War and Mexican War, among others. A collection of currency from the Confederate States opened in 1964 (*Arkansas Democrat*, May 21, 1964; *Arkansas Gazette*, September 25, 1960; *Southwest Times Record*, November 20, 1955).

Fig. 9.5: Some of the first exhibits, ca. 1955, with free-standing cases and portraits displayed along the walls, were typical of exhibit style during the middle twentieth century. *Courtesy of Arkansas History Commission.*

People did come to visit the Old State House, which was not only a symbol of Arkansas's past but also a modern tourist attraction. Throughout the 1950s and 1960s, it was regularly featured in both local and distant newspapers, and it became an expected stop for visitors to the city. School groups, convention groups, out-of-state and foreign visitors, all took Loewer's tours. Photographs in the paper regularly showed young women, such as those of the Future Homemakers of America, cooling their bare feet in the fountain or older groups lined up between the columns along the front steps. In 1964 nearly 40,000 people visited the Old State House, representing all but one state and 14 countries. Hours of operation were modest at first, beginning with "certain week days" in 1952 and expanding Monday to Friday by 1954. The museum was rarely open on weekends in the early years—just one Sunday afternoon in each of the four seasons. Those Sunday afternoons were considered special open houses, with the tour guides dressed in historic attire. By 1960 hours were expanded to include all Saturday and Sunday afternoons (*Arkansas Democrat,* April 18, 1954; *Arkansas Democrat Magazine,* October 22, 1961; *Arkansas Gazette,* May 23, 1965; *Commercial Appeal* [Memphis], August 24, 1952).

Fig. 9.6: Tour guides and reenactors dressed in period attire for Sunday open houses and special events during the 1950s and 1960s. Here Governor Sid McMath and First Lady Anne make a dashing couple. *Old State House Museum Collection.*

As a symbol, the Old State House also served as the site for special events, the most important during this period being the centennial of the state's secession from the Union on May 6, 1861, at the beginning of the Civil War. A reenactment of the secession convention was staged at the Old State House, with women dressed in hoop skirts, role-playing of historic characters, and fancy balls (*Arkansas Gazette,* May 5, 1961, May 6, 1961). The secession centennial, however, can perhaps be viewed as the last hurrah of the old order. Indeed, times were changing. The civil rights movement was already underway after the Supreme Court's ruling on *Brown v. Board of Education of Topeka, Kansas,* in 1954 and Rosa Parks's courageous rebellion on a Montgomery, Alabama, bus in 1955. By 1957 Little Rock residents were struggling with the desegregation of Central High School. Two years after the secession centennial, the modern women's rights movement would be galvanized by the publication of Betty Friedan's book *The Feminine Mystique.* The following year the Beatles arrived in America, leading changes in popular culture for the next two decades (although the closest the Beatles ever got to the Old State House was changing planes at a small airstrip in Lawrence County) (Bowman 2006). It would take more than a decade for major changes to be seen at the Old State House, but the march to that future had already begun.

The seeds of those changes were being planted in the 1960s, as interest in the preservation of historic structures grew to prominence, resulting in new laws to protect America's heritage and new agencies to manage that protection. In 1966 Congress created the National Register of Historic Places, the official list of cultural resources deemed worthy of preservation. In December 1969 the Old State House was among the first group of properties in Arkansas listed on the National Register. In March 1971 the Legislature again changed the name of the Old State House, this time to "Arkansas's First State Capitol." The renaming was short-lived, and before the end of the decade, the name had returned to the "Old State House" (*Arkansas Gazette,* March 26, 1971).

In 1971, the year before her retirement, Loewer mounted one more fight to preserve the Old State House. When the city proposed clipping a corner of the grounds to extend Ashley Street to La Harpe Boulevard, Loewer stood firm in opposing the infringement, even after city manager John Meriwether called her shortsighted. The battle took a year to resolve, but Loewer had her way and the Old State House grounds were preserved. After that last battle, Loewer knew it was time for her to retire (*Arkansas Gazette,* March 3, 1971, March 4, 1971, February 2, 1972).

At the end of 1971, the 78-year-old Loewer was injured in a fall, breaking a bone. After a few months' convalescence, she must have realized that her time as an active curator was at an end. She announced her retirement in March 1972. Loewer's management of the Old State House remained largely unchanged throughout her tenure. Her mission was to protect and promote the Old State House and interpret Arkansas's history in a manner supported by the women's patriotic organizations. In the 21 years she served as curator through the 1950s and 1960s, and right up to her last month as curator in 1972, she did that job well. At the end of her career and in the years following her retirement, Loewer received several honors for her service. The most notable among them was an award from the National Trust for Historic Preservation, presented to her by former first lady "Lady Bird" Johnson in 1974 (*Arkansas Democrat,* March 24, 1972, March 31, 1972; *Arkansas Gazette,* March 24, 1972, September 20, 1975).

The Redefinition of a Museum: 1970s

After Loewer's retirement there was a several-year period of frequent personnel changes, as the state refocused its management philosophy in regard to the Old State House and other historic resources. Betty Field took over as director in 1972 immediately after Loewer. Field was involved in historic preservation as the president of the Quapaw Quarter Association and as former director of Villa Marre, a privately owned and restored Victorian residence that was available for functions. She had been serving as director of the Old State House in an acting capacity for several months during Loewer's convalescence and continued with the manage-

Fig. 9.7: During the 1970s the Old State House was renamed "Arkansas' First State Capitol." *Photograph by Gene Prescott, Old State House Museum Collection.*

ment style Loewer had originated (*Arkansas Democrat,* March 24, 1972; *Arkansas Gazette,* March 24, 1972). Gene Richardson succeeded Field by 1975 and served for a short time as acting head of the new Department of Arkansas Natural and Cultural Heritage before a more permanent director was hired (*Arkansas Gazette,* July 3, 1975, May 20, 1976).

In the mid-1970s there was a move to professionalize the management of the Old State House in line with the methods and philosophy of professional museum management that had evolved over the years. Museums were reaching out to new audiences in new ways, while developing *mission statements* that defined their purposes and guided their methods of operations. During this period museums began a strong effort to broaden their interaction with their communities, reaching out to multiple audiences and segments of society that had been underserved or excluded from the museum. As part of this movement, education departments were established in museums, and programs changed to include hands-on learning activities, reenactments, and outreach programs. The philosophy behind exhibits changed as well. Short-term or *changing exhibits* encouraged repeat visitation. Dioramas, touch displays, and video elements allowed visitors to interact with the exhibits and enhanced learning. New exhibits drew upon the research of social historians, illuminating the stories of women, minorities, and diverse aspects of society and life. Museums were becoming more exciting places to visit and welcoming people who had previously felt little or no relationship to them. Restoration methods of historic properties also evolved during this period. Restoration was no longer based on guesswork or preconceived notions. Instead, it involved research by architectural historians and specialists in historic paints and wallpapers, building construction and architectural style.

In this context of new scholarship, historic preservation, and changes in museum management, Arkansas created the Department of Arkansas Natural and Cultural Heritage (now the Department of Arkansas Heritage) in 1975 as an initiative of Governor David Pryor. The Arkansas Commemorative Commission, which had oversight for the Old State House, became part of the new department. Anne Bartley, the stepdaughter of Winthrop Rockefeller, was appointed the director of the new department, and Lucy Robinson was hired as the new curator/director of the Old State House. Robinson came with good credentials. She had a master's degree in art history from Cornell University and had worked there for three years as a curator (*Arkansas Gazette,* July 3, 1975, May 20, 1976). Both Bartley and Robinson were young women, and their presence represented not only the rise of women into the business and professional world, but also the growing wave of college-educated baby boomers bringing new skills to the workforce. These were major differences in the way the Old State House had been managed before. In many ways, Bartley and Robinson were the personification of changes to come.

Upon accepting the directorship, Lucy Robinson was charged not only with bringing the management of the Old State House up to the standards of modern museums, she also was given the opportunity to make major changes to the public face of the Old State House—the physical structure and exhibits. This was prompted, in part, by the anticipated move of the History Commission from the Old State House to the new Capitol Mall. The move, slated for 1979, would free up space in the west wing as well as the Annex Building behind the Old State House.

Robinson began to mount new, changing exhibits shortly after she arrived. The first, "Story of Journalism," opened in February 1976. Over the next two years, other new exhibits included "Arkansas's Governors," "First State Capitol in Transition: 1833–1885," "American Cut Glass," and "Arkansas Women." Robinson hired Susan Smyer in 1976 to research the history of the Old State House, which led to Smyer's unpublished manuscript and the "First Capitol in Transition" exhibit. "Arkansas Women," which explored women's history in the state, included such topics as History is a Family Album, Suffrage: Votes for Women, If Women Were to Tell the Real Story of Their Lives, Major Breakthroughs for Women, and The Struggle Continues (*Arkansas Democrat,* September 10, 1977; *Arkansas Gazette,* February 13, 1976, April 23, 1976, October 17, 1976).

Educational programs targeted to schoolchildren also were added within the first two years of Robinson's tenure. A resource manual for teachers was developed, which included pre- and post-visit classroom activities for the students. During the class visit, students could role play and problem solve in exploring Arkansas's political history, make architectural models that studied building techniques and utilized math, and participate in hands-on activities such as brick making (*Arkansas Gazette,* September 1, 1977; *Journal of the Department of Education,* February 1977).

Despite these commendable early efforts, Robinson and Bartley quickly found themselves at odds with the women's patriotic societies. In the spring of 1976, the two held a meeting that included members of the Arkansas Pioneers Association to discuss new directions for exhibits at the Old State House. In what was described as only a "brainstorming session," suggestions were made to change the way the period rooms were handled. The Pioneers were aghast, and rumors spread like wildfire among the women's societies. Although Robinson and Bartley insisted that none of the ideas was settled yet, comments by William Stringfellow, chairman of the Commemorative Commission, suggested that the brainstorming session had not been the first discussion of such ideas (*Arkansas Gazette*, May 20, 1976).

Although the women's patriotic organizations were unable to see it at the time, there were many problems with the period rooms. The displays were static and unchanging, which did nothing to encourage repeat visitation. The rooms had little to do with most Arkansans; they didn't represent the home of any particular Arkansas family, and in some cases, the antiques contained in them had never been part of an Arkansas home. Perhaps worst of all, few records had been kept on the objects in the rooms, so by the time Robinson was director, it was unclear if the objects belonged to the state of Arkansas or the society sponsoring the room, as well as which objects were owned or simply

Fig. 9.8: Museum director Lucy Robinson, *far left*, with members of the Arkansas Commemorative Commission. *Old State House Museum Collection.*

on loan. The state of affairs was unacceptable by professional museum standards, and since the commission hoped to obtain accreditation by the American Association of Museums, the problems had to be rectified (*Arkansas Gazette,* May 21, 1976, October 8, 1977).

With the anticipated move of the History Commission, plans for reallocating space and undertaking a more historically accurate restoration of the building were developed. Already in Robinson's first two years, she had instituted a series of changing exhibits and created a dynamic educational program. The next phase was to be even more bold and exciting. To begin with, she wanted to move the period rooms out of the east wing in order to restore the original Supreme Court and eventually make room for other history exhibits. In the west wing she wanted to establish a Museum of Victorian Design that would incorporate the collections of the period rooms into changing exhibits and interpretive programs. Although the women's societies were to have space in the west wing, the designated space would be reduced in size from what they had had in the east wing, and furniture and decorative objects would be rotated between storage and display (*Arkansas Gazette,* June 9, 1979).

The women's groups, however, wanted nothing to do with the proposed changes and insisted their period rooms should remain untouched. They argued that their furniture was too old to be moved or stored, an argument that demonstrated a lack of understanding of museum curation standards and methods. They also thought their occupation of the rooms had been permanently secured by the Legislature, but Arkansas attorney general Bill Clinton ruled that the Commemorative Commission had exclusive control over the Old State House, including the individual rooms, and that objects in the museum not covered by a written agreement were the property of the commission (*Arkansas Gazette,* May 20, 1976, October 8, 1977).

While that appeared to settle matters, the displeasure of the women's societies continued to simmer. In the meantime, since the Commemorative Commission was already strongly committed to the new plans, the commission sought to open communication and build constituency in the two years preceding the History Commission's move. On February 19, 1977, the commission sponsored a day-long conference to discuss the range of possibilities for the museum's development, inviting members of the women's patriotic groups and other interested citizens. Speakers included Dr. John Ferguson of the Arkansas History Commission, Dr. Eugene Wittlake, director of ASU Museum, and Dr. William Seale, White House historian and author of a book on state capitols (*Arkansas Gazette,* February 6, 1977). Later in the year, Robinson made a presentation to the Pulaski County Historical Society, of which she was soon to become a member of the board of directors. In the same month, the *Arkansas Gazette* published an interview with the museum's exhibit specialist, Jim Watkins, who advised the public not to think the changes would be taking anything away from the museum, rather they would just be "adding a new dimension to what we already have" (*Arkansas Gazette,* September 19, 1977, September 30, 1977).

The History Commission moved out of the west wing of the Old State House in May 1979, and in early June the Commemorative Commission formally voted to adopt the new restoration and exhibit plan. A press conference was held in late June, releasing details of the plan, including a breakdown of the spaces to be allotted to the women's patriotic societies. The restoration work, which would begin in early

Fig. 9.9: John Ferguson, director of the Arkansas History Commission and State Archives, 1960–2005. *Courtesy of Arkansas History Commission.*

July with the hiring of architect Charles Witsell, would include the installation of an elevator and the repainting of interior and exterior spaces, based on research that had been done over the past three years. The plans were funded by a $275,000 appropriation (*Arkansas Gazette,* June 9, 1979, June 28, 1979, July 21, 1979).

Despite the commission's efforts to communicate with the women's groups, which had gone "further than necessary in trying to gain their support" according to one commission member, the women's opposition to the plan had not abated. One DAR member wrote to the state attorney general trying to get the plan stopped and cited the opposition of their 3,500 members, while others sent letters to local newspapers and contacted their legislators. In July the DAR and the Arkansas Pioneers Association notified Robinson that they were removing their collections from the museum rather than accept the new exhibit plan, citing the changes as "sacrilegious" (*Arkansas Gazette,* June 9, 1979, *Arkansas Gazette,* July 21, 1979).

By August the women's groups had gained state senator Knox Nelson to their cause, who spoke to the Commemorative Commission on their behalf, asking that the commission consider the women's concerns. The women presented the commission with a list of their demands, which were (1) that the period rooms and furnishings be left intact, (2) that no arts and crafts be taught at the museum, (3) that no part of the Old State House be developed as a Museum of Victorian Design, and (4) that the new elevator be placed on the outside, rather than the inside, of the building (*Arkansas Gazette,* August 25, 1979). Basically, the women really didn't want any changes at all from the way the museum had operated during the 1950s and 1960s, even going so far as to reverse the new educational program and suggest an unrealistic and visually damaging change to the architectural exterior—quite the opposite of what they claimed to be fighting for.

Overwrought by the threat to their period rooms, the women seemed to be verging on hysteria. One woman went so far as to ask whether the commission was intending to tear down the building, while another asked the commission to keep the Old State House "as a historic shrine for the people of Arkansas." Dr. Ruth Patterson, commission chairwoman, explained that the commission did not want the Old State House to become "a static museum piece" but "be preserved as a dynamic, living organism that would by changing exhibits reflect the wider spectrum of the history and culture of Arkansas," pointing out that "static parlor rooms simply cannot convey the complexity of life" in the state (*Arkansas Gazette,* August 25, 1979). Regardless of how forward-thinking the commission may have been, they misjudged the feelings and latent political power of the women's patriotic groups.

The women were irate and they hounded their state representatives until September, when the project came before a legislative council committee charged with approving the appropriation. Because of the controversy, the committee refused to completely approve the project, stopping it three times in September and October, and finally insisted that a written agreement between the Commemorative Commission and the women's groups was needed before they would grant approval (*Arkansas Gazette,* September 14, September 20, October 12, 1979).

The women had forced the commission's hand. In mid-October 1979 the commission and the women's groups came together to work out a compromise. In regard to the architectural restoration of the building, they were closer together than might have appeared. After discussion, the women's groups approved the plans, leaving only the details about the placement of the elevator until later, which eventually was constructed inside the building. In other matters, however, the commission relinquished some of their planned changes. Although the period rooms would still be moved to the west wing, the women's groups were to retain more control over their rooms, and furnishings would not be moved without the groups' consultation. The commission also agreed to end brick-making demonstrations, the only arts-and-crafts activity that had actually raised objections (*Arkansas Gazette,* October 18, 1979). With a compromise in place and feelings soothed, the Commemorative Commission finally was able to move forward with the building's restoration.

It was an unfortunate circumstance that the Commemorative Commission and women's patriotic groups found themselves at odds in the late 1970s over the management of the Old State House, since both factions ultimately shared the same goals, which were to preserve the Old State House and utilize it as a museum of Arkansas history. The youthfulness of some of the state employees may have contributed to a lack of understanding and appreciation for what the women's groups had accomplished in saving the building at the beginning of the century. From the start of planning, the women's groups should have been included as working partners in the discussion of changes to the museum, a process of community involvement whose importance to museums came to be recognized in more recent years. That inclusion of multiple voices might have led to less friction and more unified support for what was clearly a good direction for the future of the Old State House.

There comes a time in the life of an organization or movement when those who have done the most to found it must eventually step aside to allow growth and new direction. Times change, as do ideas, and holding too much to the past can destroy a once-vital movement. In many ways the success of the women's patriotic organizations created the problems they faced. The women's groups saved the Old State House and put it on a firm foundation as both a historical monument and museum of Arkansas history. They were so successful in this that by the late 1970s no one considered using the building in any other way. Their success, however, also moved the management of the Old State House in the direction of more professional museum practices, which left the amateur and volunteer management of the women's groups in the past. Their very success undermined their control. For that, the women's groups should justifiably be proud—they could have left no better monument to their accomplishment.

Moving Forward: 1980s

Despite the fits and starts caused by the controversy with the women's patriotic organizations, restoration on the Old State House began in the latter half of 1979 based on architectural research undertaken in the previous few years, including a restoration study completed by Wilson Stiles. Little Rock architect Charles Witsell, who specialized in the restoration of historic structures, was awarded the contract to oversee the restoration. Earlier work on the building had been done to preserve and maintain it, but had not been concerned with historical accuracy. As Wilson Stiles (1978) noted in his restoration study, "significant destruction of the original fabric" had occurred during the 1949 rehabilitation. The restoration of the 1980s was intended to repair the errors of previous generations and restore the building to its 1830 appearance wherever possible, although the 1885 additions would be retained, leading to a mix of Greek Revival and Victorian spaces (*Arkansas Gazette,* September 20, 1979; Stiles 1978).

Initial work included repair of the leaking roof, inspection of the foundation, and repainting of interior spaces in original colors. Architectural detective work uncovered fragments of the interior that still held original paint colors and treatments, revealing, for example, that the front hallway had been brilliant yellow and the stairwell a deeper gold with the wainscoting grained to resemble a better grade of wood. Director Lucy Robinson also wanted to restore the first House of Representatives and Supreme Court Chamber to their original appearances, which included replacing the incorrect fireplaces and mantles, and changing out inappropriate carpeting and drapery. Other work included restorations to the lighting, floors, and woodwork (*Arkansas Gazette,* September 20, 1979).

The restoration was a long, slow process that continued into the middle 1980s. The painstaking work had some surprising rewards. While installing an intercom unit in 1981, a long-hidden 1842 window in the west wing was discovered. It had been covered when the space between the center building and west wing was enclosed in 1867 for the treasurer's office. Another hidden window, this one found in the attic space, revealed remains of the original staircase. In addition to the windows, an expanse of original exterior wall hidden by the west hyphen also was uncovered. Contrary to the long tradition of a white building, restorers discovered that the brick walls of the building originally had been stuccoed and painted gray to resemble granite, which included scoring and veining to imitate large stone blocks (*Arkansas Gazette,* January 21, 1981, August 9, 1985; Roy and Witsell 1984:48).

After the controversy over the period rooms and the use of the west wing, Robinson had largely given up her ideas for a Museum of Victorian Design. The period rooms were still to be moved to the west wing, but the women's groups would retain control over them. The move did provide, however, an opportunity to rethink the displays and their contexts. By November 1981 the new period rooms in the west wing were ready for public viewing, and a special reception was held to premier them. The six period rooms were sponsored by the Daughters of the American Revolution, the United Daughters of 1812, the Arkansas Pioneers Association, the United Daughters of the Confederacy, the United Spanish War Veterans Auxiliary, and the Arkansas Federation of Women's Clubs. Working with the women's organizations, Robinson had improved the rooms by selecting the most appropriate furnishings for each time period and incorporating proper floor coverings, window hangings, woodwork, and wall treatments. Changing exhibit rooms were interspersed among the period rooms to highlight related furnishings and artifacts. The whole was arranged in chronological order, allowing visitors a logical progression on a self-guided tour (*Arkansas Gazette,* November 8, 1981).

Robinson also began to focus efforts on developing a museum friends organization. She hired Judy Thompson, who had worked on fundraising events at the Arkansas Arts Center, and the two of them organized the Old State House Museum Associates. Thompson and her staff went on to develop a large annual fundraising event for the museum, centered on the June 15 anniversary of Arkansas statehood, which came to be called the Arkansas Birthday Party (Ahart n.d.: 2). The Museum Associates proved an active and successful organization; in 1987 they presented to the museum a check for more than $61,000 that was intended to help create a permanent exhibit on Arkansas history (*Arkansas Gazette,* September 9, 1987).

Plans for the new exhibit on Arkansas history were quite ambitious. During that period, dioramas integrated with audio and video elements were all the rage in exhibit design. Robinson and Thompson were inspired by the history dioramas of the Royal British Columbia Museum and designer Jean-Jacques Andre, and with a grant from the National Endowment for the Humanities, they secured the services of Andre in 1986. It took Andre two years, to June 1988, to complete his design plan, working

Fig. 9.10: Part of the original outer walls hidden by the west hyphen were revealed during restoration work in the 1980s, showing how the brick was stuccoed, scored, veined, and colored gray to imitate stone. *Photograph by Cindy Momchilov, Quapaw Quarter Association, courtesy of Butler Center for Arkansas Studies, Central Arkansas Library System.*

Fig. 9.11: The diorama style of exhibitry used in the Wilderness Gallery, which opened in 1993, was a major shift from earlier period rooms and free-standing cases. *Old State House Museum Collection.*

within the existing space and not moving any walls. His design called for the new exhibit to be divided into three phases: wilderness, early statehood through the nineteenth century, and the twentieth century. The price tag for the full cost, however, was $2.5 million. In order to raise the money, the museum contracted with a fundraising consultant to undertake a capital campaign (Ahart n.d.:2; *Arkansas Gazette,* June 26, 1990). About this time, Robinson resigned as director and Judy Thompson was promoted into the position. Thompson served as director for only about three years, but during that time, a modified version of the first phase of the exhibit plan was completed. Problems with the fundraising consultant led to abandonment of the plans for the capital campaign, but with the money already raised Thompson proceeded with the first phase of the exhibit, hoping that its success would make future fundraising easier. The result was the Wilderness Gallery, which opened in 1993.

During Thompson's tenure as director, she also secured the museum's first accreditation by the American Association of Museums (Ahart n.d.:2–3; *Arkansas Democrat-Gazette,* July 31, 1993). The Association's Accreditation Program is a rigorous, multistep process that involves self-study, peer review, and correction of deficiencies to demonstrate "currently accepted professional standards" (O'Donnell 1996:43). It is also a process that recognizes the continual evolution of professional standards, so accredited museums must repeat the program once a decade to maintain accreditation. Receiving accreditation by the American Association of Museums is a standard of excellence that brings national recognition to a museum.

Despite the battles over control and direction of the museum during the 1970s, and the restoration, fundraising, and exhibit challenges of the 1980s, the Old State House Museum ultimately earned its place among the ranks of professional museums. With accreditation, a solid foundation of museum practice had been attained that set the course for the future.

CHAPTER 10

Archeology and the Final Restoration: Late 1980s–1990s

THE EMPHASIS ON architectural and historical accuracy of the Old State House that began to be employed in the 1970s also led to the first archeological work undertaken on the Old State House grounds. With all the historical documents available on the Old State House, a person might wonder what archeology could add to the building's history. In fact, as has been seen by studying the reports of the secretaries of state, newspaper accounts, and other documents, much information was never recorded. While details of government business transacted in the building are safely preserved in legislative minutes, details of construction and daily use of the building are not. Through the methods of archeology, the unrecorded mysteries of the past can be teased into the light of day.

A Drain and a Well

In March 1987, during the installation of a sprinkler system, archeologist Skip Stewart-Abernathy of the Arkansas Archeological Survey monitored the trench excavations. Stewart-Abernathy noted that artifacts could be found all throughout the grounds. Besides lots of window glass and brick fragments, most of the artifacts dated to the twentieth century, with occasional dark-green bottle glass and hand-painted ceramics from the antebellum years. The trenching also uncovered an unexpected French-drain system once used for carrying surface water away from the building (Guendling and Kwas 1997:46).

The following year, in September, Survey archeologist George Sabo undertook a one-day archeological investigation seeking remnants of the former nineteenth-century well house. The well had once been located in the front lawn along the walkway leading to the west wing. It was covered with a roofed open-sided house, which can be seen in photographs from the Civil War, until about 1925 when it was torn down. The well itself was sealed in 1883, on the direction of Secretary of State Jacob Frolich, after the water had gone bad, and it was replaced with a large cistern built at the back of the Old State House. As part of the restoration plans, museum staff wanted to have the well house reconstructed (*Arkansas Gazette,* July 4, 1883; Guendling and Kwas 1997:46–47).

Sabo discovered that the well shaft was sealed with limestone slabs and a filled concrete box. A layer of rubble around the sealed shaft contained fragments of brick, mortar, glass, and slate. Three concrete foundation piers, representing three corners of the well house, were located. The missing northeast foundation presumably had been destroyed when the walkway was constructed. Sabo found that each foundation pier had been poured in holes dug through the rubble, and each had a metal strap intended to be tied to their brick courses (*Arkansas Gazette,* September 2, 1988; Guendling and Kwas 1997:46–47).

The East Wing Steps

A three-day excavation was undertaken in October 1993 after a limestone slab used as a step on the east side of the east wing broke and collapsed. After the slab had been laid at an unknown time in the past, it sealed what was beneath it from modern disturbance. This provided an excellent opportunity to look into the building's past and examine the building techniques employed in the nineteenth century. Survey archeologist Skip Stewart-Abernathy directed the excavation, and museum staff members pitched in to do the earth-moving. One of the goals of the excavation was to document how the steps were constructed.

Stewart-Abernathy found that the steps were built in the shape of a hollow box with brick shoulders. The shoulders supported stone treads that overlapped so that no risers were necessary. The foundation consisted of rough stone upon which three courses of original, handmade bricks were laid. A soft lime mortar bound them together. The upper courses of brick had been replaced with modern factory-made bricks and were mortared with a modern type of portland cement. It appeared the steps had been set into a large pit that was part of the foundation preparation for the east wing. Also exposed during the excavation was the lower part of the east wall of the wing. Handmade bricks were also seen in the lower courses of the wall, as was expected, but the soft lime mortar appeared only on the lowest four courses, those above had been repaired with more modern cement mortar.

Most of the artifacts found date before 1900 and included a Henry rifle cartridge from the Civil War era, percussion caps from muzzle loaders, fountain pen nibs, Medical School debris, and sherds of earthenware dishes, including one with a tea rose pattern in copper lustre and a later decal-decorated sherd. There also were fragments of bricks, window glass, and food bones. Based on the construction techniques and the artifacts, the original stairs may well have been built at the time of the 1885 remodeling. Subsequent repairs were

Fig. 10.1: Archeological excavations at the Old State House were conducted 1996–1997 prior to repairing the building's foundation. *Photograph by Randall Guendling, Arkansas Archeological Survey.*

conducted some time after 1900 (*Arkansas Democrat-Gazette,* October 14, 1993; Guendling and Kwas 1997:47–48).

Secrets of the Foundation

In March 1994 Ronnie Nichols became the new director of the Old State House Museum. Nichols, an Arkansas native, held an art degree from UALR and a master's degree in fine arts from the Otis Art Institute in Los Angeles. He also was an expert on the experience of black soldiers in the Civil War and served as technical advisor on the film *Glory.* His previous position was as director of the Delta Cultural Center in Helena. Nichols served as director of the Old State House Museum for four and a half years (*Arkansas Democrat-Gazette,* August 16, 1998).

Shortly after Nichols became director, it was discovered that the building's foundation had deteriorated over the decades and was no longer able to safely support the structure. A plan to underpin the building with reinforced concrete beams and retaining walls was such an extensive undertaking that the Old State House had to be closed to the public and the exhibits removed during the work. The underpinning required excavation into the ground immediately surrounding the building, which would destroy any evidence of early construction techniques, renovations, and associated artifacts. It was clear that the foundation work would be the last opportunity for archeologists to retrieve and analyze the long-hidden evidence of the earliest history of the Old State House.

In November 1995, during the assessment process prior to underpinning, it was necessary

Fig. 10.2: Excavations uncovered a brick storm drain, constructed about 1855. *Photograph by Randall Guendling, Arkansas Archeological Survey.*

to expose sections of the original foundation. Skip Stewart-Abernathy returned to the site to monitor the excavations as the construction crew hand-dug six short trenches at the front of the building. Stewart-Abernathy was particularly concerned with identifying the 1830s builder's trench, documenting any architectural features, and discovering any use of the site prior to the 1830s construction. Despite disturbances to the subsoil from several generations of drain replacements, utility trenches, and other activities, intact deposits from the nineteenth century still remained around the building. It quickly became apparent, however, that monitoring the construction crew's excavations would be inadequate for recovering and interpreting what remained. Urged to undertake a more comprehensive archeological examination, the Department of Arkansas Heritage agreed and funded an in-depth archeological investigation (Guendling and Kwas 1997:48–49).

The Arkansas Archeological Survey began work in the spring of 1996. Under the direction of archeologist Randall Guendling, the five-man crew conducted most of their work during a month from mid-March to mid-April. One- and two-day return visits during the spring of 1997 allowed the crew to document additional architectural features uncovered during the underpinning. As part of the project, research of the archival record was also undertaken, which eventually led to this book (Guendling and Kwas 1997:49–50). Despite all the rebuilding and mixing of materials through the long period of the site's use, Guendling was able to discover some early evidence of the building's construction and changes.

Fig. 10.3: Behind a twentieth-century pipe can be seen the 1836 stone foundation in the wall of the east wing. *Photograph by Randall Guendling, Arkansas Archeological Survey.*

Although one was expected, no builder's trench for the Old State House was found. Instead, a huge straight-sided pit that served as the base of the foundation had been dug into the clay-filled ground. The clay was removed from the pit and used to make the bricks for the building. A rubble foundation was laid at the bottom of the pit, and the straight earthen sides provided a form against which to lay the bricks. About a foot out from the building and parallel to the foundation was a rainwater collection system. It originally was made of the same kind of bricks as the building's walls and sealed on the inside with creosote in a box shape. The ground was graded and sloped away from the building, allowing the water to flow away. During the 1885 expansion, the top of the water system was removed and stoneware pipes, called *drain tiles,* were placed on the older bricks (Guendling, personal communication).

Guendling discovered a shallow foundation for the columns of the main building, as well as leftover column bricks that had been thrown under the porch as fill. The bricks were made in several shapes that fit together like puzzle pieces to form the flutes and points of the Doric columns. Evidence for the original colonnaded walkway between the buildings was also found. Before the hyphens were built, a raised walkway enclosed by a low brick wall stretched between the main building and the wings. Guendling found a remnant of the brick footer of the walkway (Guendling, personal communication).

Two vaults were added in the late 1800s, built above ground but protruding from the building. The larger vault, located in the north-east corner of the building for the office of the

Fig. 10.4: The brick and stone foundation beneath a portico column was exposed during archeological excavations in 1997. *Photograph by Randall Guendling, Arkansas Archeological Survey.*

Fig. 10.5: The points and flutes of the columns were formed by specially shaped bricks that fit together like puzzle pieces. *Photograph by Jane Kellet, Arkansas Archeological Survey.*

commissioner of state lands, was built in 1885 during the expansion. Specifications for the work were included in the work order. It was built of stone masonry and destroyed in 1934 during the WPA renovations. A smaller vault was built for the treasurer's office and located off the west hyphen. It was built about 1898, had a brick foundation, and also was destroyed during 1934. During excavations, Guendling found the stone and brick foundations of the two vaults (Guendling and Kwas 1997:59–62).

Remnants of the 1883 cistern, which had been covered over during the 1885 expansion, also were found. The dimensions met the description of the 1883 cistern, as well as those of the cavern discovered in 1936, thus solving the mystery of the cavern.

Found Objects

The excavations around the foundation of the Old State House uncovered numerous artifacts, although almost nothing in a sealed context. Most artifacts were small fragments of glass, ceramics, and rusted metal that are not of much value in and of themselves. The real value in the artifacts is in their connection to the site and the activities that occurred there. Some of the more interesting artifacts are highlighted below.

Because of the on-site construction, expansion, and various renovations of the building, one would expect to find physical evidence of those activities. Indeed, lots of broken window glass, clumps of mortar, sewer pipe, rusted nails and other hardware, and fragments of bricks—including the specially shaped column bricks—were common finds.

All during the nineteenth century the Old State House served as the center of state

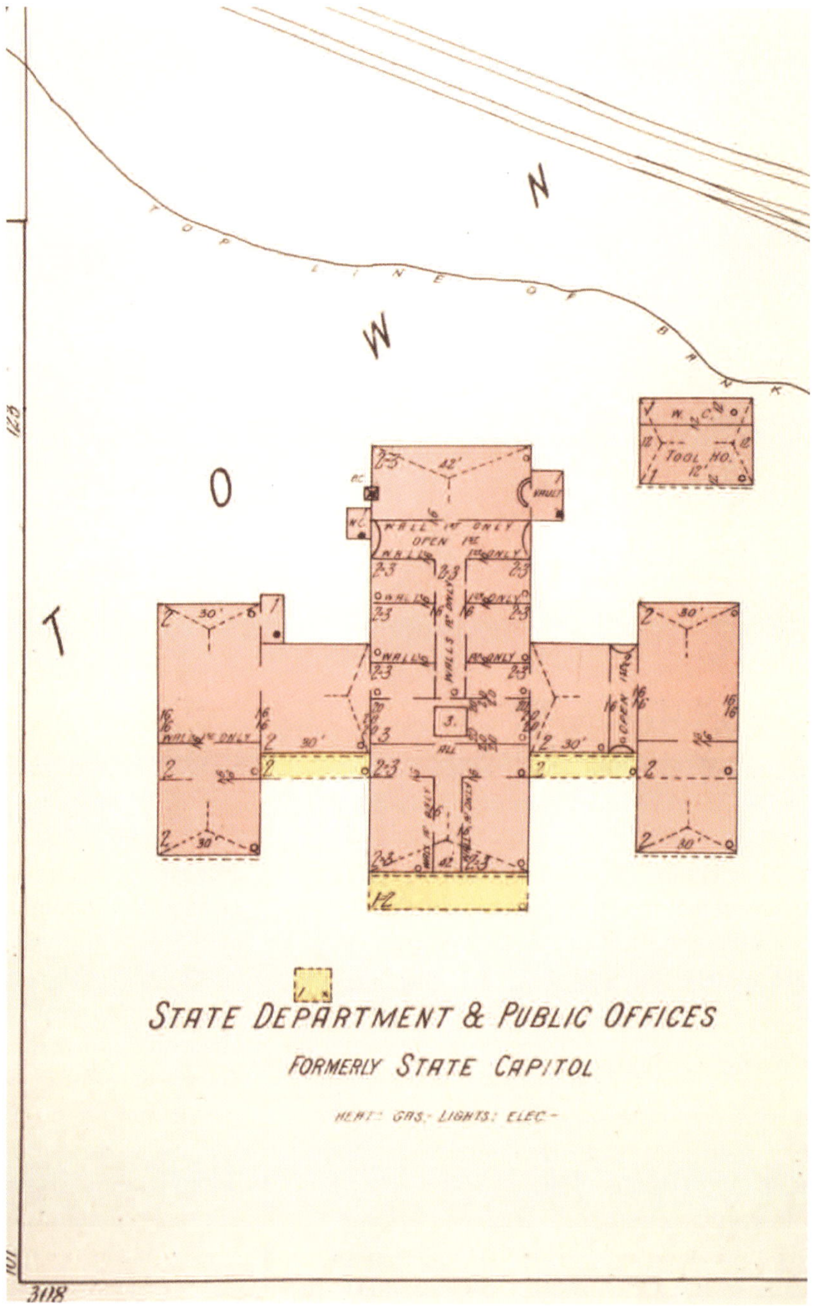

Fig. 10.6: Vaults in the northeast corner of the main building and off the west hyphen, built in 1885 and 1898, can be seen on the 1913 Sanborn Insurance Map. *Photograph courtesy of Arkansas Archeological Survey.*

government, which included offices for the governor, secretary of state, and treasurer, among others. After state government moved to the new Capitol, other agencies found office space in the building. Artifacts of various office activities were found. These included pencils, ball-point pens, paper clips, and other kinds of paper fasteners, as well as three keys, one probably for a desk and another for winding a clock. Before ball-point pens were invented, pens were dipped into inkwells. The pens had replaceable metal tips—called *nibs*—which slipped into the shaft of the pen. When the nib wore out, it was discarded and a new one fitted into the shaft. Numerous nibs were found in the excavations. Most were of a rusted metal or brass, one appeared to be made of an early hard plastic called Bakelite, and one was probably gold—perhaps it had been from the pen of a governor (Guendling and Kwas 1997:94).

Where dip pens were in use, there also had to be ink bottles and inkwells. Large ink bottles, called master inks, were used to refill the smaller inkwells. A number of sherds from master inks were found on the site; they were made of gray-colored stoneware with a brown slip finish on the exterior and were designed with a lip that formed a pouring spout. One base fragment was impressed with the potter's name of "J. Bourne & Son of Denby Pottery" and was made for the company of "P. & J. Arnold" in London. Master ink bottles from the same company were found among the cargo from the sunken steamer *Bertrand,* which went down in April 1865 on the Missouri River. Base fragments of other small stoneware bottles, measuring about 1.5 to 2 inches in diameter, were probably fragments of inkwells (Guendling and Kwas 1997:80–81).

Fig. 10.7: Pen nibs of brass, Bakelite, and gold were discovered in the excavations. *Photograph by Jane Kellet, Arkansas Archeological Survey.*

Fig. 10.8: The base of a stoneware master ink bottle includes the impressed potter's name of "J. Bourne & Son" and the company the bottle was made for, "P. &. J. Arnold." *Photograph by Jane Kellet, Arkansas Archeological Survey.*

Another long use of the building had been by the Medical Department of the University of Arkansas from 1912 to 1935, and a variety of small medical artifacts were found in the excavations (see Fig. 8.6). Most of these artifacts were parts of glass laboratory equipment, such as fragments of test tubes of various sizes, pipettes for removing small amounts of liquid, stirring rods, syringe barrels marked with gradations, and thermometers. Other glass fragments probably came from petri dishes, beakers, or bottles. Unglazed porcelain or ceramic sherds probably were fragments of mortars used to grind medicines. Six metal syringe hubs—one still containing its needle—were also found (Guendling and Kwas 1997:94–95). Among the fragments of bottles found were those with lips shaped into pouring spouts or slanted inward to keep medicine from spilling out. Another find, as discussed earlier, predated the Medical School but was associated with Dr. John J. McAlmont, one of the founders of the Medical School. The find consisted of a fragment of a glass medicine bottle from the 1872 to 1883 "McAlmont & Gibson" drugstore that once stood on the northeast corner of Markham and Main streets (Ewbank 1986:33-34; Guendling and Kwas 1997:86; Williams and Whayne 2000:183-184).

Visitors to the site unintentionally left behind artifacts as well, including two metal U.S. Infantry buttons dating to the period of the Civil War. They are shanked, two-piece buttons made of brass, with the motif of a spread eagle and the letter "I" in a shield. No doubt they were lost during the Federal occupation of Little Rock when soldiers congregated on the State House grounds. Civil War–era bullets were also found (Guendling and Kwas 1997: 91).

A particularly interesting find was a souvenir medal from the Thirty-eighth Annual Confederate Reunion (see Fig. 8.8), which was held in Little Rock with activities at the Old State House on May 8–11, 1928. The brass medal with relief images is made in three parts. The upper part has a scene of the Broadway and Main street bridges crossing the Arkansas River from Little Rock to North Little Rock. The lower

Fig. 10.9: Ammunition from the grounds of the Old State House illustrates the confrontations of the Civil War and the Brooks-Baxter War. *Photograph by Jane Kellet, Arkansas Archeological Survey.*

part, which is shield shaped, shows the state of Arkansas, the new Capitol building, and crossed flags—one Confederate and the other possibly the Arkansas state flag. The flags are enameled in red, white, and blue. The medal is embossed: "The Wonder State / Little Rock / May 8–11 1828 / S.C.V." The initials stand for "Sons of Confederate Veterans." The third piece of the medal consists of a small bar that connects the other two pieces. The medal was made by the Greenduck Co. of Chicago, Illinois (Guendling and Kwas 1997:92).

Other artifacts are more difficult to place with specific activities or occupancies of the building. Many artifacts were of such a general nature they could have belonged to anyone—visitors, government employees, office workers, students—or just represent trash that was discarded on the Old State House grounds. That doesn't make them any less interesting.

Eleven United States coins were found, all small change that perhaps fell from a pocket or slipped between fingers. The earliest was an 1842 half-dime. There were two nickels: a shield-type nickel dating to 1880 or 1883, and a buffalo nickel with a date of 1916. There were also eight pennies: an 1890 Indian-head penny, a 1942 Lincoln penny, and more recent pennies dating from 1970 to 1989 (Guendling and Kwas 1997:93).

Buttons were commonly lost on the grounds, popping off from a weak thread or catching on something while the owner worked. Most of the buttons were fairly utilitarian and made of a variety of materials. Ten bone buttons and six pearl buttons were found. The bone buttons, common in the nineteenth century, were cut from cattle bones. The pearl buttons were cut from the nacreous shells of river mussels taken from the Mississippi watershed. An extensive pearl button industry in the United States lasted from 1891 to about 1950, although the peak period for the use of pearl buttons was from 1898 to 1930. The manufacture of earthenware and porcelain buttons, made by compacting powdered clay in a mechanical press, was invented by Richard Prosser in England in 1840. Ten Prosser-type buttons were found on the site; these buttons were very common until they were replaced by plastic buttons in the twentieth century. Both the pearl and porcelain buttons were used as shirt and sleeve buttons. Seventeen metal buttons also were found, most probably from workmen's clothes. Four of the metal buttons had a thin coating of gold; these fancy buttons may have adorned a suit jacket or uniform (Guendling and Kwas 1997:88–91).

Other clothing-related items included an elastic hair band, an iron heel plate, a hose fastener, a brass eyelet, a small clothing hook, a safety pin, a straight pin, and two collar buttons, which are similar to collar studs. Miscellaneous bits of broken jewelry were found that included parts of an earring, a charm for a watch chain, and a tiebar. There were also two stickpins with imitation pearl heads, as well as several loose beads (Guendling and Kwas 1997:91–92).

Personal items included a fragment of a bone toothbrush, a couple teeth from plastic combs, a lead fishing weight, and a pocketknife. Thirteen fragments of bowls and stems from tobacco pipes were also found. The pipe bowls were made of redware or terra cotta clay and the stems of white ball clay. Decoration on the pipe bowls was limited to raised bands, cross-hatches, or dots. These pipes were most common in the nineteenth century (Guendling and Kwas 1997:92, 94, 96–98). Children who visited the site or were part of the caretakers' families occasionally lost toys on the grounds. There were four marbles, two of tan clay, one of white porcelain, and one of machine-made glass. Part of the torso of a porcelain doll was found, as well as one metal jack (Guendling and Kwas 1997:93).

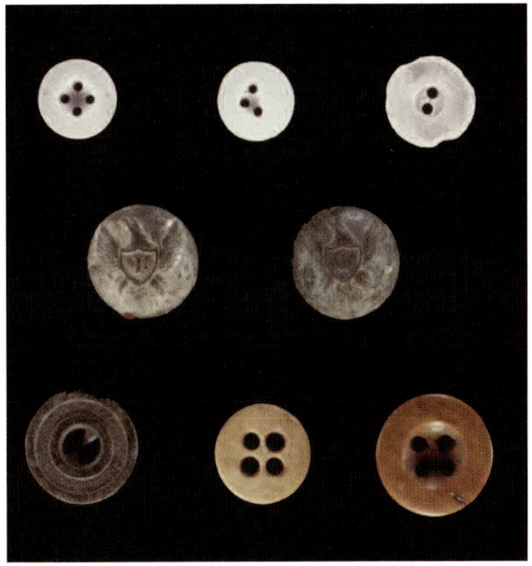

Fig. 10.10: Buttons of a variety of materials, including mussel shell, clay, bone, and metal, and two U.S. Infantry buttons from the Civil War (shown in the middle row), were recovered during excavations. *Photograph by Jane Kellet, Arkansas Archeological Survey.*

Fig. 10.11: This patent medicine bottle, embossed "W.B. Caldwell's Syrup Pepsin," dates to the turn of the twentieth century. *Photograph by Jane Kellet, Arkansas Archeological Survey.*

As can be imagined, broken pieces of glass were found all over the site, representing fragments of bottles, drinking glasses, lamps, light bulbs, window glass, and the glass artifacts from the medical lab discussed earlier. Colors ranged through shades of amber, brown, green, and aqua, as well as cobalt blue, milk glass, and colorless glass. Fragments of bottles included parts of the body, base, neck, and lip. The distinctive finish on bottle lips often suggests the contents the bottles once held, as the lips usually vary for soft drinks, liquors, medicines, foods, or nonconsumable products, such as ink or cleaning fluids (Guendling and Kwas 1997:82–88).

Besides the McAlmont & Gibson medicine bottle described above, two other bottles were able to be identified. One was a whole patent medicine bottle, embossed with the following information: "Dr. W.B. Caldwell's / Syrup Pepsin / Pepsin Syrup Company / Monticello, Illinois." Dr. William Burr Caldwell introduced his Syrup Pepsin about 1889 and used embossed bottles with cork closures from 1895 to 1942. The other was a base from a colorless bottle from the Lambert Pharmacal Company, makers of Listerine. The company was founded in St. Louis, Missouri, in 1878, and Listerine was introduced by Jordan Lambert the following year (Guendling and Kwas 1997:84, 86).

Numerous ceramic sherds, representing small fragments of dinner dishes, utilitarian kitchenwares, and even flowerpots, were found throughout the excavations. Types of ware and decorative treatments spanned the range of nineteenth-century ceramics. Sherds of white earthenware were found in blue shell edge, in spatter and sponged wares, with colored banded slips, and with hand-painted florals done in both broad strokes and fine sprigging. Transfer prints on white earthenware came in dark blue, light blue, flow blue, brown, green, purple, gray, and black patterns. One rim sherd with a dark-blue transfer print was identified as being from the "Large Scroll Border Series" made by potters John and Richard Riley of Burslem, Staffordshire, England, between 1813 and 1828. The series featured views of British and Irish buildings, and the sherd may be one of the earliest found on the site. Other ceramic sherds came from relief-molded ironstone. Fragments of porcelain and fine-grained black stoneware, known as Egyptian Black, represented teawares. Sherds of yellow ware and a variety of stonewares came from kitchen mixing bowls, crocks, and other storage vessels (Guendling and Kwas 1997:72–82).

One might wonder why the site of a state capitol would have so many fragments of ceramic dishes and glass bottles. But consider your own work space—we all bring coffee mugs and lunch plates and drinking glasses to work with us. We have the advantage of plastic and disposable dishes to use at work, but during the nineteenth century, ceramics and glass were the most common materials for table use. In addition, caretakers, workmen, and soldiers lived on the grounds and made use of dishes, and various special events, such as balls and dinners, added their broken dishes to the debris.

Although not of great value, the artifacts found in the excavations around the Old State House represent the many and diverse activities that were held on the grounds. These fragments of lost and broken objects are a tangible part of Arkansas's past.

The Last Renovation

When the Old State House closed on April 1, 1996, so that work on the building's foundation could begin, it was anticipated the museum would reopen in 14 months. Unexpected problems and delays expanded that time to more than three years at a cost exceeding $3 million. But the work was crucial to the building's survival, since the structural integrity of the building was threatened by the deteriorating foundation. In 1830 the foundation had been constructed of fieldstones, handmade bricks, and soft mortar, all of which over time had cracked and crumbled. As the foundation shifted, cracks appeared in the outer walls. Repeated stresses and minor structural damage over the years also affected the wooden joists that supported the second floor. These joists, which fitted into hollow places in the brick walls, had shifted in their sockets, causing the brick around them to crumble. Over time, this action led to a bowing in the center of the second floor (*Arkansas Democrat-Gazette,* March 30, 1996).

The renovation project proceeded in phases, the first of which was to reinforce the foundation with concrete beams sunk ten feet deep. Work stopped periodically to let the archeologists examine in-ground evidence of the building's construction and recover artifacts. The foundation work took a year to complete, longer than originally expected. The second phase repaired the supports on the second floor, but a discovery of asbestos in the building again slowed the renovation. Repairs, plastering, and painting of interior and exterior walls followed. During the renovation process, a new annex building also was constructed behind the Old State House to serve as staff offices (*Arkansas Democrat-Gazette,* March 30, 1996, August 7, 1998, August 16, 1998).

The Old State House had been on the National Register of Historic Places since 1969, but during the 1990s it earned an even higher honor recognizing its importance. In December 1997 the Old State House was designated a National Historic Landmark.

Once the physical work on the building had been completed, it was expected to take about six months to restore exhibits and prepare for a grand opening. Those plans were delayed by a near-tragedy, when the roof of the building caught fire on September 21, 1998, just as the staff was beginning to reinstall the exhibits. Workers attempting to loosen old paint on the tin eaves with a propane torch inadvertently ignited timbers in the attic. The building's sprinkler system kept the fire from spreading, and firefighters extinguished the fire within an hour, but much damage had been done to the newly renovated building. Firefighters had to cut holes into the roof and second-floor ceiling to access the attic, and broke windows to ventilate the building. Damage from water was worse than that from the fire, especially in the original House of Representatives, where part of the plaster ceiling had collapsed. Concerns about the plaster walls and ceilings in other areas, and possible damage to the pine floors and hollow Doric columns, raised early damage estimates as high as half a million dollars (*Arkansas Democrat-Gazette,* September 22–23, 1998).

Luckily, only two exhibits were in the building at the time: the Wilderness Gallery, which was far enough from the fire to be unaffected, and the President Clinton exhibit, which largely consisted of replicas and which was quickly covered by plastic for protection. Although the fire was a setback—and a frightening potential threat to the Old State House—it was not as bad as it could have been. When the Old State House reopened in June 1999, it was clean, polished, and standing on a firm foundation—ready to face a new millennium of service to the state and people of Arkansas.

Fig. 10.12: Water shoots out of the roof of the Old State House as firefighters contain the blaze in the building's attic on September 21, 1998. *Photograph by Steve Keesee, courtesy of* Arkansas Democrat-Gazette.

Programs and Projects for the Future

As the museum reopened to the public, behind-the-scenes changes to the management of exhibits and programs were underway. Themes and topics for exhibits continued to grow out of the diverse history of Arkansas. There were new permanent exhibits, as well as ones designed to change periodically, on display long enough to give state residents ample opportunity to see them, but short term enough to keep interest alive and encourage repeat visitation. *Pillars of Power* introduced Arkansans to the history of the Old State House itself. Other exhibits explored Arkansas women, music, political history, architecture, African American quilts, Arkansans in the U.S.-Mexican War, and the early years of Arkansas archeology.

The museum began to incorporate new technologies into the exhibits, introducing videos and interactive computer kiosks, as well as on-line access through a Web site that displays images and information from current and past exhibits. Adjuncts to the exhibits have included scholarly books and popular items to sell in the gift shop. Exhibit development has been enhanced by seeking community input and expertise from scholars through advisory committees and guest curators (Ahart n.d.:4–5).

Changes in the museum's education department included staff expansion, additional tours, and living history programs. The

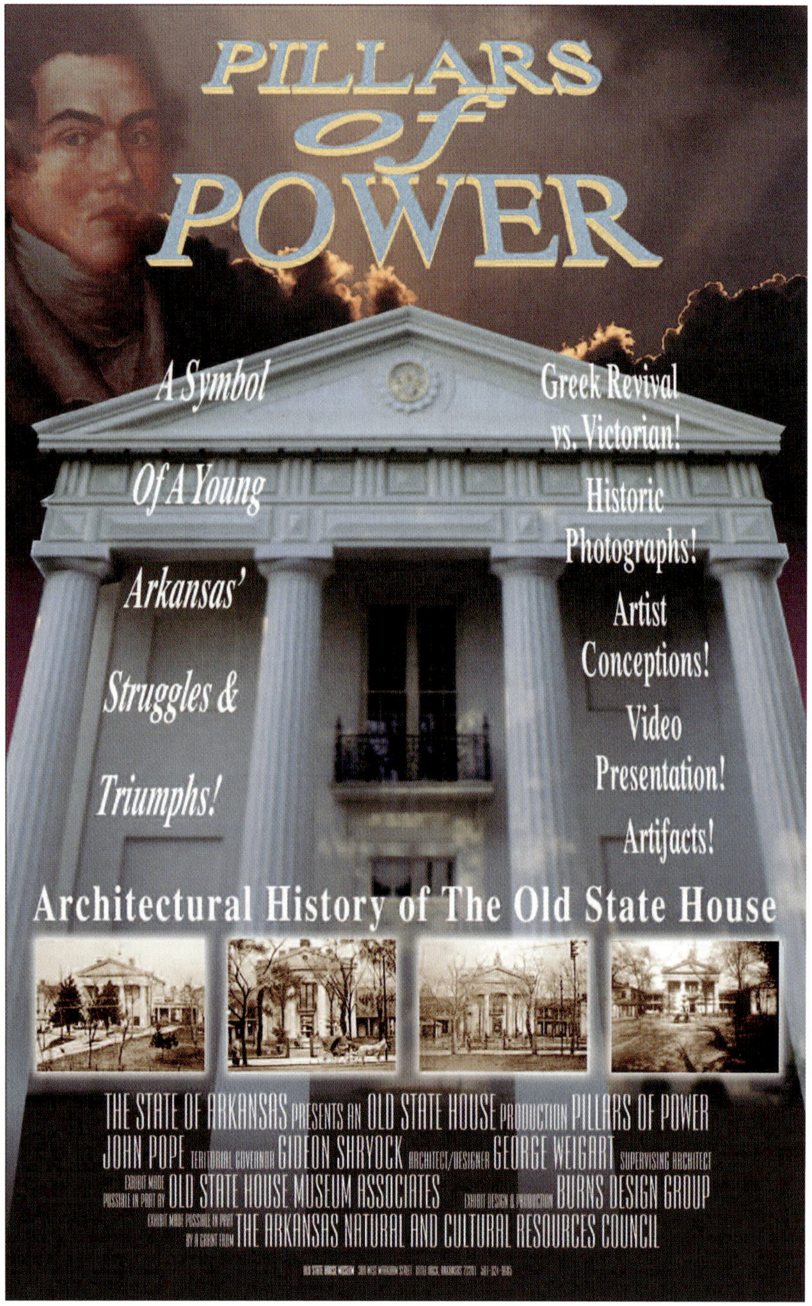

Fig. 10.13: Designed to imitate the poster of a blockbuster movie, this poster was used to advertise the museum's *Pillars of Power* exhibit. *Courtesy of Dennis Oxley, Oxley Art Graphic Designs, Little Rock, Arkansas.*

museum's education staff provided workshops for teachers and educational programs and tours for students. Other programs included Civil War seminars and special events, such as the *Big Boo!seum Bash.* Educational activities and games can also be found on the museum's Web site. Museum staff worked toward improving collection records through a computerized database and fine-tuned professional management of the museum to retain accreditation by the American Association of Museums.

The Old State House Museum is one of the premier museums in Arkansas. The management of the Old State House Museum continues to preserve and promote this important historic building, and the museum's programs and exhibits embrace and expand its purpose as an embodiment of the history of Arkansas.

CHAPTER 11

A Living Legacy

THE OLD STATE HOUSE has survived 175 years of both tribulations and honors. It stands as a monument to all of Arkansas's history—from territorial times on to the present. In the nineteenth century the building served as the seat of state government. In the twentieth century its purpose was recreated several times—as an office for federal agencies and patriotic organizations, a medical school, a war memorial, a shrine, and finally a museum of Arkansas history. As the Old State House now crosses into a third century, it continues to provide a vital service to Arkansas.

Its purpose as a museum of Arkansas history is a fitting one. This grand building that participated in so much Arkansas history now serves as a home to educate and inform Arkansans, while doing so in a way that brings the past alive through historical collections, informative exhibits, and outreach activities.

Even more than as a museum, however, the Old State House serves as a symbol of Arkansas's history. It embodies the aspirations of Greek Revival architecture and forms a bridge between the past and the future. Perhaps the most elegant expression of the Old State House's symbolism came on a night in 1992 when Arkansas governor Bill Clinton won the election to the presidency of the United States.

Fig. 11.1: President-elect Bill Clinton celebrates victory on election day, November 3, 1992, at the Old State House in Little Rock. *Photograph by David Turnley, courtesy of CORBIS.*

The Old State House served Clinton as election night headquarters, and at about 11:25 P.M. on November 3 he delivered his victory speech in front of the historic building.

Clinton thanked his supporters and told the people who stood on the Old State House grounds: "My fellow Americans, on this day, with high hopes and brave hearts, in massive numbers, the American people have voted to make a new beginning" (*Arkansas Democrat Gazette,* November 4, 1992). Not only Arkansans saw the beautiful Old State House, but viewers throughout the United States and around the world also caught a glimpse of Arkansas's most historic symbol. In 1996 for President Clinton's reelection campaign, the Old State House again served as election night headquarters.

The Old State House has continued through both quiet times and exciting times in Arkansas history. With the care and esteem of the people of Arkansas, the Old State House will continue to be the site of many new beginnings to come.

SECTION 3

Biographical Sketches of Old State House Personalities

Anthony, Joseph J.

State Representative, 1836–1837

Joseph J. Anthony had only been a resident of Arkansas for about two years, not long enough to be well known in the state, when his homicide in the House of Representatives at the Old State House catapulted him to an infamous immortality. The act also besmirched the good name of the state, giving Arkansas a long-lasting image as a place of uncivilized violence.

Anthony was born about 1780 in Virginia, the son of the Reverend Joseph Anthony and Jane Ferris. Shortly after the death of his father, Anthony, his mother, and three brothers moved to middle Tennessee, settling in Sumner County by 1805. Three years later Anthony was living in nearby Smith County, where he was probably engaged in the mercantile trade. He joined the Twenty-fourth U.S. Infantry in 1812 and was appointed a second lieutenant. He later participated in the battle of Fort Sandusky on August 1–2, 1813, but was arrested shortly after the battle by his commander on charges that included cowardice and dereliction of duty. He maintained his innocence on all but one of the charges—sleeping at his post—citing personal animosity from his commander, but resigned his commission to avoid a court marshal. After returning to Tennessee, he enlisted under Andrew Jackson and fought in the campaign against the Creek Indians in Alabama, where he apparently conducted himself honorably, although the previous charges continued to haunt him throughout his life. When he again returned to Tennessee, he went back into business, and his name is found frequently in the court records pursuing the prosecution of those who owed him debts. By 1830 he left Tennessee, following his brothers to Missouri.

In 1835 Anthony moved to Arkansas Territory, settling in the Current River Township of old Lawrence County. The following year he purchased some land on the east side of the river in Randolph (now Clay) County, and in August was elected to the first state House of Representatives. Anthony became embroiled in Arkansas politics, which during that period often erupted in volatile verbal battles, accusations in the newspapers, and even duels. A scandal involving the Arkansas Real Estate Bank occupied the legislators during 1837 and led to the fatal argument.

On December 4, 1837, in a special session of the General Assembly during a debate over a bill pertaining to bounties for wolf scalps, Anthony alluded to the Real Estate scandal in an insult against Speaker of the House John Wilson, who recently had been elected president of the Real Estate Bank. Wilson ordered Anthony to take his seat, but when Anthony refused, Wilson stormed toward him insisting he would physically make him, despite the fact that Anthony was a large man over six feet tall and weighing over 200 pounds and Wilson was rather smaller. The two men drew large Bowie knives from their jackets as they approached one another. Representative Grandison Royston, sitting near Anthony, threw up his chair between them, but Anthony and Wilson grabbed the chair and began thrusting at each other over and under it. Anthony made the first strike, cutting halfway through Wilson's left wrist. After a few more jabs, Anthony finally threw his knife at Wilson, cutting him to the bone above his right wrist but disarming himself. Anthony then grabbed a chair to strike Wilson, but the latter pushed the chair up with his shoulder, which exposed Anthony's chest. Seeing an opening Wilson lunged forward with his knife and plunged it into Anthony's heart. Anthony died instantly on the floor of the House of Representatives. The fight lasted less than two minutes.

Despite the wild and unruly conditions of life in early Arkansas, the incident shocked both fellow representatives and residents of the state, and the affair was widely publicized. For further details on the aftermath, see the entry on John Wilson.

A funeral for Anthony was held two days later in the Representative's Hall, after which he was buried in Little Rock's Old Burial Ground, located at Capitol and Gaines streets, where the Federal Building now stands. Anthony was about 57 years old when he died, unmarried and without children. His brothers came to Randolph County to settle his estate. Recent mythology purports that Anthony's ghost haunts the Old State House.

(*Arkansas Gazette,* November 15, 1836, March 14, 1837, May 23, 1838, June 4, 1882; Baker 1998:74–79; Dalton 1981:142–143, 207)

Armistead, Henry Beauford

Secretary of State, 1893–1897

Henry Beauford Armistead was born October 19, 1833, in Upperville, Fauquier County, Virginia, a member of a prominent military family with numerous officers. He was the son of John Carter Armistead and Ann S. Harrison. He graduated from the Virginia Military Institute in 1853, having studied under Stonewall Jackson, and then spent some years in the Creek Nation, Indian Territory, and in Utah. He was in the Rocky Mountains when the Civil War began, but made his way back to the South and in 1862 enlisted in the Confederate army with the Sixteenth Missouri Regiment in Clinton, Mississippi. He was paroled in 1865 with the rank of second lieutenant. After settling in Arkansas he served in the Arkansas State Militia, rising to the rank of brigadier general.

Armistead settled in western Arkansas. He was a farmer and a dry-goods merchant in business with his brother-in-law John P. Falconer in the town of Charleston, Franklin County, and also in Fort Smith. He was elected to the state Senate for two terms from 1877 to 1879, representing the Twenty-fifth District of Crawford and Franklin counties. He served as deputy secretary of state from 1889 to 1893, before winning two terms as secretary of state beginning in 1893. His reports as secretary of state are signed "H. B. Armistead."

As the General Assembly continued to discuss plans for a new Capitol, little money was allotted to the State House for its maintenance. Armistead, like his predecessors, pleaded for the money necessary to do his job properly. He was left to patch the building as best he could, but he warned the legislators that the governor and other officials were at risk if the library room collapsed.

Following the completion of his term as secretary of state, Armistead was appointed district clerk and commissioner of the U.S. District Court at Fort Smith under Judge H. M. Rogers, a position he held for 12 years. Armistead died February 7, 1914, at the age of 80, at his home in Charleston. He is buried in Burt Cemetery in Charleston, beside his mother. He never married, but had a sister, Fannie Armistead Falconer, and cousins living in the state.

(Anon. 1974; *Arkansas Democrat,* February 7, 1914; *Arkansas Gazette,* February 8, 1914, February 9, 1914; Herndon 1922a:986–987; Leonard 1901:30; Priest 1998:205, 241, 243; VMI 2007;)

Beavers, Benton B.

Secretary of State, November 13, 1874–January 17, 1879

Benton B. Beavers was born October 3, 1841, in Shelby County, Tennessee, the son of Saline County judge William E. Beavers and Margaret E. Brown. In the following year his family moved to Saline County, where he was raised. Beavers studied medicine at the Louisville Medical College, graduating in 1868. He served in the Trans-Mississippi department during the Civil War and then was elected to the state Senate in 1872 from the Twenty-first District, representing Dallas, Saline, Perry, and Grant counties. At the end of 1874 he was elected secretary of state and served two terms. His reports as secretary of state are signed "B. B. Beavers."

By the time Beavers was secretary of state, Arkansas was so burdened by debt that the Legislature was reluctant to provide any money for the care and upkeep of the State House. In fact, in 1878 Beavers reported that the money allotted for repairs in the previous year had not even covered expenses. During Beavers's term, however, Arkansans were looking for ways to promote the state, encourage immigration, and boost prosperity. To that end Arkansas participated in the Centennial Exposition in Philadelphia in 1876, receiving an award for the Arkansas Building. Items returned to Arkansas from the exhibition and displayed on the State House grounds and buildings were the great seal of Arkansas, a three-tiered fountain, and a group of statues representing Law, Mercy, and Justice. Also during Beavers's term, some unused barracks behind the State House were converted into a charity hospital that became the foundation of the Pulaski County Hospital.

Beavers ran again for the office of secretary of state in 1878, but lost in the state Democratic Convention by only six votes to Jacob Frolich. In 1882 Beavers purchased the newspaper the *Benton Digest,* changing its name to the *Review,* and continued to edit it for a year or more. Beavers married Fannie Moore about 1868, and the couple had six children. Beavers died February 1, 1886, at his home in Benton, Saline County; he was 46 years old.

(Allsopp 1922:541; *Arkansas Methodist* [Little Rock] May 1, 1886; Goodspeed 1889a:757; Priest 1998:205, 237–238; 1850 U.S. Census, Saline Co., Arkansas)

Chism, Benjamin Boone

Secretary of State, 1889–1893

Benjamin Boone Chism was born March 12, 1845, in Booneville, Logan County, Arkansas, the son of physician and state senator S. H. Chism and Jennatta Logan. When still a teenager, Chism enlisted in the Fifth Arkansas Infantry and then the Seventeenth Arkansas Infantry of the Confederate army, serving from 1861 to 1865, and participated in the battles of Wilson's Creek (Oak Hills), Missouri, and Elkhorn, Arkansas. When only 18 years old, he commanded a company at the battle of Corinth, Mississippi, and eventually rose to the rank of captain. After the war he went into farming and then into the mercantile business in Logan County. Chism was admitted to the Arkansas bar in 1873. He was elected to the state constitutional convention in 1874, and in the same year he was commissioned a colonel of the state militia by Governor Elisha Baxter. He was elected to the state Senate, serving in 1877, representing the Eighth District of Yell and Logan counties. Chism won the election for secretary of state on the Democratic ticket in 1888. His reports as secretary of state are signed "B. B. Chism."

Chism served as secretary of state beginning four years after the completion of the State House expansion that tied the wings into the central building. The advanced age of the State House, however, meant that the building had reached a point where repairs were constantly needed. Chism had to repair gutters, lay tile, repaint part of the roof, and overhaul the heating apparatus. He also was short of space to accommodate an increase in the number of Supreme Court judges, juggling their offices depending on whether the General Assembly was in session or not.

After his term as secretary of state, Chism continued in commercial and political activities in Logan County. He retired in 1904 and moved to Fort Smith in 1907, but maintained a residence in Paris, Logan County. Chism married Addie Titsworth in 1871, and the couple had six children. He died at the home of his daughter in Fort Smith on January 15, 1924, at the age of 78. He is buried in Paris, Arkansas.

(Goodspeed 1889a:434–435; Hempstead 1890:1138–1139; Priest 1998:205, 241; *Southwest American* [Fort Smith] January 16, 1924)

Conway, James Sevier

Governor, 1836–1840

James Sevier Conway was born December 4, 1796, in Greene County, Tennessee, the son of Thomas Conway and Anne Rector. The family was well-to-do, raising corn, cotton, and livestock on their plantation and hiring private tutors for their ten children. When Conway was 21, the family moved to St. Louis, Missouri, where he was taught land surveying by his uncle Elias Rector. In 1820 Conway was appointed a federal land surveyor for the Arkansas Territory, and in 1832 he was named surveyor general of the territory by President Andrew Jackson. His income allowed him to purchase over 2,000 acres of land along the Red River, as well as a summer cottage at Magnet Cove and a bathhouse at Hot Springs. In 1828 he entered state politics, but was defeated in a run to represent Lafayette and Union counties in the Territorial Legislature. Three years later he successfully won the seat to fill an unexpired term. In 1836, following Arkansas's entrance into the Union, Conway won election as Arkansas's first state governor.

Conway took over from territorial governor William Fulton, who believed that Pope had exceeded his authority in supervising the construction of the State House and refused to push the project to completion. By the fall of 1836, when Conway succeeded Fulton, the main building was nearing completion and the west wing was ready to be roofed. Things were far enough along that the first session of the first General Assembly of the new state was able to meet in the main building on September 12, 1836. The following day Conway was inaugurated the first state governor in the Representatives' Chamber, and immediately after his inauguration Governor Conway made a plea to the state Legislature to complete the construction of the State House buildings. The Legislature responded by passing an act allowing him to sell five additional sections of land that had been granted by Congress to raise funds. Conway also appointed Elijah A. More as commissioner of public buildings in the fall of 1836 to superintend the construction and straighten out the finances. Work continued on the State House throughout his term.

When Conway became ill in the summer of 1838, he took leave from office from May to September and seriously considered resigning, although he remained governor to the end of his term in 1840. Ill health and political factors influenced his decision not to run for a second term. He returned to his plantation in Lafayette County, built a new home, and remained active in civic affairs. He was a strong advocate of education and led efforts to establish Lafayette Academy.

In 1826 Conway married Mary Jane Bradley, the daughter of a prominent Red River pioneer family, and the couple had ten children, half of whom died young. In 1855 Conway became ill with pneumonia and died on March 3, 1855, at the age of 58. He is buried in the family cemetery on his plantation "Walnut Hill."

(Donavan et al. 1995:3–7; Williams and Whayne 2000:72–73)

Crockett, John Wesley

Secretary of State, 1901–1905

A great-grandson of Davy Crockett, John Wesley Crockett was born May 24, 1860, in Mount Adams, Arkansas County, Arkansas, the son of Robert H. Crockett and Mary B. Lewis. He studied law and was admitted to the bar at DeWitt in 1882. Crockett served as clerk of Arkansas County from 1894 to 1898 and was elected to the state House of Representatives from Arkansas County, serving in 1899. He won the election to secretary of state the following year, serving two terms.

With a new Capitol being built during Crockett's term in office, the future of the State House was uncertain, with suggestions including disposal of the old building and sale of the grounds. Crockett did what he could to maintain the building, while continuing to report on its deteriorating condition. During his term, he served as secretary of the Second Capitol Commission.

In 1906 following his term, Crockett was elected as one of three railroad commissioners for Arkansas and was reelected in 1908. In 1910 he was elected state treasurer, serving from 1911 to 1915. Crockett married Lillian Sutliff Allen of Des Arc on July 23, 1907, and they had one daughter. Crockett died April 8, 1920, at his home in Little Rock; he was almost 62 years old. His remains were brought to DeWitt, where he is buried.

(*DeWitt Enterprise*, April 15, 1920; Hempstead 1911b:866–867; Priest 1998:205, 208, 259;)

Crosson, George D.

Caretaker, 1925–1946

George D. Crosson was born July 29, 1898, at Board Camp, near Mena, in Polk County, Arkansas. He served as a private in the U.S. Army from Texas during World War I and as a veteran became a member of the American Legion. On April 5, 1921, he married Frances Morgan in Alto, Texas, and the following year the couple moved to Little Rock.

In 1925, when Crosson was 27, he was hired as caretaker for the Old State House, then known as the Arkansas State War Memorial. Oversight for the building was with the American Legion, and Crosson's membership probably helped him gain the position. He worked as caretaker for about 21 years, living with his family in the caretaker's cottage behind the Old State House. His five children—Chyrline, Lorraine, Jewell, Morgan, and Kelly—were raised on the grounds, the two boys assisting their father in his work. Besides his regular duties as caretaker, Crosson earned extra money by providing custodial services for a number of the agencies housed in the building. In 1936 Crosson discovered the remains of Jacob Frolich's forgotten 1883 cistern, which was mistaken for a mysterious cavern. Crosson retired or resigned his position as caretaker about 1946, when he was 48 years old, and moved to Texas. His sister's son, Austin Metzger, replaced him as caretaker.

After leaving Little Rock Crosson spent two years in Texas before moving to Phoenix, Arizona, in 1950. He lived there for 12 years before moving back to Mena, Arkansas, where he spent the rest of his life. Crosson died on November 18, 1972, at the age of 73, in De Queen. He is buried in Liberty Cemetery near Board Camp, Polk County, Arkansas.

(Brown et al. 1978:100, 168–169, 186–187, 213–214; Kannaday and Daniel 1984:155; *Mena Weekly Star,* November 25, 1971)

Donaghey, George Washington

Governor, 1909–1913

Born July 1, 1856, in Union Parish, Louisiana, George Washington Donaghey was the oldest child of Christopher Columbus Donaghey and Elizabeth Ingram. Shortly after his birth, the family moved across the state line to Arkansas where five additional children were born. Donaghey worked on the family farm and at 15 left for Texas were he worked odd jobs, including a several-month stint as a cowboy on the Chisholm Trail. In 1880 he settled in Conway, Arkansas, where an uncle lived, making it his home for the next 30 years. He became a carpenter, partnering with John A. Pence, and in 1886 when a large part of downtown Conway burned, Donaghey's fortune was made as he expanded his business into construction and contracting. Among the many buildings Donaghey constructed over his lifetime were the first bank building in Conway, the main building of Hendrix College, courthouses in Texas and Arkansas—including the Washington County Courthouse in Fayetteville and the second Faulkner County Courthouse—ice plants and roads in Arkansas, office buildings in Little Rock, and railroad stations and water tanks for the Choctaw, Oklahoma, & Gulf Railroad. Thus, it is no surprise that he was appointed by Governor Dan Jones to serve on the First Capitol Commission in 1899 for the construction of the new Arkansas Capitol.

The idea of a new Capitol for Arkansas won Donaghey's heart so that despite ten years of setbacks, political controversy, and construction fiascos, Donaghey eventually parlayed his business experience and devotion to the cause into a successful run for governor. He served two terms, beginning in 1909, during which time he oversaw most of the completion of the Capitol. Wanting to see the project to the end, Donaghey tried for a third term, losing to Joseph Robinson, but when Robinson resigned his position as governor after only two months to fill a vacated U.S. Senate seat, acting governor J. Marion Futrell quickly appointed Donaghey to the Fourth Capitol Commission, which allowed him to remain in full charge of the construction until the end.

Although Donaghey's focus was understandably not on the Old State House, his attitude toward the building is uncertain. There is some suggestion that during his term in office he may have supported the sale of the Old State House; however, in his book *Building a State Capitol,* published in the year of his death, he indicates the bill to sell the Old State House came from another faction. Instead, Donaghey praised the "farseeing and active women"—one of whom happened to be the wife of Judge John I. Moore, another of the Capitol commissioners and a Donaghey ally—who rallied support for the preservation of the Old State House. Donaghey was the last governor to have an office in the Old State House and the first to have one in the new Capitol.

While Donaghey is best known for his role in the Capitol construction, he made other significant contributions as governor. He saw the creation of state boards of health and education, supported an Arkansas Tax Commission, and initiated an amendment to the state constitution that allowed for public initiative and referendum. In a bold move just before leaving office, he set the course that abolished the corrupt convict lease system. After leaving office, he served on many boards of businesses, charities, and public commissions in Little Rock.

Despite having little formal education himself, he was a strong supporter of education in the state. While in Conway he was involved in securing three colleges: Hendrix College, Central College, and what later became the University of Central Arkansas. While governor he established four agricultural high schools that eventually became Arkansas State University, Arkansas Tech University, Southern Arkansas University, and the University of Arkansas at Monticello. After leaving office, he provided a large endowment to the college that became the University of Arkansas at Little Rock.

Donaghey married Louvenia Wallace of Lonoke County on September 20, 1883; the couple had no children. He died December 15, 1937, at the age of 81, of heart disease at his home in Little Rock and is buried in Roselawn Memorial Park.

(Brown et al. 1978:18–20; Donaghey 1937:269–277, entire book; Donovan et al. 1995:134–138; Williams and Whayne 2000:86–87)

Frolich, Jacob

Secretary of State, 1879–1885

As reported by the *Encyclopedia of the New West* in 1881, it was commonly said that "Arkansas never had a better secretary of state than Jake Frolich." Following that superlative, the *Encyclopedia* went on to praise his sterling integrity, obliging disposition, and efficiency as a public officer, noting that the records under his charge were properly classified and correspondence was promptly answered. Whether or not that flattering account is accurate, Frolich is certainly one of the more interesting of Arkansas's secretaries of state.

Jacob Frolich was born November 15, 1837, in Oberndorf, Bavaria, Germany, the son of John Frolich and Marie Elizabeth Herrman. When he was 9 years old, the family emigrated to America, staying in New Orleans for a few months before settling in Indiana. At the age of 14, Frolich decided to enter the printer's trade, beginning in Evansville, Indiana, and then moving on to St. Louis and New Orleans while still a teenager. He worked for several years clerking in mercantile establishments in New Orleans, before returning to printing in Baton Rouge and elsewhere in Louisiana. He lived a rather itinerant life during this period, undertaking state printing during the winters and traveling in the summers, including a trip into the Nebraska territory to see Indians. He supported the Confederacy from the beginning of the Civil War, the first two years in special service with the Army of Tennessee and the last two years with the Washington Artillery of New Orleans. He suffered slight wounds several times and made several hair-breadth escapes. After the war he purchased a printing outfit in Memphis and headed to Searcy by boat on the White River. Unfortunately, the boat hit a snag and sank, taking his equipment with it. He returned to Memphis and took a position at the Memphis *Appeal* for a year until he could save enough money to buy another supply of type and a press.

Frolich established the *White County Record* in November 1866 in Searcy. The paper was staunchly Democratic and hard on the Radical Reconstructionists, being considered a "rebel sheet" by the Republicans. In 1868 White County became embroiled in virulent political intrigue. Albert Parker, a secret agent sent out by Governor Powell Clayton to gather information to justify martial law, was found murdered. A year and a half later, several local men were accused of being members of the Searcy Ku Klux Klan and responsible for the murder, Frolich among them. Frolich was identified as the Head Cyclops of the Searcy den and said to have planned and ordered the murder. A bench warrant was issued for his arrest with no bail allowed, and a $500 bounty was put on his head. Tipped off to the accusation, Frolich fled Arkansas and made his way to Windsor, Ontario, where he worked as a printer for 14 months until the case was made bailable and he could return to Arkansas to stand trial. Frolich insisted the charges were trumped up and demanded an immediate trial. When no evidence was presented to connect him with the charges, the prosecuting attorney directed the jury to acquit him, and so he was found not guilty. He then returned to running the paper, which he continued until April 1878. In 1874 he was elected assistant secretary of the state Senate and in 1877 chief secretary of the same. In 1878 Frolich won the election for secretary of state.

Frolich served three terms as secretary of state, and through his reports he seems to have been particularly conscientious—and bluntly outspoken—regarding the care and needs of the State House. Frolich encouraged the General Assembly to provide necessary funds for the upkeep of the buildings, framed in the terms of promoting the state to visitors, encouraging immigration, and fueling prosperity. He had a new gate made for the main entrance, which was designed by Little Rock civil engineer George Rumbough and manufactured by local firms. He also asked Rumbough to inspect the buildings, reporting in detail on the potentially dangerous conditions.

Frolich removed the barracks after they were vacated by the county hospital, and he had the ground sodded and planted in ornamental trees. He recommended fireproof vaults for the offices to protect the state records, and he suggested the Legislature enact building codes for private development in the area surrounding the State House to further reduce risk from fire. He commented wryly on the situation of the state battling Pulaski County for possession of the east wing, and he had a cistern dug in 1883 at the back of the State House, which later was forgotten and rediscovered as the mystery cavern.

As secretary of state, Frolich investigated the means for deriving a state revenue and drafted a general revenue bill that was adopted by the General Assembly. He also began a program of acquiring portraits of distinguished Arkansans. After concluding his term as secretary of state, Frolich moved to Washington, D.C., and was made chief clerk of the Mineral Division of the Interior Department in President Grover Cleveland's administration. Within the first year he was promoted to the office of chief financial clerk of the Patent Office and held that position through the end of Cleveland's administration. In 1889 he returned to Little Rock and became the business manager of the *Arkansas Gazette,* but resigned in early 1890 to go into the mercantile business of J. H. Sannoner & Co., a cotton factor and general commission merchant. At the same time, he announced his candidacy for the position of state treasurer, but died before the election.

Fred Allsopp, writing in *Twenty Years in a Newspaper Office,* described Frolich as "a mighty good man and about the foxiest one I have ever known," but also noted that he had a "peculiar way of crossing his fingers and batting his eyes" when worried. The *Encyclopedia of the New West* said he had "a genial and pleasant face, with the look and air of a business man." Frolich married Mollie Gaines Finley on September 2, 1869, in Clarksville, Tennessee, and the couple had three children. Undergoing surgery for the illness that took his life, Frolich described the ordeal to Allsopp in a note that said the "doctors had come and gone, with their bulge pumps, crowbars, saws, pinchers, corkscrews, knives, gimlets, and augurs—an armful of them—and he did not know whether he would survive an attack with so many weapons." Frolich died at his home on April 25, 1890, at the age of 52. He is buried in Oakland Cemetery in Little Rock.

(Allsopp 1907:131–139; Allsopp 1922:16–17, 329, 474–477, 494, 571–572; *Arkansas Gazette,* April 25, 1890, April 26, 1890, April 27, 1890; Counts 1977:133; Goodspeed 1889a:453; Priest 1998:205; Ross 1972:157–165; Speer and Brown 1881:26–28)

Fulton, William Savin

Territorial Governor, March 9, 1835–1836

William Savin Fulton was born June 2, 1795, in Cecil County, Maryland. He served as private secretary to Andrew Jackson and fought against the Seminole Indians in the Florida everglades and in the 1812 Battle of New Orleans. He was appointed by territorial governor John Pope to secretary of the Arkansas Territory in 1829, then succeeded Pope as territorial governor in 1835, serving for less than two years.

Fulton believed Governor Pope had exceeded his authority involving the sale of the ten sections and the construction of the State House, so refused to push the project to completion. By the time Governor James Conway took office, the architectural plans were lost, the record of accounts was in Kentucky with Pope, and general confusion about the construction of the State House reigned.

Fulton went on to serve Arkansas as U.S. senator from 1836 to 1844, dying in office. Fulton County is named after him. He married Matilda Frances Nowland in 1825, and they had a number of children. Fulton died August 15, 1844, at the age of 49, and is buried in Mount Holly Cemetery in Little Rock.

(Crawford and Worthen 1993:88–89; Priest 1998:179, 201).

Greer, David Buford

Secretary of State, November 12, 1840–May 9, 1842, and August 9, 1842–September 3, 1859

David Buford Greer was born about 1802 in Tennessee, the son of Andrew Greer and Sarah Burke. He emigrated to Arkansas about 1828 and became secretary of state in 1840. Greer served 19 years as secretary of state from 1840 to 1859 (with John Winfrey serving in an acting capacity from May 9 to August 9, 1842), the longest time in office of any Arkansas secretary of state. During 1848 Governor Thomas Drew offered him the seat of U.S. senator Ambrose Sevier on his resignation, but Greer declined, preferring to remain secretary of state. He was embroiled in a debate in the Little Rock newspapers during 1851–1852 over perceived irregularities in awarding printing contracts, but the Legislature must have been satisfied with his explanations for they reelected him as secretary of state in January 1853.

During his term in 1846 the General Assembly abolished the position of commissioner of public buildings, assigning the care of the buildings and grounds to the duties of the secretary of state, thus making Greer the first secretary to hold those responsibilities. His reports as secretary of state are signed "D. B. Greer." During his long term in office, the State House went from a new building to one needing serious repairs. In 1858, near the end of his term, he reported that the building was rapidly going to decay and needed "thorough, substantial, and permanent repairs" beyond the "mere patch-work" that had previously been undertaken. Thus, Greer became the first of many successive secretaries of state to plead for money from the Legislature to adequately care for the State House.

Greer had been in ill health for some time in 1859 and a few months before his death suffered a stroke. He was taken to the house of his sister, the wife of Capt. C. W. Jackson, near Nashville, Tennessee, for medical care and nursing. Greer died there on August 29, 1859, while still holding office as Arkansas secretary of state. He was 57 years old. There is no evidence he was married or had any children. His body was taken to Lebanon, Wilson County, Tennessee, for burial beside his brother.

(*Arkansas Gazette*, January 7, 1853, September 10, 1859, September 17, 1859, and various issues in 1851–1852; Priest 1998:205; Ross 1969:281–182; *True Democrat* [Little Rock, Ark.] September 14, 1859)

Hawkins, Richard Clay

Commissioner of Public Buildings, 1841–1843

Richard Clay Hawkins was born about 1797 in Tennessee and served in the War of 1812 as a teenager. He married Sylvana (or Sylvinia) McDonald on December 9, 1819, in Jefferson County, Mississippi, and they had a number of children. In 1830 the family moved to Hot Springs, Arkansas, and in April 1831 Hawkins was appointed clerk of the circuit court by the governor. The following year he won election for the same position. In 1832 the family moved to Little Rock, and while having a new frame house constructed in front of their log cabin in January 1834, the two buildings caught fire and were destroyed, causing a loss not only of the buildings but also of much of the contents and clothing. Stemming from the loss, the *Arkansas Gazette* made a plea for the town to organize a fire company. Down but not out, in 1835 on 36 acres Hawkins had purchased southeast of town, he built a race track and viewing stand for horse racing. He also bred race horses, bringing good blood stock into the state, most notably the sire Black Hawk. In December 1837 Hawkins served as one of three justices on the court of investigation in the case of John Wilson for the murder of J. J. Anthony, setting bail at $10,000. In April of the following year Hawkins provided an affidavit to the Grand Jury supporting Wilson's motion for a change of venue.

Hawkins served as the fourth commissioner of public buildings from 1841 to 1843, following W. W. Stevenson. Elected by the General Assembly in late 1838 to serve the two-year term from 1839 to 1841, he found himself holding the same position as Stevenson, who had been appointed by Governor Conway for the same term. After the Arkansas Supreme Court decided in Stevenson's favor, Hawkins was forced to step down until the next term became available. He may have been selected by the General Assembly for the position because of his experience in building and developing the race track, although it is clear from his involvement in the John Wilson trial that Hawkins had political connections.

Most of the work on the State House was completed by the time Hawkins took office. He oversaw the completion of the north portico, and finished the grading and beautification of the grounds. His report to the Legislature mostly described the settling of accounts and the construction of a new penitentiary. The State House was officially declared complete by Governor Archibald Yell during Hawkins's term.

In June 1843, while serving as commissioner of public buildings, Hawkins's 14-year-old son, Henry Clay, drowned in the Arkansas River near the State House. A year later Hawkins's wife died. He then married Louisa Hudgens on December 9, 1844, in Little Rock. In 1846 Hawkins made an unsuccessful run for a seat in the state Legislature, coming in last out of six candidates. He then moved to Prairie County, where the couple's first child was born, and went into farming. Eleven more children eventually were born to them. About 1853 the family moved to Texas, settling first in Bexar County and then about 1861 in Goliad County, where Hawkins continued as a prosperous farmer. Hawkins died in Goliad County in March 1870 at the age of 73.

(*Arkansas Banner,* July 31, 1844; *Arkansas Gazette,* April 6, 1831, January 11, 1832, January 28, 1834, December 19, 1837, December 26, 1837, February 13, 1838, April 23, 1838, August 10, 1846, February 13, 1938; Arkansas Reports 1841:260–281; *Arkansas Times and Advocate,* June 12, 1843; Clay 2006; Sherwood 1938)

Hempstead, Samuel Hutchinson

Commissioner of Public Buildings, 1839

Samuel Hutchinson Hempstead was born November 26, 1814, in New London, Connecticut, the son of Joseph Hempstead and Celinda Hutchinson. His parents moved to St. Louis, Missouri, when he was about 6 years old, and he grew up there. He studied law under Thomas H. Benton and was admitted to the bar in St. Louis in 1835. The following year he came to Little Rock, where he was elected as chief clerk of the Arkansas House of Representatives during the sessions of 1836–1838.

Hempstead was appointed the second commissioner of public buildings in early 1839 by Governor Conway, following Elijah More. Hempstead held the position for less than seven months, resigning midyear, and was replaced by W. W. Stevenson. He left no reports of his time as commissioner.

Hempstead continued in the legal profession, partnering with Robert W. Johnson about 1840 and being appointed U.S. attorney for the district of Arkansas by President Polk in 1844. In 1848 he made an unsuccessful run for the U.S. Senate. In 1856 Governor Elias Conway appointed him solicitor-general for the state, and in the same year he published a volume of legal decisions known as *Hempstead's Reports.* He served frequently as special judge of the Arkansas Supreme Court.

Hempstead married Elizabeth Rector Beall on August 10, 1841. They had at least six children, among whom was noted Arkansas historian and attorney Fay Hempstead. Hempstead died in Little Rock on June 25, 1862, at the age of 48, and is buried in Mount Holly Cemetery.

(*Arkansas Gazette,* August 21, 1839, August 18, 1841; Arkansas Reports 1841:260281; Crawford and Worthen 1993:110; Hallum 1887:286–288; Priest 1998:216–217)

Hodges, Earle William

Secretary of State, 1911–1917

Earle William Hodges was born September 27, 1881, in Newark, Independence County, Arkansas, the son of Jesse Beane Hodges and Teresa J. Humphreys. His parents moved to Fulton County when he was still a toddler. While in school he began to learn typesetting at the local newspaper office. He continued in newspaper work, serving as foreman in the office of the *Monitor* in Mammoth Spring and publishing a weekly newspaper at Imboden. After working in the U.S. Census Department in Washington, D.C., in 1900 he went to St. Louis, Missouri, where he worked as a reporter for the *Post-Dispatch* and the *Star.* Following that, he was half owner and editor of the *Pocahontas News-Herald.* In 1904 he was appointed state printer, a position he held for six years. In 1906 he accepted the position of secretary of the Arkansas Press Association, which he held for 12 years.

In 1910 Hodges ran for secretary of state on the Democratic ticket and held the office for three terms. At the time he was the youngest person ever elected to the office, being only 28 years old. His election was fortuitous for the State House, for Hodges was also the president of the State Historical Museum Association and a strong supporter for preservation. In order to keep the building safe while discussion of its fate continued, Hodges paid some expenses out of his own pocket and borrowed money for a watchman. As soon as state government vacated the old building, Hodges located agencies and organizations wanting space, which he provided in exchange for maintenance of their assigned areas at their own expense, thus giving the building a continued purpose and ultimately ensuring its survival.

At the end of his third term in 1916, Hodges made an unsuccessful run for governor against Charles H. Brough. During World War I, Hodges served as a member of Exemption Board No. 2 in Little Rock and in 1919 was put in charge of raising funds for the American Jewish Relief Committee, headquartered in San Francisco. In 1922 he returned to Arkansas as publicity director for the Public Utility Association of Arkansas and was appointed a member of the State Capitol Beautification Committee by Governor Thomas McCrae. In 1925 he accepted the position of public relations manager for Henry L. Doherty Co., a utilities investment firm that controlled the Cities Service Corporation of New York, and served as an executive of Cities Service for many years. In 1930–1931 Hodges served as the president of the International Association of Lions Clubs.

Hodges married Nell Gamel of Maynard, Arkansas, on March 3, 1901, in Hoxie, and they had one son. Hodges died of a heart attack October 14, 1941, at age 60, at his home in Fieldstone, New York. He is buried in New York City.

(Allsopp 1922:584–585; *Arkansas Gazette*, October 15, 1941; Hempstead 1911b:854–855; Priest 1998:205; Schwitalla 1921:75; Thomas 1930:642)

Hull, Alexander C.

Secretary of State, 1897–1901

Alexander C. Hull was born April 20, 1858, in Marion County, Arkansas, the son of John E. Hull and Matilda A. Killough. His father served in the state House of Representatives from Marion County in 1862 and rose to the rank of captain in the Confederate army before he was killed in action when Alex was only 7 years old. His mother moved Alex and his brothers to Flippin Barrens, Marion County, after the war, where she operated a boardinghouse. Hull began his career clerking in a mercantile establishment, then served as deputy clerk of Boone County from 1878 to 1880. Following that, he went into newspaper work, founding the *Baxter County Citizen* at Mountain Home. He did a stint as chief clerk of the United States Land Office in Harrison before becoming editor and owner in 1887 of the *Harrison (Boone County) Banner.*

In 1892 Hull ran in the state Democratic primary for secretary of state, coming in second in a four-man race. Four years later, he won the office and served two terms. Hull's reports as secretary of state are signed "Alex. C. Hull." Hull faced the same problems with a deteriorating building that his predecessors had, but the legislators made his job even more difficult by reducing his budget. Repairs were needed on nearly a weekly basis. The roof was so old and worn that rain was leaking into the rooms, and the records and books of the library continued to be threatened. Hull's reports indicate he was mighty annoyed with the situation. Only after the waterlogged plaster ceiling of the Senate Chamber collapsed on the senators, however, was the legislation authorizing a new Capitol passed.

After completing his term as secretary of state, Hull remained in Little Rock for several years, where he organized the Security Fire Insurance Company. In 1907 he moved to Oklahoma City and then to Edmond, Oklahoma, but returned to Harrison in 1912. There he opened an insurance and loan office, and established the *North Arkansas Herald.* Hull also served as historian, committeeman, and recording secretary of the Arkansas Press Association. In 1893 he was appointed by Governor William Fishback as an accountant to examine the condition of the state treasurer's office.

Hull married Lucy Mary Cory of Harrison in 1884, and they had five children. He died January 28, 1914, of a cerebral hemorrhage at his home in Harrison; he was 56 years old.

(Allsopp 1922:586; *Arkansas Democrat*, January 29, 1914; Goodspeed 1894:92–96; Priest 1998:205, 230; Shiras 1939:125–126)

Johnson, James Madison

Secretary of State, March 14, 1871–November 12, 1874

James Madison Johnson was born December 8, 1829, 1832, or 1833, in Warren County, Tennessee, the son of James Martin Johnson and his first wife, Elizabeth Dunagin. The Johnson family moved to Madison County, Arkansas, about 1836. Johnson was educated at Arkansas College and the Ozark Institute, then taught school for two years before he began the study of medicine in 1855 under practitioners in Fayetteville. He subsequently attended the St. Louis Medical College and in 1859 began practicing medicine at Huntsville, Arkansas, until the beginning of the Civil War. He was a Unionist, and in 1862—along with Isaac Murphy, who became the Unionist governor in 1864—he joined General Curtis's army, later joining General Scofield's army at Springfield, Missouri. In 1863 he was authorized to raise troops and raised all of the Union troops furnished by Arkansas except for two regiments. He then took command of the First Arkansas Infantry and was commissioned colonel. He was made brevet brigadier general by President Andrew Johnson in 1867 upon the recommendation of General U. S. Grant.

In 1864 Johnson was elected to Congress from the Third District and was reelected in 1866 but was not allowed to take his seat. In 1867 he was elected lieutenant governor of Arkansas. In 1870 he was embroiled in political controversy with Governor Powell Clayton, who questioned his authority to hold the office of lieutenant governor. Apparently, Clayton persuaded Johnson to resign his position in March 1871 in order to run for U.S. Senate. Clayton then decided to run for the Senate seat himself and instead appointed Johnson to fill the unexpired term of secretary of state, which was open after the resignation of Robert J. T. White. Johnson subsequently was elected secretary of state in 1872 and served through 1874.

It was during Johnson's term as secretary of state that the Brooks-Baxter War was waged on the State House grounds. The coup lasted only a month, but in that time the buildings had been occupied by hundreds of men who destroyed the books and records in the library and damaged the physical structure of the building. In addition, their construction of earthworks and barricades made a mess of the grounds. Johnson was responsible for cleaning, disinfecting, and repairing the damage.

After his service as secretary of state, Johnson returned to Madison County with his family and lived in a log house on land he owned near Wesley. He raised sheep, hogs, and fine riding and carriage horses, and probably continued as a physician. His daughter Kate studied medicine under him and assisted Johnson and other doctors with surgeries and other medical services. Johnson also served on the board of trustees of the University of Arkansas beginning in 1874.

Johnson married a cousin, Elizabeth Johnson, in Madison County on September 10, 1850, and the couple had seven children. After Elizabeth's death, he married Mrs. Jennie Mullins Wilson of Whitener, Arkansas, on October 15, 1893. Johnson died February 15, 1913, and is buried in the family cemetery a few hundred feet from the log house on the plantation near Wesley.

(*Arkansas Gazette,* December 6–7, 1870, March 14–15, 1871; Goodspeed 1889b:1098; Priest 1998:205; Reynolds and Thomas 1910:107, 396–397; Weideman 1984a:30–31, 1984b:91–102)

Loewer, Agnes McDaniel

Curator, 1951–1972

Agnes McDaniel was born June 26, 1893, in Searcy, Arkansas, the daughter of William Green McDaniel and Etta Aunspaugh. Her father engaged in the mercantile business and moved the family to Little Rock in 1900. In 1912 when Agnes was 18, she began her business career, beginning as an assistant bookkeeper and cashier for the Underwood Typewriter Company and quickly was promoted into management. In 1914 she accepted the position of secretary to the mayor of Little Rock, and the following year she started as the first office secretary of the Little Rock YWCA, quickly rising into positions of greater responsibility. She pioneered much of the Little Rock YWCA's progress throughout the First World War, establishing programs in social work and services, leading campaigns to raise funds, preparing the first budget, and serving as treasurer and then president. On August 27, 1919, at the age of 26, she married Charles F. W. Loewer in Little Rock. The couple had only one child, a son, who died very young in 1923.

Throughout the years, Agnes McDaniel Loewer was active in numerous civic organizations, devoting her business and organizational skills to a great many causes. She served as secretary, treasurer, and president of various organizations, and filled leadership roles in accomplishing goals and missions. Loewer was a member of the Arkansas Federation of Women's Clubs, the Business and Professional Women's City Club, the Women's Division of the State Fair, the Arkansas Conference of Welfare Legislation, the National Youth Association, the Canteen Corps of the American Red Cross, and the Arkansas Federation of Garden Clubs, among others.

Loewer's work with the Arkansas Federation of Women's Clubs undoubtedly focused her attention on the preservation of the Old State House, but her interest in Arkansas history was reflected in her involvement in other organizations as well. She was a member of the United Daughters of the Confederacy, the Pulaski Chapter of the Arkansas Pioneers Association, and the Quapaw Quarter Association of Little Rock. She was a member of the Arkansas State Historical Society, director of the Pulaski County Historical Society, and executive secretary of Arkansas Landmarks, Inc. Beginning about 1939 Loewer and Louise Loughborough lobbied daily in the halls of the State Capitol for the preservation of the Old State House. Successful in this endeavor, Loewer was appointed a member of the Arkansas Commemorative Commission in 1947, which was formed that year to oversee the restoration of the Old State House and create a future museum of Arkansas history. She served as secretary to the commission, a position that later evolved into director. She was a perfect choice for the commission with her strong support for preserving Arkansas's history, her active involvement in so many women's organizations, and her business skills.

When the restoration was completed, Loewer was hired as the first curator of the Old State House, beginning July 1951. At 58 years old, she already had 40 years of business and management experience that she brought to the position. She supervised a support staff of five and trained numerous volunteers as guides and hostesses, instructing them in dress, diction, and a scripted presentation. She also began to build a collection and exhibits for the new museum. She worked with the various women's patriotic organizations to furnish period rooms and developed exhibits on the gowns of Arkansas's first ladies, battle flags from the Civil War and Mexican War, and Confederate money. Throughout her curatorship, she promoted the Old State House as a historic shrine and tourist attraction, and continued to battle threats to its preservation.

In late 1971 Loewer was injured in a fall that ultimately led to her retirement in March 1972, at the age of 78. She had served 21 years as curator. Among the honors she received were a commendation from the Arkansas Legislative Council in 1971 for her public service; a certificate of appreciation from the Arkansas Parks, Recreation and Travel Commission in 1974; and an award from the National Trust for Historic Preservation in 1974, presented by former first lady Mrs. Lyndon B. "Lady Bird" Johnson.

Loewer died just three and a half years after her retirement, on September 18, 1975, at the age of 82. She is buried in Roselawn Memorial Park in Little Rock.

(Allard 1959:162–163; *Arkansas Gazette* 20 September 1975; Arkansas History Commission, Manuscript Collection, Notes; Herndon 1947:1446–1448; Social Security Death Index)

Loughborough, Louise Watkins Wright

Preservation Activist, 1930s–1940s

Louisa Watkins Wright, who went by the name "Louise," was born January 23, 1881, in Little Rock, Arkansas, the daughter of William Fulton Wright and Louisa Watkins. The family had a long history in Arkansas and included as a direct ancestor William Savin Fulton, the last territorial governor of Arkansas in 1835–1836, who was in office during the construction of the Old State House. Louise married James Fairfax Loughborough, an attorney at the Rose Law Firm, on October 21, 1902. As a nonworking spouse she began to focus her energies on the civic activities undertaken by the various women's organizations to which she belonged. Her interest in local history was engendered as a child and found an outlet through her civic work. She was a charter member of the Little Rock Garden Club, a member of the National Society of the Colonial Dames of America and the National Trust for Historic Preservation, and served as vice regent of the Mount Vernon Ladies Association of the Union, which was the organization that preserved and maintains the home of George Washington.

Loughborough's interest in preserving historic structures in Little Rock began in the early 1920s when the Little Rock Garden Club took on the project of improving the grounds of the Old State House, planting a great variety of trees, shrubs, and flowers. Although their work was done under the approval of the War Memorial Commission, over the decade the Garden Club gradually gained authority for the appearance of the grounds. By 1928, led by Loughborough, the club began an effort to return the grounds and exterior portions of the building to historical accuracy. They replaced the granite gateposts with the original eagle-topped ones and relocated many stone memorials to places with less impact. In a bold and controversial act, Loughborough orchestrated the removal of the three Greek statues, which had been brought back from the Philadelphia Centennial Exposition, from the roof of the Old State House and had them destroyed. In 1931 the Garden Club appointed her chairwoman of the Old State Capitol Restoration Committee.

In 1935 Loughborough was appointed to the Little Rock Planning Commission, and it was in this role that the planned demolition of an original section of territorial Little Rock came to her attention. In 1938 she started a campaign to save and restore the buildings, lobbying for money from the General Assembly and mounting a private campaign to raise funds. She coined the phrase "town of three capitols" to inspire supporters. In 1941 the Arkansas Territorial Restoration opened, with four museum houses on their original half-block. Loughborough became founding chair of the Arkansas Territorial Restoration Commission and directed daily operations at the museum complex through its first 20 years. The museum complex continues today as Historic Arkansas Museum.

Loughborough remained a strong advocate for the preservation of the Old State House, even though her main efforts were concentrated on the Territorial Restoration. Her success with that work set a precedent for what could be done with the Old State House. During the 1940s Loughborough joined with Agnes Loewer lobbying daily in the State Capitol for the money to save the Old State House.

Loughborough retired in 1961 as director of the Arkansas Territorial Restoration due to failing health and died in Little Rock the following year, on December 10, 1962, about six weeks shy of her eighty-second birthday. In her will she left $2,000 to restore a room in the Old State House to honor her great-grandfathers. She is buried in Mount Holly Cemetery in Little Rock.

(*Arkansas Gazette,* December 11, 1962, December 12, 1962, December 21, 1962; Brown et al. 1978:103–108, 144–160, 243; Williams and Whayne 2000:171–172;Worthen 1992:26–33)

Ludwig, Oswald Cross

Secretary of State, 1905–1911

Oswald Cross Ludwig, the son of German immigrant Fred Ludwig and Mary Hoxter, was born in Decatur, Alabama, on September 16, 1858. He moved to Atkins, Pope County, Arkansas, in January 1880, when he was 21 years old, working as publisher and editor of the *Atkins News.* Following that he worked at papers in Eureka Springs, Clarksville, and Conway. He also served as postmaster in Conway from 1884 to 1887.

Ludwig began his political career in 1891, when he was elected to the position of assistant clerk of the House of Representatives, being reelected in 1893. From 1893 to 1895 he served as secretary of the State Board of Charitable Institutions, and in 1897 he became chief clerk of the House of Representatives, at which time he moved his residence to Little Rock. From 1899 to 1901 he served as secretary to the First Capitol Commission, resigning to accept the position of deputy secretary of state under John W. Crockett. In 1905 Ludwig was elected secretary of state, serving three terms. His reports as secretary of state are signed "O. C. Ludwig."

Although not much is mentioned of the State House in Ludwig's reports, he was in office when the Legislature moved from the State House to the new Capitol. He apparently sided with the political alliance opposed to Governor George Donaghey's efforts to complete construction of the new Capitol. Ludwig was critical of the State Capitol Commission's expenditures for heating and lighting the still-unfinished Capitol so the Legislature could meet there in 1911, and he debated Governor Donaghey in the newspapers over the move. The papers reported that Ludwig planned to prepare the rooms of the Old State House, placing the chairs and desks in the positions they had since 1836, so the General Assembly could meet there on January 9, and that he intended not to "deviate one jot or tittle from the precedent set by his predecessors in office." The legislators met one last time on January 8, 1911, in the Old State House and voted to move to the new Capitol.

During his time in state office Ludwig also wrote for the *Little Rock Daily Press* and other papers and was a member of the Arkansas Press Association, holding the position of poet laureate. Ludwig was married three times. He married Kate Roberts of Atkins on April 22, 1880, and the couple had a daughter before Kate died the following year. In 1882 he married Theodosia Wilson of Springdale, who died ten months after their wedding. On January 7, 1885, Ludwig married Lizzie E. May of Clarksville, and the couple had ten children. Ludwig died October 17, 1918, at the age of 60, in Little Rock, Arkansas, from pneumonia after contracting the deadly Spanish flu. His body was sent back to his hometown of Decatur, Alabama, where he is buried.

(Allsopp 1922:599–600; *Arkansas Democrat,* October 21, 1918; *Arkansas Gazette,* October 18, 1918; Donaghey 1937:269–277; Hempstead 1911b:635–636; Priest 1998:205, 257)

Moore, Elias Bryan

Secretary of State, 1885–1889

The son of William Ward Moore and Isabella Bryan, Elias Bryan Moore was born in Sparta, Tennessee, on January 23, 1842. His father moved the family to Fayetteville, Arkansas, in 1858, where he operated a sawmill and a store. The following year, Elias

Moore began work in the Fayetteville printing office of the *Arkansian,* founded by James Pettigrew and Elias Boudinot. In 1860 he and his brothers established the *Fayetteville Democrat,* and he also was appointed Fayetteville postmaster. In 1861 Moore enlisted in the Third Arkansas State Regiment from Washington County and on August 10 was severely wounded in the battle of Wilson's Creek (Oak Hills), Missouri. After recuperating, he joined Captain Palmer's company of Confederate Scouts operating in northwest Arkansas and participated in the battle of Fayetteville. His efforts aggravated his wound and he was required to take another leave, but he ended the war with Cabell's brigade in Texas and the rank of colonel. After the war, in 1868, Moore and his brothers reestablished the *Fayetteville Democrat,* and he continued as editor until 1884.

During the 1870s Moore served as a Fayetteville alderman and as a delegate to the Democratic State Convention and in 1878 was elected to the state House of Representatives from Washington County, serving three consecutive terms. In 1884 he won the election for secretary of state and served two terms. His reports as secretary of state are signed "E. B. Moore," which has caused him to be confused in earlier writings on the Old State House with Commissioner of Public Buildings E. A. More.

Moore served as secretary of state during the period of the 1885–1886 renovations of the State House, in which the central building was expanded to the north and connected to the wings by two-story hyphens. An armory was also built behind the east wing, and additional shade trees were added to the grounds. Despite the expansion the state library was still cramped for space.

At the end of his term, Moore tried several business ventures in Little Rock, including a private investigation agency, and became president of the Famous Life Insurance Company of Little Rock. In 1895 he accepted an appointment as warden of the Arkansas State Penitentiary, but the following year returned to Fayetteville where he established the *Mountain City Gazette* with his youngest brother. He continued at the paper until his death the following year.

Moore was married to Emma Jane North on February 9, 1869, in Fayetteville, and the couple had four children. Moore died in Fayetteville on May 19, 1897, at the age of 55, and is buried in Evergreen Cemetery.

(Allsopp 1922:605; *Arkansas Gazette,* January 16, 1885; Campbell 1928: 14, 27–28, 45, 83, 114; Easley and McAnelly 1996:141; Goodspeed 1889a:488–489; Priest 1998:205, 243,245–246; Speer and Brown 1881:85–87; Williams and Whayne 2000:200–201)

More, Elijah A.

Commissioner of Public Buildings, 1836–1838

Elijah A. More was born in Danville, Kentucky, on January 20, 1799. He was in Arkansas by the 1830s and followed the law profession. In 1834 he was elected mayor of Little Rock. In 1836 he was named director of the Bank of Arkansas, and late in that year More was appointed the first commissioner of public buildings by Governor James Conway. More's reports as commissioner of public buildings are signed "E. A. More," which has caused him to be confused in earlier writings on the Old State House with Secretary of State E. B. Moore.

More walked into a tangled mess of records and construction work when he accepted the position. After the death of supervising architect George Weigart and the replacement of territorial governor John Pope with William Fulton, who let the State House project languish, there had been little oversight of the work, and no one seemed to know who had been paid and who was owed money. With the architectural plans also lost, More had no idea what was intended. To try to solve the problems and move the project forward, More undertook a trip to Kentucky in 1837 to meet with former governor Pope and architect Gideon Shryock. Pope discussed with More all the accounts, vouchers, and papers pertaining to the State House and turned the records over to him. During the same trip, More made arrangements to purchase building materials and hire additional craftsmen, which he intended would meet him in Danville and accompany him back to Arkansas.

Back in Little Rock, More had increasing problems with the workmen hired to build the State House. He was untrusting of the contractors and suspicious of their accounting claims and methods for calculating expenses. He further annoyed local workmen by advertising out of state for additional craftsmen and contractors. By late 1838 relations between More and the contractors completely broke down, and charges of misrepresentation and inattention to duties were made against More to the legislators.

Considering the later evidence of construction problems and the confused state of accounts that More inherited, his efforts to put the building project back on track seem reasonable and commendable. But he may have been overzealous and needlessly suspicious of his craftsmen, ultimately leading to his problems and the failure to win reappointment at the end of 1838.

After his term as commissioner of public buildings ended, he was elected to the board of the Real Estate Bank and to the position of Pulaski County probate judge, both in early 1839. While serving as Little Rock mayor, More married Caroline Owens on May 8, 1834, in Conway County, and the couple had two sons before Caroline died in 1839. More left Arkansas sometime after 1840, eventually settling in Missouri. He was living with his son in Columbia, Boone County, Missouri, in 1870. More died on May 15, 1878, in Boone County, at the age of 79, and is buried in Columbia Cemetery.

(*Arkansas Gazette,* January 8, 1834; May 13, 1834; November 8, 1836; January 9, 1839; January 16, 1839; January 30, 1839; *Columbia Missouri Herald,* Death Role, January 9, 1879; Evans and Thompson 1992:36; Western Historical Co. 1882:777–778; 1870 U.S. Census, Columbia, Boone County, Missouri)

Pendleton, Henry F.

Commissioner of Public Buildings, 1844–1846

A carpenter by trade, Henry F. Pendleton was born about 1805 in Virginia. He came to Kentucky, where he probably was married before 1836 to a woman named Sarah and began a family. Pendleton was hired by Elijah More in late 1837, probably coming from the Kentucky area in response to More's advertisement, to serve as the contractor for the carpentry and to take over as superintending architect. Along with John Wassell, Pendleton accused More of false statements and inattention to his duties in two 1838 reports to the Legislature. More countered that Pendleton was doing more expensive work when cheaper had been directed. In 1840 Pendleton was elected a Little Rock alderman.

Pendleton's quality of work may have won over the Legislature, for he was appointed the fifth and last commissioner of public buildings, following Richard Hawkins, in 1844. With the buildings essentially completed, Pendleton's duties appear to have been to provide minor repairs and maintenance, although he did replace the plastering on the north and south porticoes with a wood finish. In 1846, at the end of his term, the position of commissioner of public buildings was abolished, and care of the buildings and grounds was turned over to Secretary of State David B. Greer.

After his work on the State House was completed, Pendleton left the state, moving to Iowa in 1846 and then to Memphis, Tennessee, by 1848. The family then moved to Campbellsburg, Henry County, Kentucky, where Pendleton died on November 29, 1855, at the age of 50 or 51. He and his wife had at least eight children, three of whom were born in Arkansas.

(*Arkansas Gazette,* January 8, 1840; *Arkansas Gazette and Democrat,* December 28, 1855; 1850 Census, Shelby County, Tennessee; 1860 U.S. Census, Henry County, Kentucky)

Pope, John

Territorial Governor, March 9, 1829–1835

John Pope was born in 1770 in Prince William County, Virginia, the son of Colonel William and Penelope Pope. In 1779 the family moved to Kentucky. While still a boy, Pope lost his right arm in an accident in a cornstalk mill. He became a lawyer and began in politics in his early thirties, becoming one of the most prominent politicians in Kentucky in the early nineteenth century. He served in the Kentucky Legislature before being elected to the U.S. Senate from Kentucky in 1806. In 1819 he was appointed Kentucky secretary of state by Governor Gabriel Slaughter. He served as a Kentucky state senator from 1825 to 1829, during the period when Gideon Shryock won the commission to rebuild the Kentucky State House. In 1829 Pope was appointed the third territorial governor of Arkansas by General Andrew Jackson.

After arriving in Arkansas, Pope began a campaign to build a proper state house for the Territory, seeking funds from the United States Government and asking Shryock to provide a suitable plan. Shryock sent the plan to Arkansas with George Weigart. After Pope and Weigart abridged the plan to suit the funds available, Weigart took over as supervising architect, and the work began in 1833. Unfortunately, Weigart died in July 1834 and Pope lost his position as governor in March 1835, with the building still unfinished.

During his time in Arkansas, Pope also became involved in political controversy, both in Arkansas and with the Jackson administration, which eventually led to his loss of the governor's position. In one circumstance, Pope got into a bitter quarrel with C. F. M. Noland, which would have led to a duel, except that Noland was unwilling to fight a one-armed man. Pope's nephew and personal secretary, Fontaine Pope, sought out the duel and lost his life, resulting in a severe censure of Pope by his acquaintances and family. When he was not reappointed as territorial governor in 1835, Pope had only a few weeks' notice to settle his affairs and papers. He was ill during that time and one of his daughters was on her deathbed back in Kentucky. So Pope quickly left Arkansas with things unsettled for his successor, William S. Fulton.

Fulton refused to push the State House project to completion, believing that Pope had exceeded his authority in supervising the construction. It wasn't until James S. Conway was elected the first state governor in 1836 that the project again moved forward. Conway appointed Elijah A. More as commissioner of public buildings in the fall of 1836, and the following year More visited Pope in Kentucky to try to untangle the business of the State House construction. Pope went over all the accounts, vouchers, and papers pertaining to the State House fund with More and then turned them over to More to bring back to Arkansas. In the meantime, Pope had been elected from Kentucky to the U.S. Congress, serving three terms from 1837 to 1843. Misunderstandings about the Arkansas State House construction accounts dragged on until 1844, when Pope returned to Arkansas to defend himself against a lawsuit regarding the funds. The return to Arkansas allowed him to see his vision of the State House finally completed.

Pope was married three times, first to Anne Christian, ca. 1795, probably in Fayette County, Kentucky; second to Eliza Johnson, on February 11, 1810, in Washington, D.C.; and third to Frances Watkins Walton, widow of General Matthew Walton, on May 1, 1820, in Springfield, Kentucky. He had two daughters by his second wife. Pope died at his home in Washington County, Kentucky, on July 12, 1845, at the age of 74. He is buried in Cemetery Hill in Springfield, Kentucky.

(Jacoway 1941:31–44; Rose 1917:284–292; Williams and Whayne 2000:226–227)

Rumbough, George Philip Cowles

Civil Engineer, 1880s

George Philip Cowles Rumbough was born October 23, 1834, in Lynchburg, Virginia, the son of Jacob Rumbough and Ann Dandridge. He graduated from the Virginia Military Institute in 1856 with a degree in civil engineering and came to Arkansas in 1860 to work as a locating and construction engineer for the Little Rock and Memphis railroad. He also located routes for the Rock Island line. When the Civil War broke out, Rumbough returned to Virginia to join General Robert E. Lee's army, where he served in the engineering corps. He returned to Little Rock at the end of the war.

In Little Rock he held the position of city engineer for many years, supervising sanitary improvements in the city. He also did contracting and consulting work for laying sewer systems and building levees on the Arkansas and Mississippi rivers. The historian Carl H. Moneyhon considers Rumbough one of the "creators of the New South," men who differed from the agricultural elite and who urged economic change and the development of industry following the Civil War. He was among the first to support the organization of a cotton factory at Little Rock and was one of the founders of the Arkansas State Horticultural Society.

In 1880 Rumbough designed a new iron gate for the main entrance of the State House grounds, as part of Secretary of State Jacob Frolich's goals to promote Arkansas. He was also asked by Frolich to inspect the buildings, and he found serious problems with the chimneys and the roof over the House Chamber. His findings are included in Frolich's 1882 report.

Rumbough retired after he lost his hearing, and his deafness contributed to an accident that led to his death. On December 26, 1916, he was crossing Markham Street near State in Little Rock when he stepped in front of an oncoming streetcar and was struck down. He died shortly afterward at his home; he was 82 years old. Rumbough was married to Anna Frances Trezevant and had four sons and four daughters, but only two daughters survived him. He is buried in Oakland Cemetery in Little Rock.

(*Arkansas Gazette,* December 27–28, 1916; Moneyhon 1996:383, 389, 408; Rothrock 1975:243–344; VMI 2007; Worthen 1987:337–338, 340)

Shryock, Gideon

Architect

Gideon Shryock was the architect from Kentucky who designed Arkansas's Old State

House. See chapter 2 for a detailed treatment of his life and work.

Stevenson, William Wilson

Commissioner of Public Buildings, 1839–1840

The Reverend William Wilson Stevenson was born January 29, 1797, in South Carolina, the son of James Stevenson and Jane Wilson. After his father died in 1802, his mother remarried and the new family moved to the Arkansas Territory in 1811, settling near Batesville, in Independence County. Stevenson was educated for the Cumberland Presbyterian ministry and preached throughout the state. He was married in 1821 to Ruanna Trimble of Batesville, and the couple had a daughter and two sons before she died. After his wife's death, while in Little Rock conducting a religious meeting, he met Maria Toncray Watkins, the widow of early settler Isaac Watkins, and married her on March 29, 1831. Mrs. Watkins had two children from her previous marriage, and the couple had two additional children. Although originally a minister of the Cumberland Presbyterian church, Stevenson was invited to hold services at the First Baptist church of Little Rock. In 1832 the congregation moved toward the reformation and converted en masse into the Christian church with Stevenson as their leader.

In addition to his religious work, Stevenson was active in the formation of Little Rock. He presided over the meeting to obtain a charter for the town and was promoted as a candidate for first mayor, although he declined to run. In 1837 he was elected a vice president of the first Antiquarian Association and in 1842 was elected president of the Antiquarian and Historical Association. He helped to build a collection of fossils and Native American artifacts. Travel-author G. W. Featherstonhaugh stayed with him on his visit in Little Rock.

Governor James Conway appointed Stevenson as the third commissioner of public buildings on July 31, 1839, to fill a vacancy left by the resignation of Samuel H. Hempstead. His status as a minister, in addition to his recognition as a public figure, may have been viewed as qualities that could help defuse the volatile situation with the workmen that had been engendered by the contentious Elijah More. Besides bringing the State House close to completion, Stevenson made efforts to secure and beautify the grounds, putting up a fence, grading the land, and planting trees. He also recommended that the Legislature formally designate the uses for each part of the buildings. Stevenson's reports as commissioner are signed "W. W. Stevenson."

After his term as commissioner ended, Stevenson continued to be active in the public sphere. In 1841 he attempted to start an agricultural society and experimented with culturing silkworms. In 1843 he served as chaplain in the state House of Representatives, and in 1846 he was elected an officer of the Arkansas Temperance Union and served as register of the land office.

In 1849 Stevenson and two of his sons, John and Robert, left Arkansas for the California gold fields. Stevenson was selected as geologist for the Little Rock Company, probably due to his involvement with the Antiquarian Association. He sent several letters from Los Angeles describing the agricultural opportunities of California to friends in Arkansas in the winter of 1849–1850, which were published in the *Arkansas Gazette.* By the fall of 1850, he was in Stockton, California, running an eating-house, while his son Robert hauled goods in the mines. But life was not easy for the Forty-Niners. Stevenson's wife remained behind in Little Rock, and they eventually became estranged. He also lost his son John in Stockton. A pocket diary that made it back to Little Rock with Robert has an entry dated December 20, 1858, that reads:

> Tomorrow I expect to leave for Santa Rosa. Have been quite sick. Robt and W. will leave in March or April for Little Rock it is not probable that we will ever meet again. I am truly lonely all all gone and alone on the Pacific Shore. It is my intention to begin anew in every thing—I would not have them remain on my account. No not an hour. I shall yet succeed.

Apparently he did succeed, as Stevenson married a third time to Helen Radison about 1863 when he was about 66 years old and she was only about 22. (His second wife, Maria Toncray Watkins, died in Little Rock in 1874 and was buried in the tomb of her previous husband, Isaac Watkins.) In the 1880 census, Stevenson was living in Santa Clara, California, and listed his occupation as physician. He and Helen had five children, the last twin daughters born when he was about 74 years old. Stevenson died November 16, 1886, two and a half months shy of 90, in Santa Clara. He is buried there in the Mission City Cemetery.

(*Arkansas Gazette,* May 5, 1841, August 4, 1841, January 26, 1842, February 22, 1843, March 3, 1846, June 15, 1846, March 15, 1850, March 29, 1850, October 25, 1850, January 1, 1887; Arkansas Reports 1841:260–281; Featherstonhaugh 1844:46–47; Jordan 2006; McArthur 1986; Mission City Memorial Park Index, Santa Clara County Historical and Genealogical Society; Ross 1954:5–16; Tunnah 1913:23–16; 1880 Census, Santa Clara County, California)

Thorn, Thomas

Contractor, Construction Superintendent, 1830s

Thomas Thorn was born July 25, 1806, in Bordentown, New Jersey, the son of Enoch Thorn and Catherine Nagle. He was in Little Rock by the early 1830s and was involved in the construction of a number of buildings. Along with partner William Cook, he contracted to do the brick and stone work for the construction of the Old State House, hiring bricklayers, stonemasons, and other laborers in 1833, and publishing a report on the progress of the work in the *Arkansas Gazette* in the same year. He continued to work on the building through the loss of Governor John Pope and supervising architect George Weigart, and it appears he served as superintendent until Elijah More was appointed commissioner of public buildings. At the end of 1836 he proposed to the Arkansas House of Representatives that they hire him to complete the public buildings within two years in exchange for five sections of land, but they did not take him up on the offer. In May 1837 he sent another letter to the *Arkansas Gazette* defending Governor Pope's handling of the State House construction. In August of the same year, he was chosen chairman to represent the laborers in their dispute with Elijah More over out-of-state hirings.

Thorn's business dealings extended beyond that of the State House. In 1836 he became part owner of the DeBaun building, which was one of the homes of the *Arkansas Gazette,* and in 1838 purchased the Hinderliter house from Chester Ashley. He was also part owner of a stagecoach line that ran between Little Rock and Hot Springs in 1841. In the 1840s he was in partnership with Edward Walden as brick contractors. He served as Little Rock alderman in 1838 and 1840, and in the latter year also unsuccessfully sought a seat in the state Legislature. In 1840 he was elected one of the directors of the State Bank of Arkansas by the Arkansas House of Representatives.

Thorn married Mary Fisher Sherman in Little Rock on February 10, 1835, and the couple had at least four children born in Little Rock, three of whom died before the age of 3. About 1844 the family moved to Texas, where Thorn bought land in Leon (formerly Robertson) County and possibly Bexar County. By 1849, however, he was smitten by gold fever, and the entire family, along with ten slaves, moved to California. They spent the winter of 1849–1850 in Los Angeles, meeting up with W. W. Stevenson. In the spring of 1850 they moved to Mariposa County. The Thorns founded the short-lived town of Quartzburg, near Hornitos, which Mary Thorn named for the county's quartz mines. Thorn opened a store and lodging house and also served as postmaster. By 1851 a school was in operation in the town. Thorn had additional children in Texas and California, bringing the total to eight, but only two children survived to adulthood. Thorn died November 25, 1854, in Quartzburg at the age of 48. He is buried there in the Thorn family cemetery.

(*Arkansas Banner,* December 2, 1843; *Arkansas Gazette,* February 3, 1833, July 10, 1833, May 23, 1837, August 29, 1837, January 2, 1838, June 6, 1838, August 29, 1838, August 21, 1839, December 11, 1839, January 8, 1840; House Journal 1840:470; Jones 1955:17; Klein and Chapman 2006; McArthur 1986: 117, 125, 228; Morgan 1992:46; Ross 1966b:140; Ross 1969:272; Ross 1971:184–185; Quartzburg 2006; Thorn 1837:179–181; Walden 1954:9–11; 1850 U.S. Census, Bexar County, Texas)

Wassell, John

Carpenter, 1830s

Representing a real-life Horatio Alger story, John Wassell rose from a humble carpenter to a lawyer and businessman of distinction in Little Rock. He was born in Kidderminster, Worcester County, England, on February 10, 1813. At the age of 18 he emigrated to America, intending to join an uncle in Philadelphia. By the time Wassell arrived, the uncle had left and Wassell followed him on foot to Pittsburgh and then Cincinnati. Arriving in Cincinnati he discovered the uncle had returned to England, but there Wassell apprenticed himself to a carpenter and thoroughly learned the trade. After finishing his apprenticeship, he answered an ad in the city paper and won a contract to build a house in Grand Gulf, Mississippi. He subsequently answered a second ad, probably the one placed by Elijah More in 1837 for carpentry work on the construction of the State House in Little Rock. The ad appeared in papers in Kentucky and Ohio, and those desiring to work for More were instructed to meet him in Danville,

Kentucky, by October 1 to accompany him back to Little Rock. This, along with Wassell's Louisville marriage, suggests he may have returned to the Cincinnati area after his work in Mississippi was finished.

Wassell came to Arkansas with More, probably in October 1837, and was hired as carpentry foreman by Henry Pendleton. Wassell made a trip back to Kentucky in the spring of 1838 to marry and brought his new wife back to Arkansas with him, setting up housekeeping in the west wing while work continued. By late 1838 he and Pendleton may have become partners for contracting the carpentry, as indicated by their report to the General Assembly complaining about More's handling of his duties. With his contract nearing an end but much work remaining due to delays in receiving materials, he set his crew to hammering above the Legislative halls, creating such a din that he was called before the Senate and told to desist. He negotiated for an extended contract, and the problem was settled to everyone's peace and satisfaction.

After Wassell completed work on the State House, he remained a Little Rock resident, working on the construction of both private and public buildings, including two early bank buildings. He then moved to Lonoke County, where he farmed for seven years, before returning to Little Rock and becoming part owner of the newspaper the *Old Line Whig*. He later became a merchant and opened a general supply and steamboat store, while also purchasing land along the Arkansas River below Lewisburg and erecting a sawmill. He sold the sawmill in 1863 after Federal occupation of the state and returned to Little Rock, where he became a party in a suit and defended himself so brilliantly he not only won the suit but was encouraged to study law, which he did and then began a law practice about 1870. By the time of his death, he was a judge and a member of the bar of the Supreme Court of Arkansas.

Identified by Carl H. Moneyhon as one of the "creators of the New South," Wassell promoted economic change and the development of industry following the Civil War. He was one of the originators of the Memphis & Little Rock Railroad, president of the Home Water Company, director of the Little Rock Gas Company, and vice president of the First National Bank. During Reconstruction, in 1868, he was appointed mayor of Little Rock by President Andrew Johnson and under his administration city hall was built, the first fire engine was purchased, and the first grading of streets begun. He also was a founder of Christ Episcopal Church and founder and first president of the Deaf Mute Institute.

Wassell married Margaret Spotts in Louisville, Kentucky, April 18, 1838, and the couple had eight children. Wassell died January 29, 1881, in Little Rock, a few weeks shy of his sixty-eighth birthday, and is buried in Mount Holly Cemetery.

(*Arkansas Gazette*, August 15, 1837, January 30, 1881; Cantrell 1900:38–41; Cook 1996:74; Crawford and Worthen 1993:242; *Daily Arkansas Democrat*, February 2, 1881; Goodspeed 1889a:514–516; Moneyhon 1996:408; Woodward 1960:19–22)

Weaver, Samuel Montgomery

Secretary of State, January 21, 1860–October? 1860

Samuel Montgomery Weaver was born October 1, 1805, in Kentucky. At the age of 27 in 1830, he moved to New Orleans, where he became associated with the Rose family and came with them to Little Rock later that year. The group then moved to the countryside near Paris, Arkansas. In 1836 he married the eldest Rose daughter, Mary Eliza, and later that year the couple moved back to Little Rock, where he became a merchant.

After David Greer's death in office, Alexander Boileau served as secretary of state for five months, followed by Samuel M. Weaver. Priest's *Historical Report* shows him serving for only two months (to March 20), but his report to Governor Elias Conway is dated October 30, 1860. His reports as secretary of state are signed "S. M. Weaver."

Weaver reiterated Greer's warnings about the condition of the State House, especially noting the deteriorating condition of the passageways between the buildings, which he referred to as "wood houses," and suggesting that they be removed and the passages rebuilt. He also reported on the condition of the library in the west wing, which was by then outgrowing its space. Although a joint committee on public buildings looked into the matter and recommended the removal of the west wing to erect a fireproof building, the Civil War intervened and the work was never begun.

Weaver married Mary Eliza Rose in 1836, and the couple had at least six children. Weaver died April 21, 1864, in Little Rock, at the age of 58. He is buried in Mount Holly Cemetery.

(Crawford and Worthen 1993:245; Field 1951:328–338; Priest 1998:205)

Weigart, George

Supervising Architect, 1833–July 25, 1834

George Weigart was born about 1807 in Kentucky, possibly the son of Phillip Adam Weigart. Although little is known of his early years, he went into the building trades. He was in Lexington in 1829 when the main building at Transylvania University burned, and for his assistance in saving college property the night of the fire, the university awarded him a scholarship for one of his sons. Direct evidence of his association with architect Gideon Shryock in the construction of the Kentucky capitol or Morrison College at Transylvania University has not been found, but Shryock was working on Morrison College when he received the request from Governor John Pope for a design for the Arkansas State House. Shryock prepared the plans and sent them with Weigart to Arkansas, recommending Weigart to supervise the work.

When Pope discovered the plans were too elaborate for the money he had available, Pope and Weigart abridged them, and Weigart remained in Little Rock to serve as supervising architect. A letter from him in the *Arkansas Gazette* describes the work in progress. Weigart brought his wife, America, and two sons, Horace Anthony and Oliver Perry, with him to Little Rock.

In the midst of his work on the State House, Weigart suffered an untimely death on July 25, 1834, when he was only about 27 years old. America Weigart and Isaac Sutton were named administrators of his estate, and items offered in the public sale included a clock, a watch, a dining table, a bedstead, a feather bed and mattress, brass andirons, a set of china, a set of mantel ornaments, one cow, a lot of glassware, chairs, a set of architect books, a complete chest of carpenter's tools, a set of drawing instruments, a lot of bed clothing, and a lot of household and kitchen furniture. The abridged plans for the State House were probably lost or disposed of at this time. Weigart's wife and children moved to Tennessee after Weigart's death, where America remarried.

Although descendants think George Weigart may be buried in an unmarked grave in Mount Holly Cemetery, this is unlikely since the land for it was not acquired until 1839. Weigart was probably buried in Little Rock's first public cemetery, used from ca. 1828 to 1843, known as the Old Burial Ground, located at Capitol and Gaines streets, now the site of the Federal Building. In 1860 the Peabody School was built on the cemetery, and at that time only recent graves with markers were moved to Mount Holly Cemetery.

Weigart married America Monks on October 11, 1827, in Fayette County, Kentucky. They had three sons, two of whom probably died as children. Interestingly, three of Weigart's grandchildren through his son Oliver Perry moved to Arkansas around 1888, and descendants can still be found in Arkansas today.

(*Arkansas Advocate,* August 29, 1844; B. Brittain letter, 1997; Crawford 1993:1–6; Fayette County, Kentucky, marriage records; Peter and Peter 1896:159; Thomas 1930:566; L. D. Weigart letter, 1997)

White, Robert J. T.

Secretary of State, January 20, 1864–January 1871?

Robert J. T. White was born about 1822 in Loudoun County, Virginia, where he spent most of his life. He was educated at Benjamin Hallowell's school in Alexandria, Virginia, and Dickinson College in Carlisle, Pennsylvania. He then went into public life, serving Loudoun County in the Virginia General Assembly—in the House of Delegates from 1847 to 1850, as a delegate to the constitutional convention of 1850–1851, and in the state Senate from 1852 to 1854, a seat he won in a celebrated contest against the popular John Janney. White married Mary Louisa Taylor, on February 17, 1859, in Hillsborough, Loudoun County, Virginia. Shortly after the marriage, they left Virginia, stopping first in Ohio, where their first son was born, and then on to Arkansas by 1861, where at least three more children were born.

During the Civil War, White was a Unionist and subsequently identified with the Republican party. Although John I. Stirman (1860–1862) and O. H. Oates (1862–1864) served as secretaries of state during the war years, White held the position in a provisional capacity beginning in January 1864, being elected in the Constitutional Convention. He then was elected to the position by popular vote in March of that year. He served terms under governors Isaac Murphy and Powell Clayton, which ran from 1864 to 1873, but resigned sometime after the death of his wife in 1870. James M. Johnson then completed White's term prior to his own election to office.

The beginning of the Civil War in 1861 delayed any further plans for expansion or major work on the State House. When White took the position as secretary of state, he found the buildings in "wrecked condition," but set to work making repairs, with the assistance of work orders by General Steele and General Reynolds. It was under his watch that the renovations of 1867 took place, which closed the passageway to the west wing, creating the first hyphen. With space at a premium, White was faced with the Legislature's growing resentment over the occupation of the east wing by Pulaski County.

White's wife, Mary, died in March 1870 of complications from the birth of their daughter, who was named for her. After Mary's death, White resigned his position as secretary of state and moved his family back to Loudoun County, where he took up agriculture. Four years before his death, he suffered a bad accident when he was violently thrown from his horse after running into a clothesline. The accident resulted in some paralysis, which progressed over the years and contributed to the deterioration of his health. White died at the home of his sister in Hamilton, Virginia, on June 14, 1890, at the age of 68 or 69.

(*Arkansas Gazette,* March 15, 1870; *Democratic Mirror* [Virginia], February 23, 1859; Leonard 1978:426, 431, 436, 441, 453, 458; *Osceola Times* [Arkansas], June 14, 1890; Priest 1998:205; Ross 1969:387–389; Weideman 1984b:94; 1870 Arkansas Census, Pulaski County;)

Wilson, John

Speaker of the State House of Representatives, 1836–1837

John Wilson's killing of Joseph Anthony in the House of Representatives on December 4, 1837, was an act that thrust Wilson into the ranks of Arkansas's most notorious figures. Because of that, it is difficult to find the truth of Wilson's character and life. To his friends and supporters, he was a man of honor and good will; to his enemies, he was a heartless ruffian.

John Wilson was born March 16, 1787, in Virginia. The family moved to Kentucky when he was a boy, and as a young man he lived in Missouri, where he married Sarah (Sally) Byrd in 1810 in Cape Girardeau. The first 4 of their 12 children were born in Missouri. About 1818 the family moved to the Red River area of southwest Arkansas and lived consecutively in Hempstead, Clark, and Pike counties. In addition to farming, Wilson also built a gristmill in Clark County before 1830 and held a term as judge in 1838–1840. In land speculation Wilson was one of the founders of the towns of Manchester, originally in Clark County, and St. Martin, in Pope County. By 1837 he owned 15 parcels of land in Pike County.

Wilson was elected to the Third Territorial General Assembly in 1823, serving as representative from Hempstead County and held that position until 1831, when he was elected representative from Clark County. During a special session of the Fifth Territorial General Assembly in 1828, he became Speaker of the House, a position he held, except during 1831, through the remainder of the Territorial General Assemblies and into the First State General Assembly. He was also elected the first president of the Real Estate Bank of Arkansas. He was 50 years old at the time of his fight with Anthony.

Wilson's 14-year tenure in the Arkansas House of Representatives and repeated selection to serve as Speaker of the House suggests he was both well known and well respected. Grandison Royston, who was an eyewitness to the Wilson-Anthony fight, described Wilson as "a fine parliamentarian—a gentleman of good common sense, possessing a high sense of honor, amiable and courteous in his demeanor." An account written after his death and published in Goodspeed's *Biographical and Historical Memoirs: History of Arkansas* described him as having "not the shadow . . . of the bully or desperado about him" with a "nature inclined to peace and good will." All of which only raises the question as to what possessed Wilson on that fateful day in December 1837 that would incite him to such a terrible act of violence as to lead to the death of Joseph Anthony?

As president of the Real Estate Bank, Wilson had been taking some heat from the bank's opponents, which included Anthony and state senator Robert McCamy. Just before his fight with Anthony, Wilson had stepped out of the Representatives' Hall to settle a disagreement with McCamy, through the intercession of their friends, but which probably left Wilson without much patience for Anthony's insult and challenge. Nonetheless, that hardly could excuse the subsequent violence. For a description of the fight, see the entry on Joseph J. Anthony.

It was three days before a warrant for Wilson's arrest was issued, but during that time the severe injuries he incurred during the fight had confined him to his bed. He subsequently tendered his resignation as a member of the House, but the Representatives refused his resignation and expelled him instead. Wilson was charged with murder and brought before a court of investigation in Pulaski County, where bail was set at $10,000. Eminent lawyers Chester Ashley and Absolom Fowler represented him. In April a change of venue was requested on the argument that Wilson would not receive a fair trial in Pulaski County. The request was granted, and the trial was moved to Saline County.

The trial was held in early May and lasted several days, ending on May 11. Wilson's guilt or innocence of the murder of Anthony seemed to hinge on which man first drew his weapon and which made the first strike. The entire fight lasted less than two minutes, and the drawing of knives was so close to simultaneous that the witnesses could only report on which man they happened to be watching at that moment. It was clear, however, that Anthony delivered two serious and debilitating cuts to Wilson before Wilson managed the single stab that took Anthony's life. The jury found Wilson not guilty of murder, ruling in favor of excusable homicide.

The verdict did not sit well with many people. James C. Anthony, a kinsman of J. J. Anthony, sent a long diatribe to the *Arkansas Gazette*, which appeared on May 30, 1838, claiming that the trial was tainted and that Wilson had won the good will of the judge and local residents in the dram shops. He also included his version of the fight, introducing sensational and grisly details that later were used in popular retellings. A rebuttal to James Anthony's account appeared as an "extra" in the *Arkansas Gazette* on June 20.

Not long after the trial, Wilson and his family moved from Clark County to Pike County, perhaps because of ill-feeling among his neighbors or for financial reasons, although Pike was formed out of Clark and Hempstead counties in 1833, so it was not a substantial move. In 1839 he borrowed money from the Real Estate Bank. After sitting out a term, Wilson again was elected to office, serving this time as representative from Pike County during the Third General Assembly in 1840, during which he participated fully in the business of the House. During that session, according to one memoir written over 50 years later, Wilson supposedly was restrained from attacking another Bank critic, thus ending his Arkansas political career, although no mention of the purported altercation has been found in the 1840 House Journal or in the *Arkansas Gazette*. By 1841 Wilson was keeping a "public house" on Wolf Creek in Pike County on land with two mineral springs. About 1842–1844 Wilson's fortunes sunk even lower. His wife died and he found himself in financial ruin, defaulting on his Real Estate Bank loan, after which he left Arkansas.

Wilson and several of his children moved to Texas, where he married Emily Brown in 1845 and began a second family. Six children were born to them. The family was living in Cass County, Texas, in 1850 while Wilson did a stint in the California gold fields during the 1849–1850 gold rush. After he returned from California the family settled in the Cedar Hill community of Dallas County, Texas, and he reestablished himself. Hardly a crushed man, in 1860 Wilson owned personal property and real estate valued into the thousands of dollars. Wilson died in Dallas County, Texas, on September 11, 1864, at the age of 77. He is buried there in the Little Bethel Cemetery.

(*Arkansas Gazette*, May 2, 1837, June 20, 1837, April 25, 1838, May 16, 1838, May 23, 1838, May 30, 1838, June 13, 1838, June 20, 1838, June 4, 1882; Boyd 2006:233; Dodd 1990; Gems of Pike County 1995:1–2; Goodspeed 1890:141–142; Goodspeed 1978:104–105; Heath 2007; House Journal 1837:299–302; Pope 1895: 261–264; Priest 1998: 213–218, 512; Richter 1992:10, 71, 782–783; Whayne et al. 2002:113; Worley 1950:408–411; 1850 U.S. Census, Cass County, Texas; 1860 U.S. Census, Dallas County, Texas)

SECTION 4

From the Collection of the Old State House Museum

AN IMAGE GALLERY

The Old State House is one of Arkansas's most prominent and most recognized buildings. It has been the focus of interest throughout its history as the seat of state government, an Arkansas historic building, and a tourist attraction. Because of this, the Old State House has been the subject of drawings and photographs, has been pictured on brochures and objects promoting Arkansas, and has spawned numerous souvenirs. These images and objects are a physical part of the history of the Old State House.

The staff of the Old State House Museum has selected the following images and objects from its collection that they feel are representative of various periods and activities that involve the building, and to fulfill their obligation to make these collections available to the public. Like an exhibit, this Image Gallery provides a visual tour of the Old State House.

Architecture and Artifacts

The physical structure of the Old State House, which spanned some 175 years, went through numerous changes and modernizations during that time. Thus, early pieces of the building, interior hardware, and furnishings expand our understanding of the structure's architectural history. Artifacts recovered from below ground also contribute to the story.

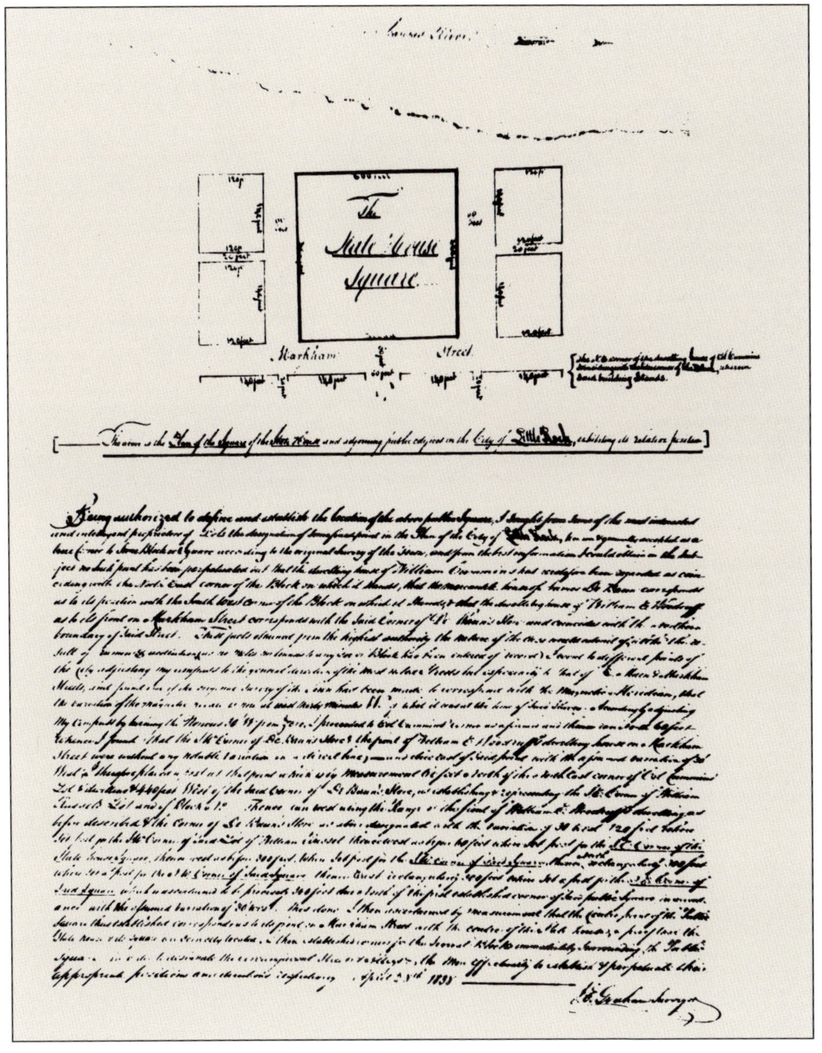

Fig. G.1: This photocopy of a document from Little Rock City Hall records shows the April 1835 plat for the lots upon which the Old State House sits. *Old State House Museum Photo Collection.*

Fig. G.2: The Arkansas state seal was first placed in the center of the pediment in 1877, after being brought back from the Arkansas Building at the Philadelphia Centennial Exposition. *Photograph by Gail Moore Stephens, Old State House Museum Photo Collection.*

Fig. G.3: An acanthus leaf pilaster decorates the central stairway in the main building of the Old State House. *Old State House Museum Photo Collection.*

Fig. G.5: This bit of wood trim from underneath window paneling in the original House of Representatives dates back to the construction of the building and reveals the original trim color. It was discovered during the 1990s renovation. *Old State House Museum Collection.*

Fig. G.4: Door latches used in the Old State House were intricately detailed. *Old State House Museum Collection.*

Fig. G.6: This window panel, part of the vertical jam that fits inside the window frame, had been covered by the 1885–1886 addition. It was rediscovered during the 1990s renovation in the landing of the central stairway. The panel is original to the construction of the building and reveals a hand-painted grain pattern. *Old State House Museum Collection.*

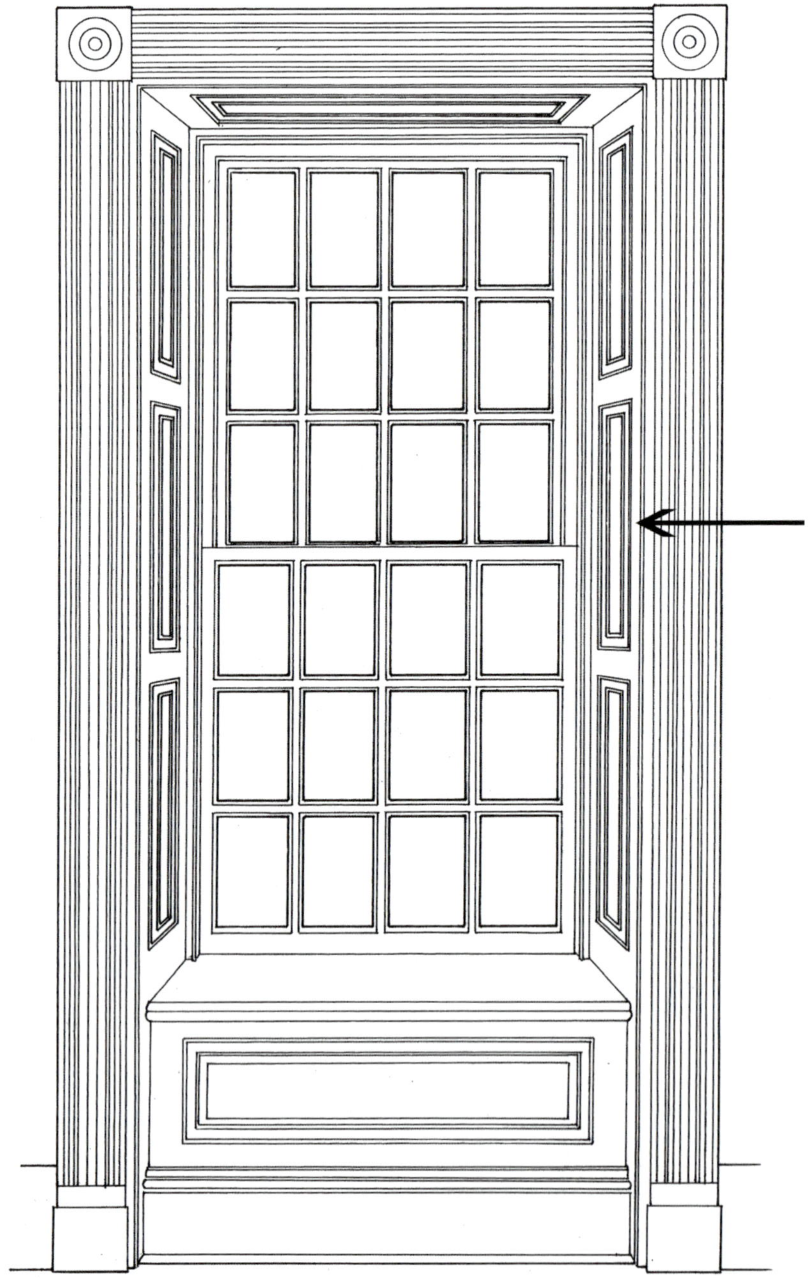

Fig. G.7: The drawing indicates the location of the window panel within the window frame. *Illustration by Bill Reames, Old State House Museum Photo Collection.*

Fig. G.8: The Old State House was originally heated by woodstoves, like this one found in the attic. It measures 3 feet long by 11½ inches wide, and stands just over 2 feet tall. *Old State House Museum Collection.*

Fig. G.9: A view of the fountain looking south down Center Street, from a ca. 1905 photograph. Cast by Janney Ironworks of Montgomery, Alabama, the fountain was purchased by the ladies of the Centennial Club of Arkansas for the Arkansas Building at the Philadelphia Centennial Exposition in 1876. It was installed at the Old State House in 1878 and began operating the following year. *Courtesy of Arkansas History Commission.*

Fig. G.10: This middle section of the three-tiered fountain, decorated with cranes, was found in 1998 during excavation of the cistern. Other wildlife sculptures were arrayed around the base of the fountain. *Old State House Museum Collection.*

Fig. G.11: Terra-cotta chimney pots were used on the Old State House to improve the draft from the chimneys. When this one was found during the 1947–1949 restoration, it was believed it had been made in France, although it now appears that England was the more likely source, where similar styles have been found. Changes in heating technology eliminated the need for chimney pots. *Old State House Museum Collection.*

Fig. G.12: John Quinn, superintendent of construction for the Baldwin Company, which had the contract for the 1947–1949 restoration, examines two chimney pots removed from the building. The pot on the left is marked with what appears to be an 1832 date and initials, probably those of the maker. The architectural presentation painting (Fig. 3.6), possibly by Shryock, seems to show chimney pots at the tops of the chimneys. *Courtesy of Arkansas History Commission.*

Fig. G.13: The ca. 1955 museum interpretation of the 1885 House Chamber. *Old State House Museum Photo Collection.*

Fig. G.14: The ca. 1955 museum interpretation of the 1885 Senate Chamber. *Old State House Museum Photo Collection.*

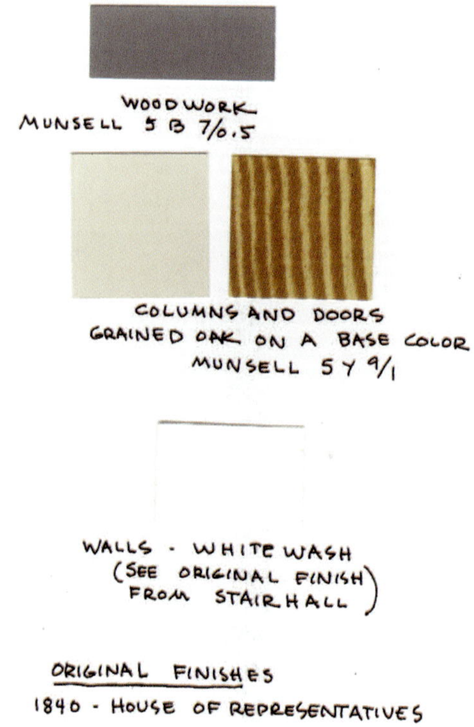

Fig. G.15: Based on paint samples found on hidden woodwork, the 1998 restoration was able to replicate the original colors used in the 1840 House of Representatives. *Old State House Museum Photo Collection.*

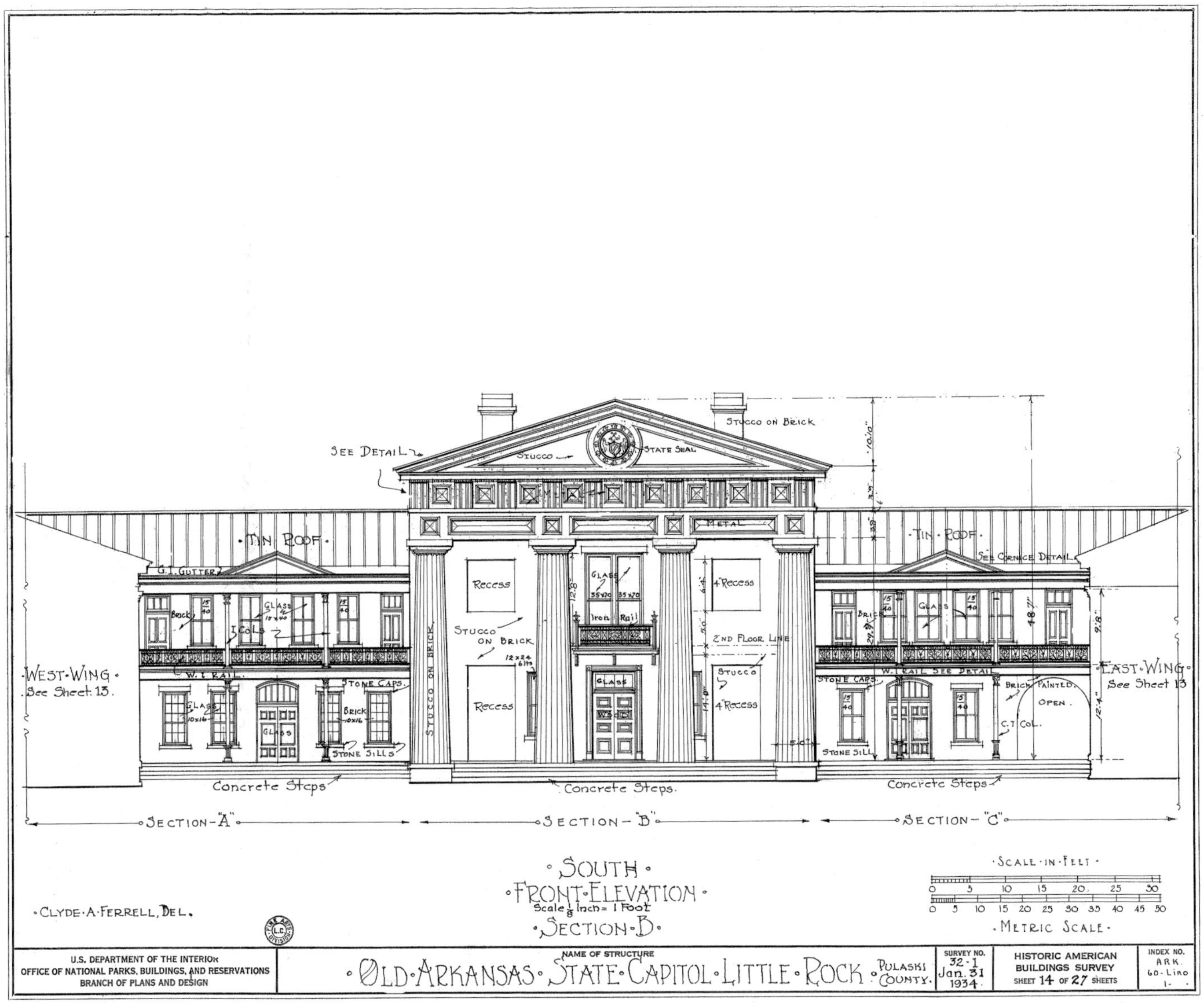

Fig. G.16: Begun during the Great Depression in December 1933, the Historic American Buildings Survey put hundreds of architects to work documenting America's historic buildings in detailed drawings and photographs. The HABS program, administered by the National Park Service, documented the Old State House in 1934, as the building looked after the 1885–1886 expansion. The HABS documents can be viewed on-line at http://hdl.loc.gov/loc.pnp/hhh.ar0016.

South (front) elevation of the main building and hyphens. *Courtesy of Historic American Buildings Survey, U.S. Library of Congress.*

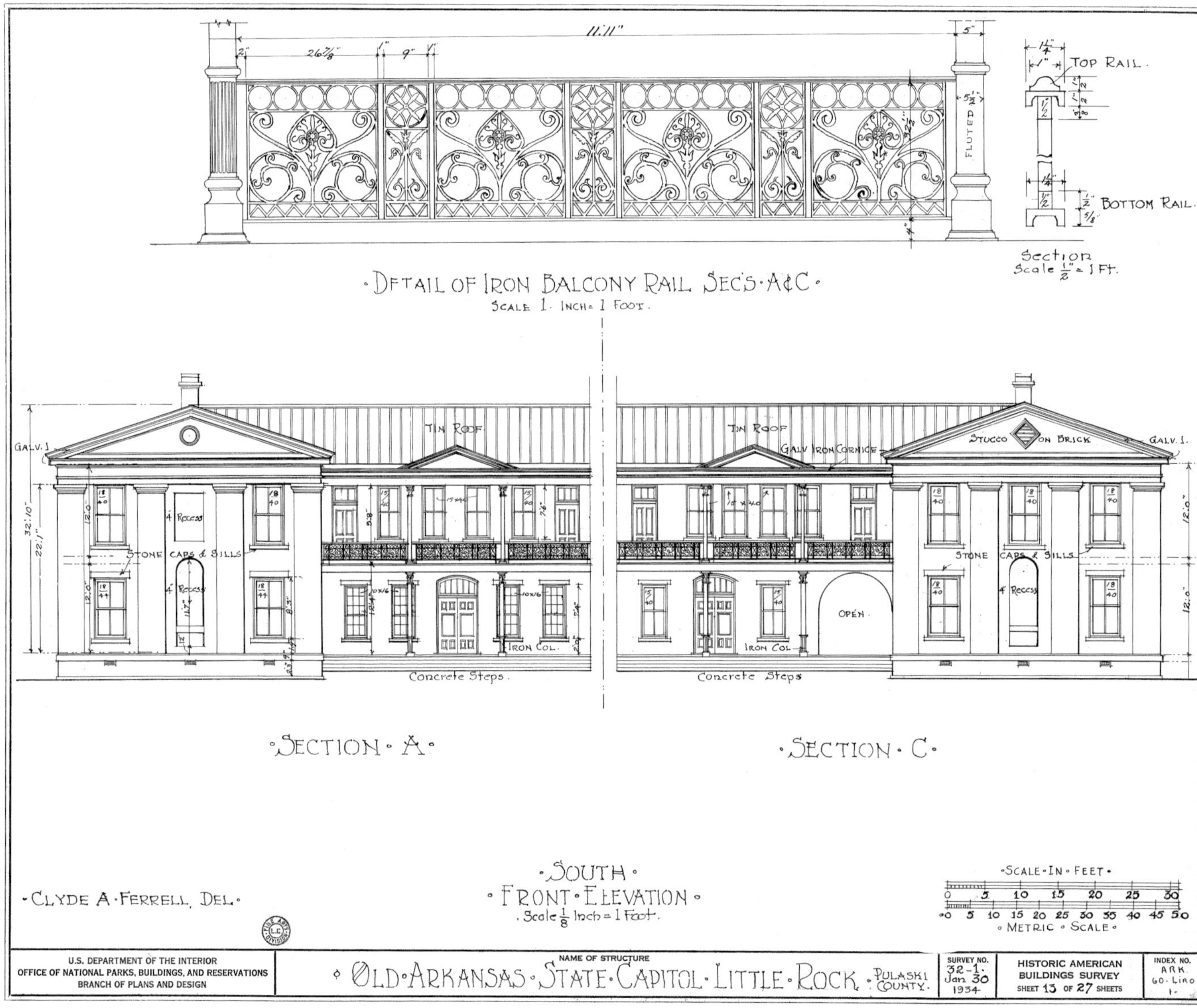

Fig. G.17: South elevation of the hyphens and wings. Notice that the east hyphen has an arched passageway and differs from the west hyphen. *Courtesy of Historic American Buildings Survey, U.S. Library of Congress.*

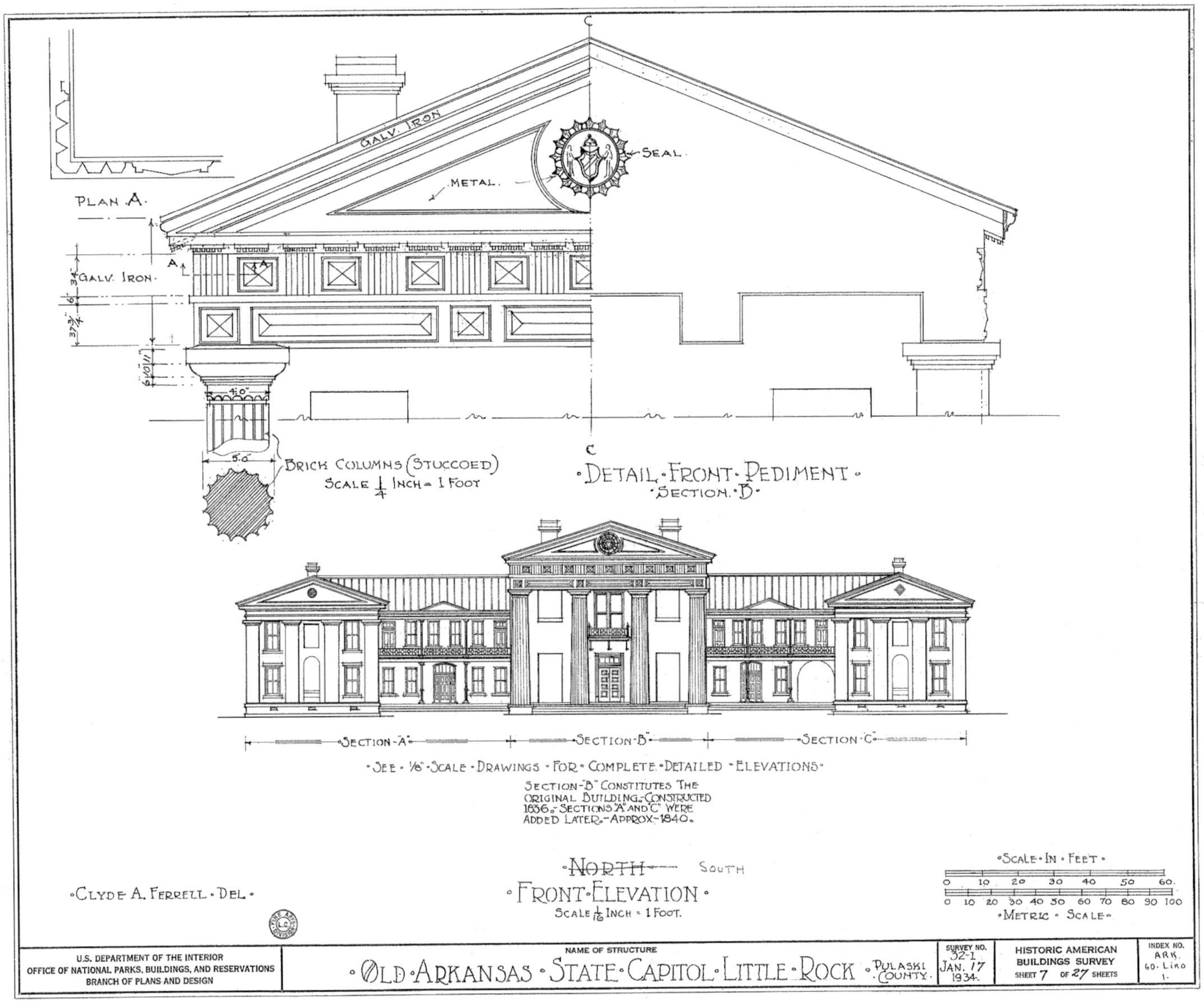

Fig. G.18: South elevation of the entire building with a detail of the pediment. *Courtesy of Historic American Buildings Survey, U.S. Library of Congress.*

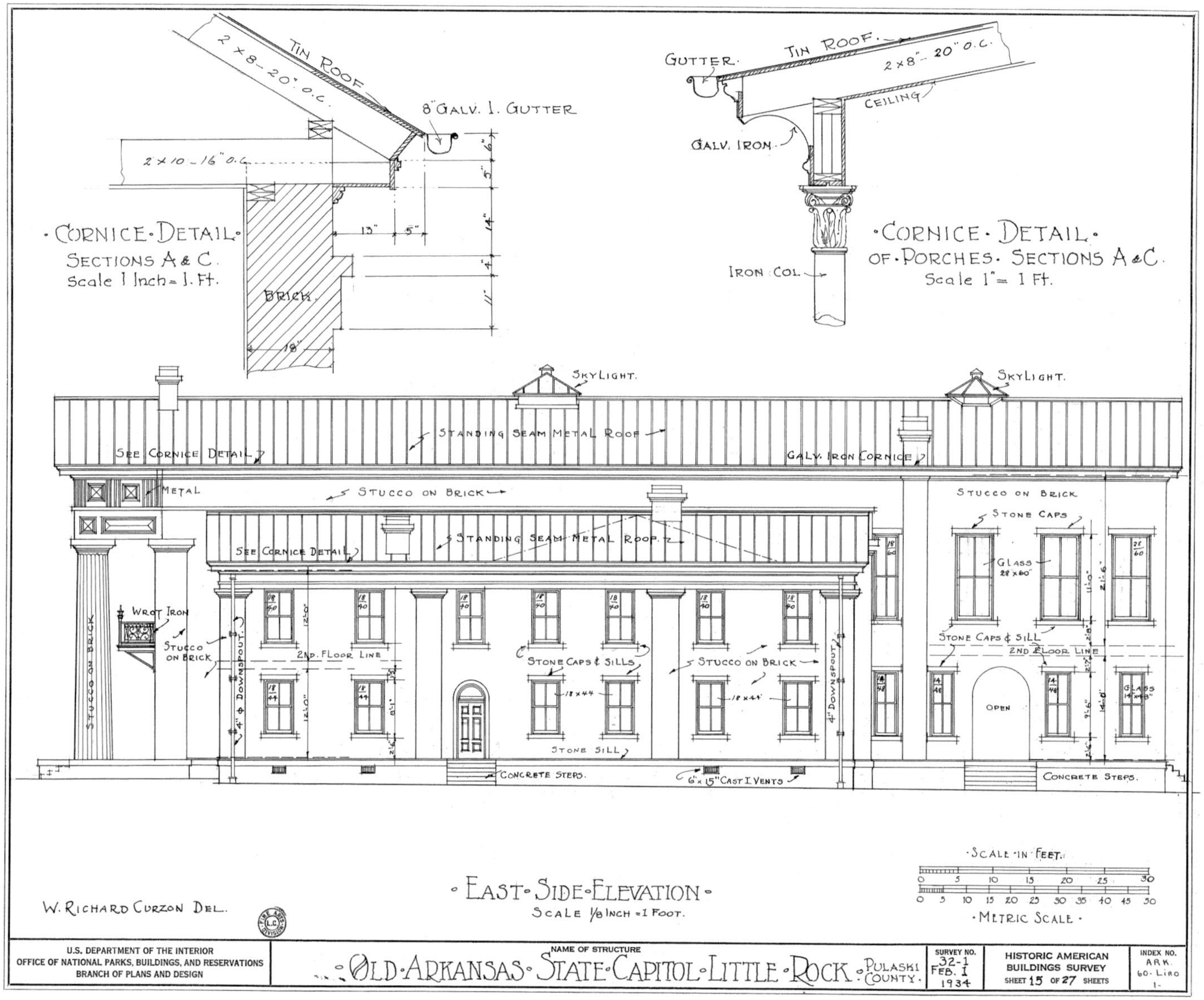

Fig. G.19: East side elevation showing the main building behind the east wing. *Courtesy of Historic American Buildings Survey, U.S. Library of Congress.*

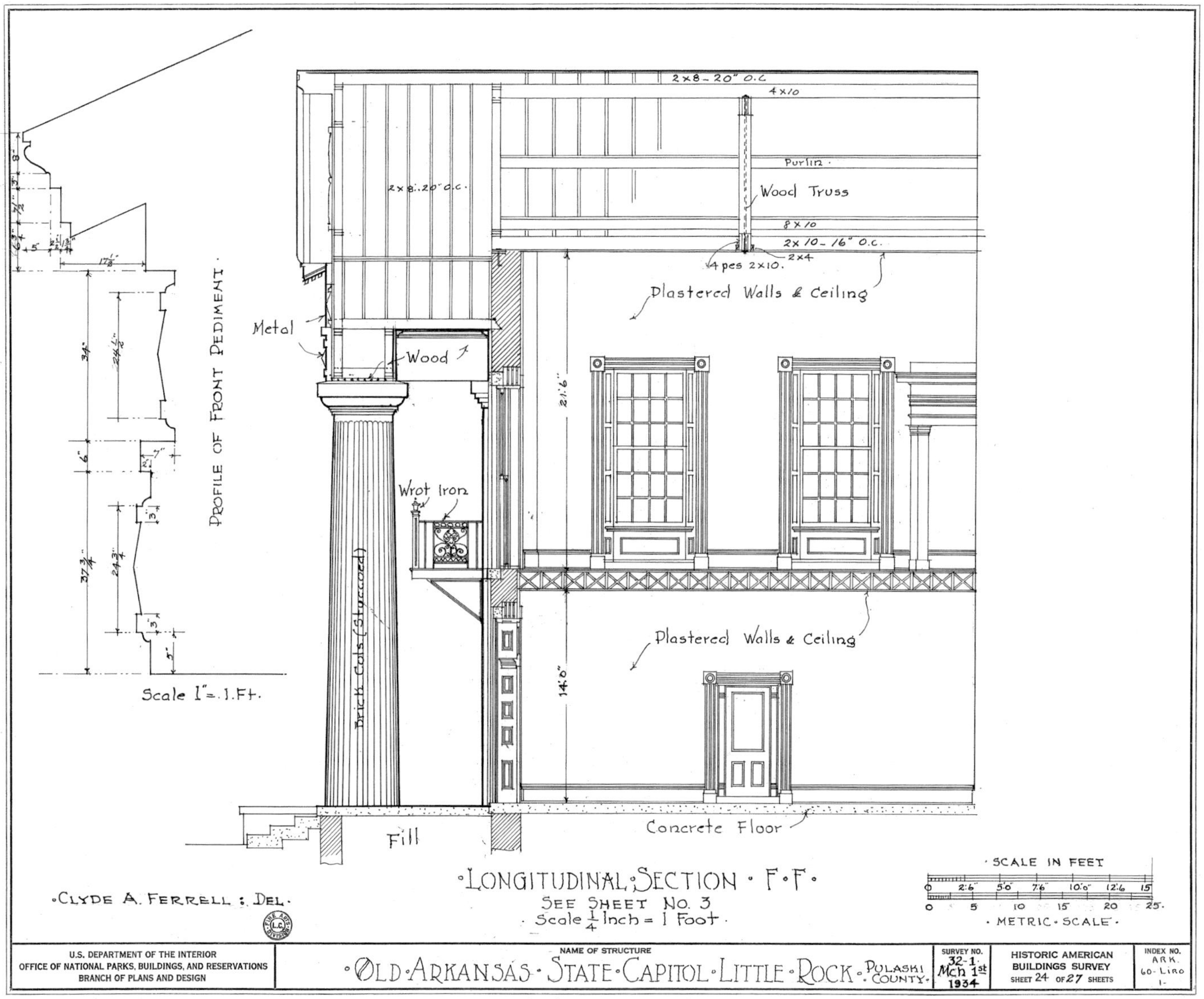

Fig. G.20: Longitudinal section details. *Courtesy of Historic American Buildings Survey, U.S. Library of Congress.*

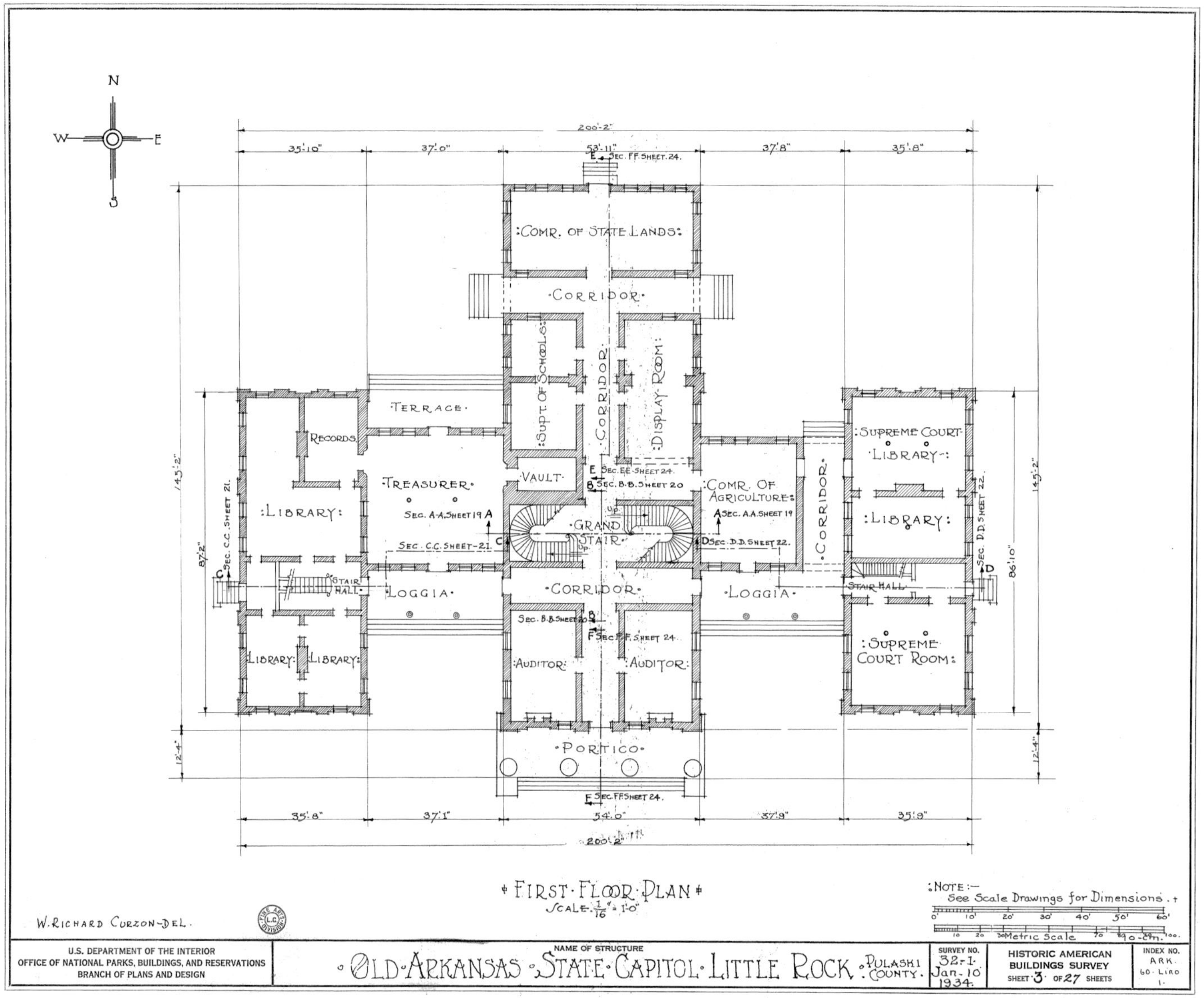

Fig. G.21: First-floor plan, including use of the rooms by state government. *Courtesy of Historic American Buildings Survey, U.S. Library of Congress.*

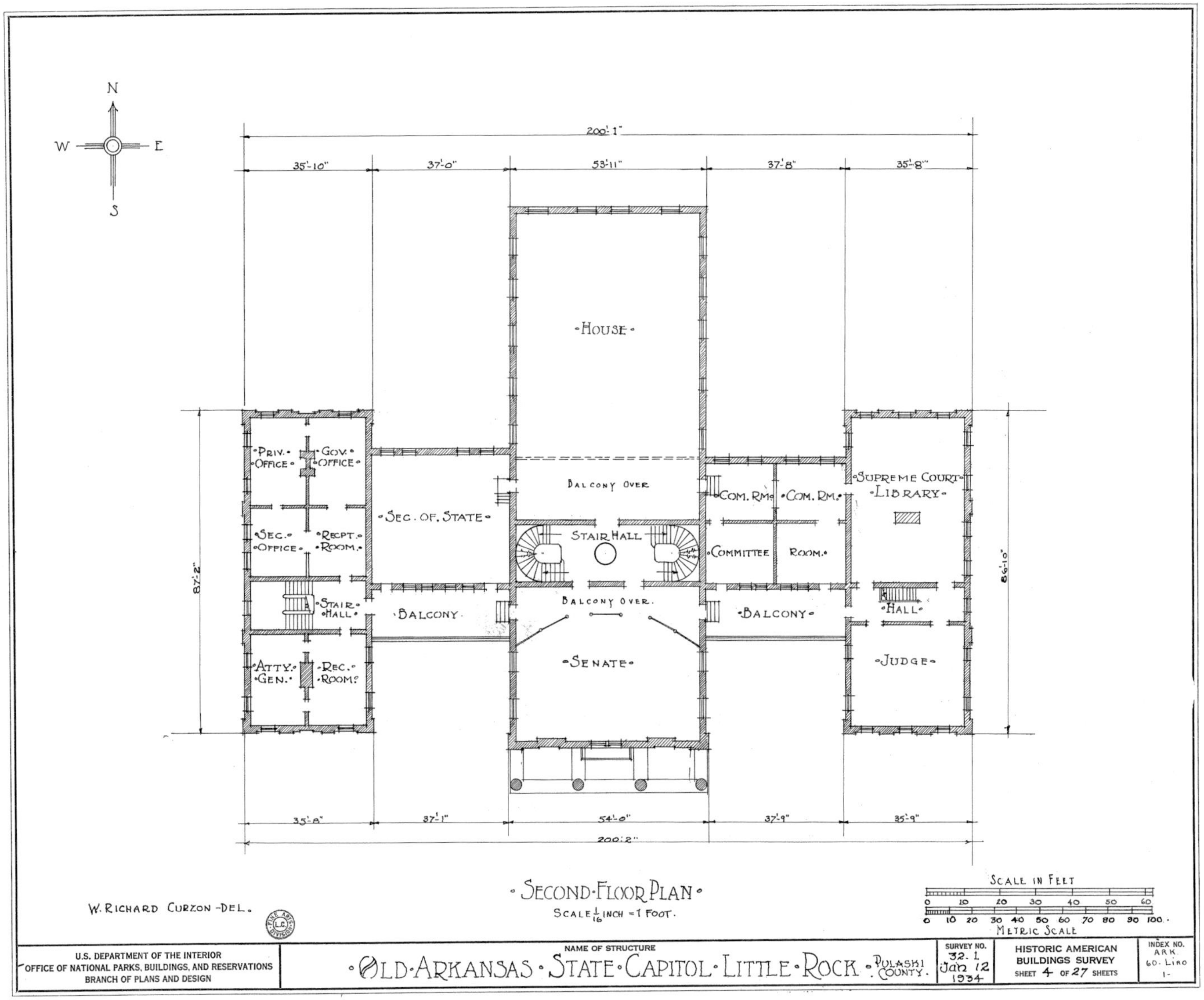

Fig. G.22: Second-floor plan, including use of the rooms by state government. *Courtesy of Historic American Buildings Survey, U.S. Library of Congress.*

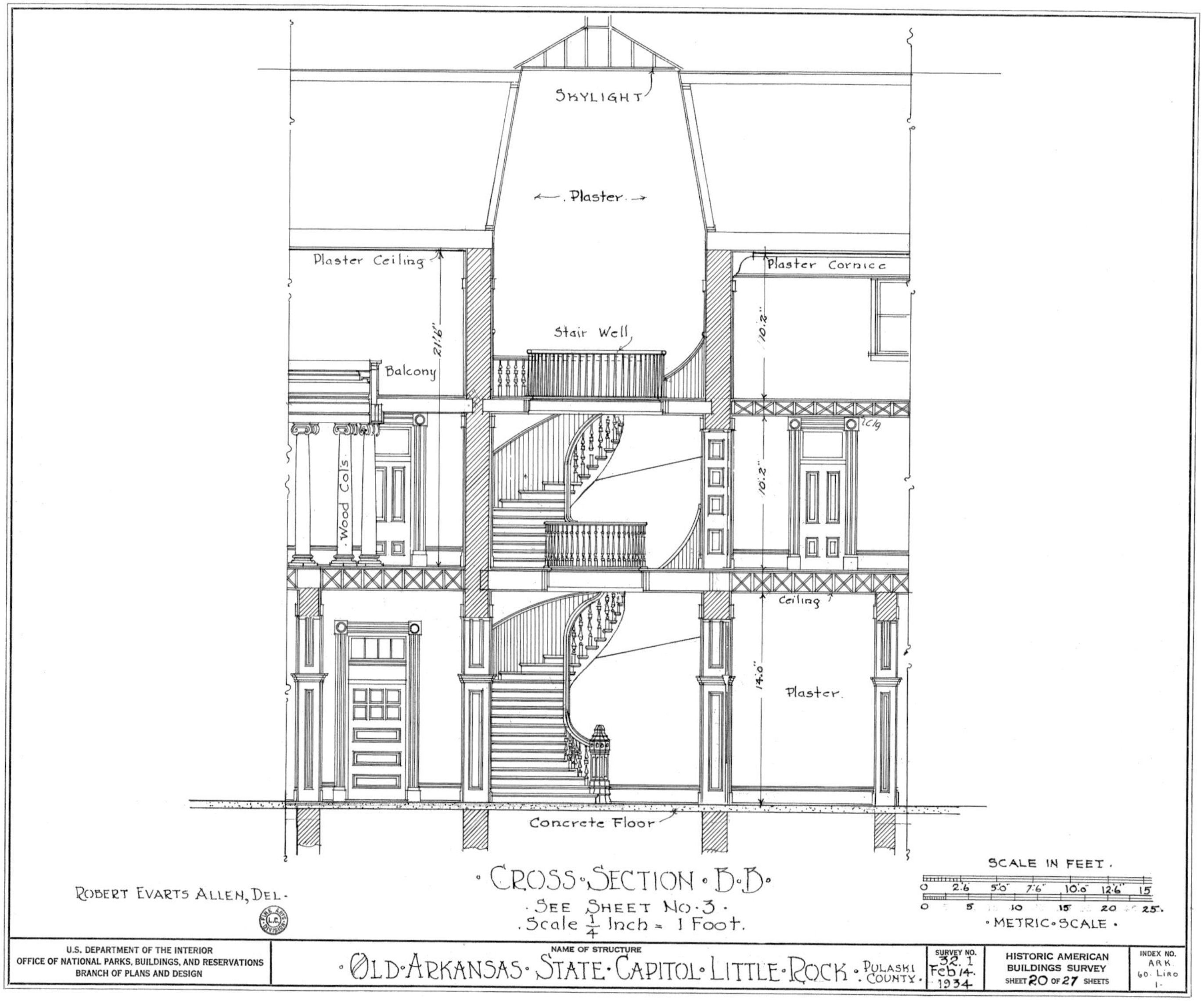

Fig. G.23: Cross section of the main stairwell. *Courtesy of Historic American Buildings Survey, U.S. Library of Congress.*

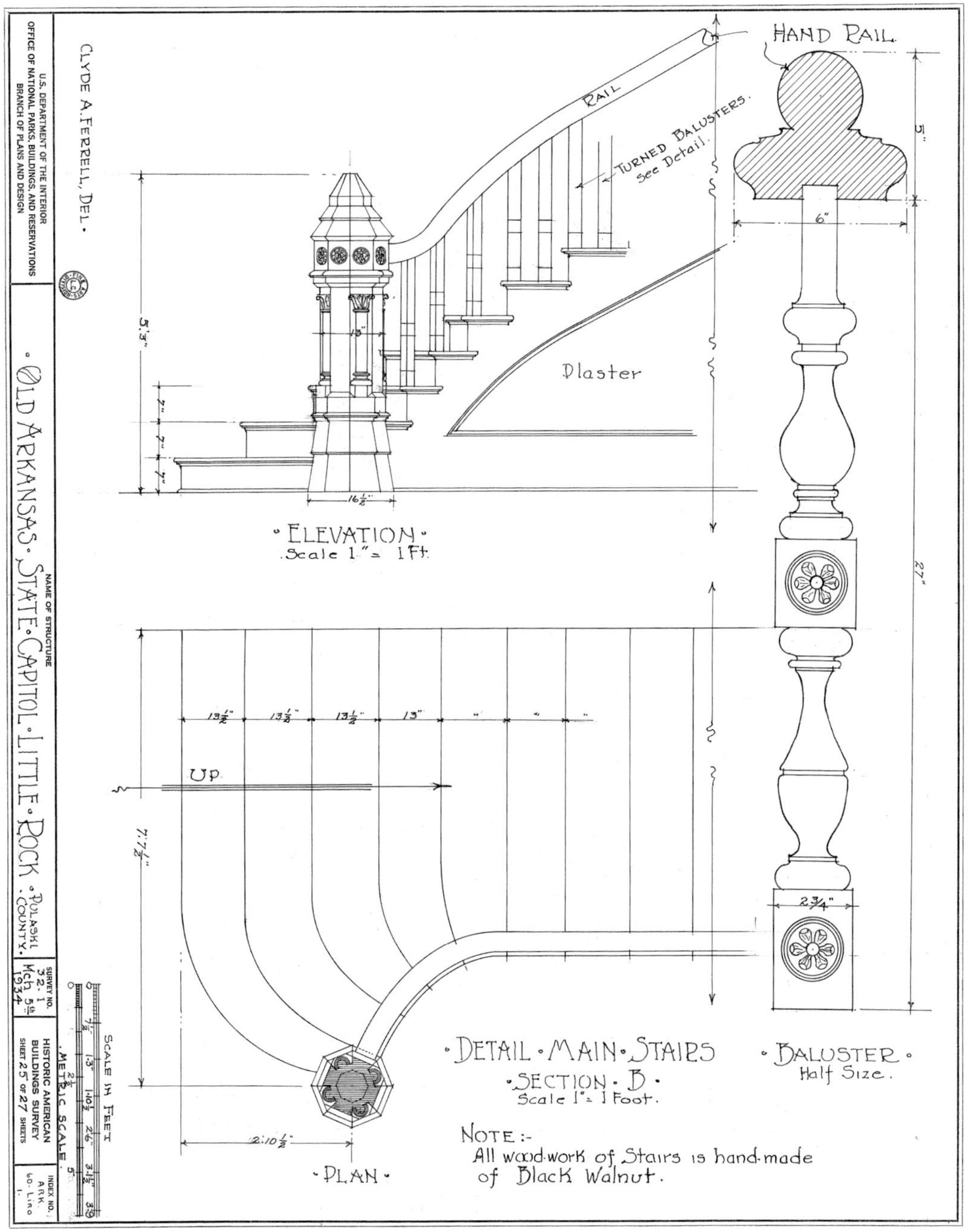

Fig. G.24: Details of the main stairwell. *Courtesy of Historic American Buildings Survey, U.S. Library of Congress.*

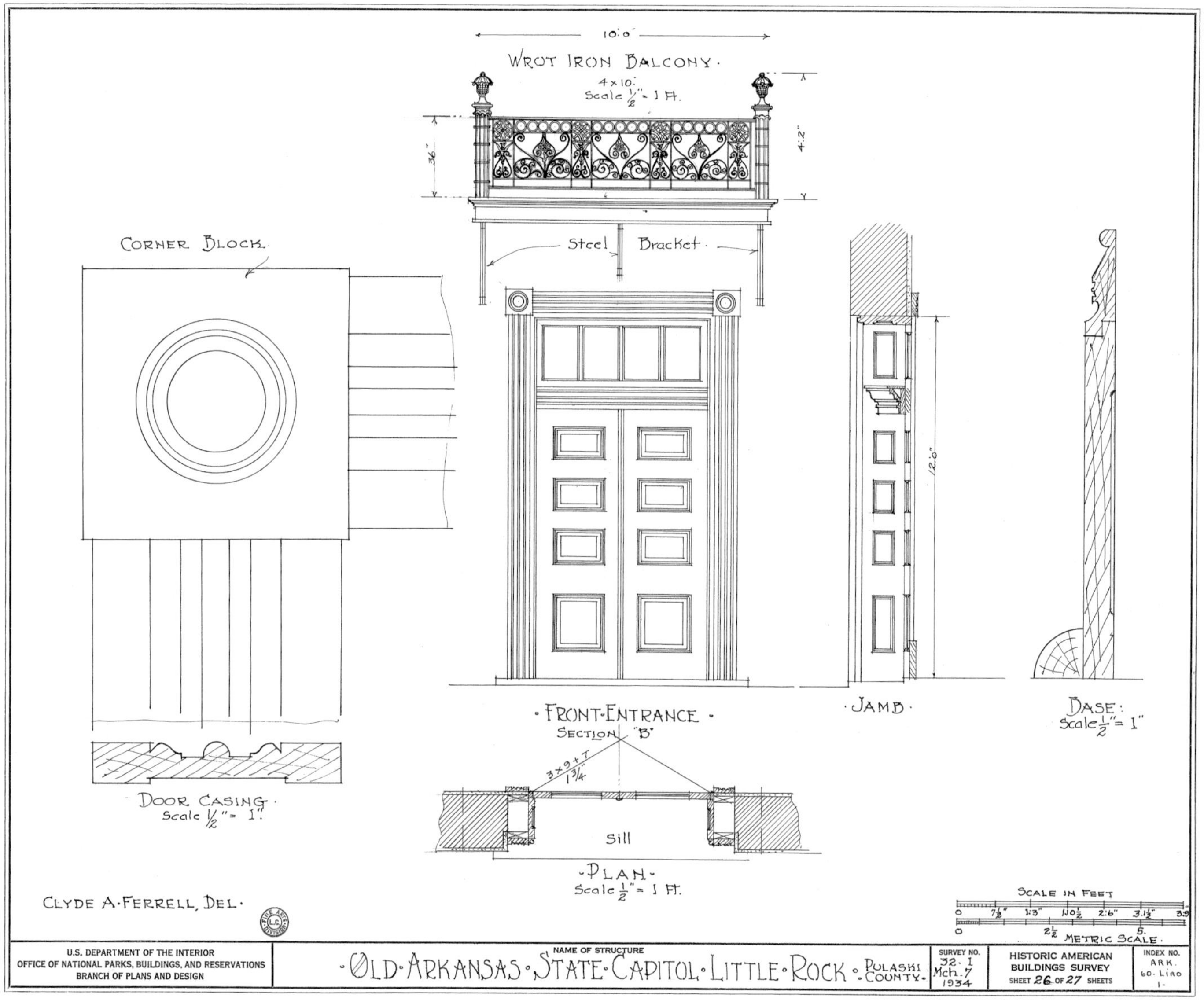

Fig. G.25: Front entrance details. *Courtesy of Historic American Buildings Survey, U.S. Library of Congress.*

Fig. G.26: HABS photograph shows details of the west hyphen, including the decorative balcony railing. *Courtesy of Historic American Buildings Survey, U.S. Library of Congress.*

Fig. G.27: HABS photograph of the north (river) side of the building. *Courtesy of Historic American Buildings Survey, U.S. Library of Congress.*

Fig. G.28: HABS photograph of the south (city) side of the Old State House, looking slightly from the west, with period cars parked on the street. *Courtesy of Historic American Buildings Survey, U.S. Library of Congress.*

Fig. G.29: HABS photograph of the south (city) side of the Old State House, looking slightly from the east, with period cars parked on the street. *Courtesy of Historic American Buildings Survey, U.S. Library of Congress.*

Any work that breaks the ground surface at the Old State House—such as utility lines, foundation repair, or even gardening—can turn up discarded artifacts from earlier years. The following objects were found within the Old State House grounds.

Fig. G.30: This ceramic tobacco pipe, dating to the nineteenth century, was smoked with a reed stem. *Old State House Museum Collection.*

Fig. G.31: The color and design of these transfer-printed ceramic sherds suggest they date to the 1830s or 1840s. *Old State House Museum Collection.*

TFig. G.32: his blue bottle, 4 inches tall by 2½ inches in diameter, might have held medicine. *Old State House Museum Collection.*

Fig. G.33: This 7¼ inches tall chemical bottle was probably used by students at the Medical School. *Old State House Museum Collection.*

Fig. G.34: The inscription on this bottle reads "Dr. Price's Delicious Flavored Extract." The company, located in Chicago, Illinois, manufactured food flavorings during the late nineteenth and early twentieth centuries. *Old State House Museum Collection.*

Fig. G.35: Early L-headed cut nails are of the type used in the construction of the Old State House. *Old State House Museum Collection.*

Postal Commemoratives

In celebration of Arkansas's centennial in 1936 and sesquicentennial in 1986, the Old State House was featured on United States postage stamps and first-day covers. During the centennial, several different styles of first-day covers were issued, all released on June 15, 1936, one hundred years to the day after Arkansas became a state.

Fig. G.36: Commemorative three-cent stamp for the 1936 Arkansas centennial features the Old State House in the center, flanked by Arkansas Post and the State Capitol. *Old State House Museum Collection.*

At least eight different designs (see also Fig. 8.14) of first-day cover envelopes were made to celebrate Arkansas's centennial in 1936. All feature various images of the Old State House, along with the commemorative postage stamp.

Fig. G.37: Nineteen thirty-six first-day cover. *Old State House Museum Collection.*

Fig. G.38: Nineteen thirty-six first-day cover. *Old State House Museum Collection.*

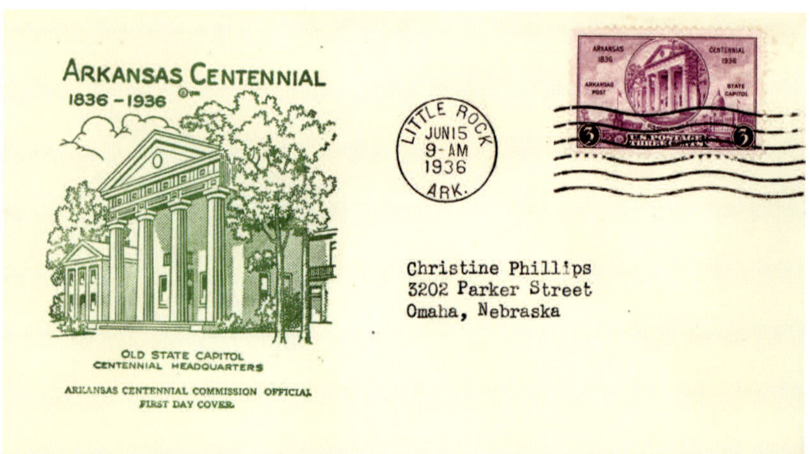

Fig. G.39: Nineteen thirty-six first-day cover. *Old State House Museum Collection.*

Fig. G.40: Nineteen thirty-six first-day cover. *Old State House Museum Collection.*

Fig. G.41: Nineteen thirty-six first-day cover. *Old State House Museum Collection.*

Fig. G.42: Nineteen thirty-six first-day cover. *Old State House Museum Collection.*

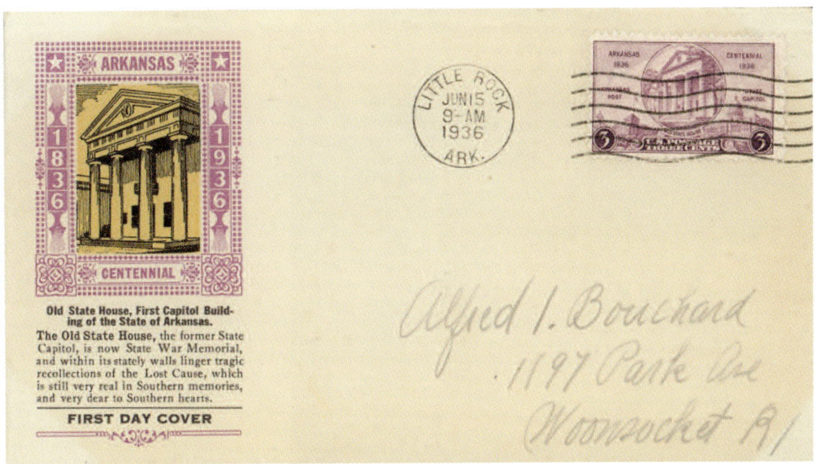

Fig. G.43: Nineteen thirty-six first-day cover. *Old State House Museum Collection.*

Fig. G.44: This first-day cover with stamp celebrates Arkansas's sesquicentennial in 1986. *Courtesy of Gail Moore Stephens.*

Postcards

Postcards have been popular souvenirs beginning after 1898 when private printers were first allowed to issue postcards. Providing a way to send short messages, the cards served as advertisements, holiday greetings, and souvenirs of travel. Postcards did not always carry a printed date and remained available for sale for a number of years after they were printed. Unless a postmark or printing date is provided, an approximate date is given for the cards below.

Fig. G.45: This early postcard, postmarked 1909, and the next three postcards may have originated as black-and-white photos that were color tinted. Because they identify the building as the "Old State Capitol" or "Old State House," they indicate the new State Capitol was already under construction or in use. In fact, groundbreaking for the new Capitol occurred in 1899 and state government moved to the new Capitol in 1911. The well house is visible in the three springtime pictures. *Old State House Museum Collection.*

Fig. G.46: Postmarked 1911. *Old State House Museum Collection.*

Fig. G.47: The Old State House is hidden behind sleet-covered trees on this card, postmarked 1914. *Old State House Museum Collection.*

Fig. G.48: Postmarked 1916. *Old State House Museum Collection.*

Fig. G.49: Postmarked 1921, this postcard dates from the first year the Old State House was designated as the War Memorial Building. *Old State House Museum Collection.*

Fig. G.50: Photo postcards allowed people to have their snapshots printed on postcard weight paper, with a postcard design on the back. This image is dated June 4, 1923. *Old State House Museum Collection.*

Fig. G.51: Postmarked 1945, the Old State House is still identified as the War Memorial Building. *Old State House Museum Collection.*

Fig. G.52: After the Old State House was designated a museum, postcards featuring interior rooms and exhibits became available, such as this one showing the Senate Chamber, postmarked 1962. *Old State House Museum Collection.*

The Period Rooms, sponsored by various women's patriotic organizations, were a major focus of the exhibits during the 1950s and 1960s. Each room featured a different historical period, outfitted with furnishings appropriate to the period. The following six postcards all date ca. 1960.

Fig. G.53: Daughters of the American Revolution Room, furnished by the Arkansas Society of the DAR. *Old State House Museum Collection.*

Fig. G.54: Daughters of 1812 Room, furnished by the Arkansas Division of the United States Daughters of 1812. *Old State House Museum Collection.*

Fig. G.55: Pioneer Room, furnished by the Arkansas Pioneer Association, featured a mix of antiques. *Old State House Museum Collection.*

Fig. G.56: United Daughters of the Confederacy Room, representing the 1860s. *Old State House Museum Collection.*

Fig. G.57: Spanish-American War Room, representing the 1890s, furnished by the Auxiliary of the Spanish-American War Veterans. *Old State House Museum Collection.*

Fig. G.58: Women's Federation Club of Arkansas Room. *Old State House Museum Collection.*

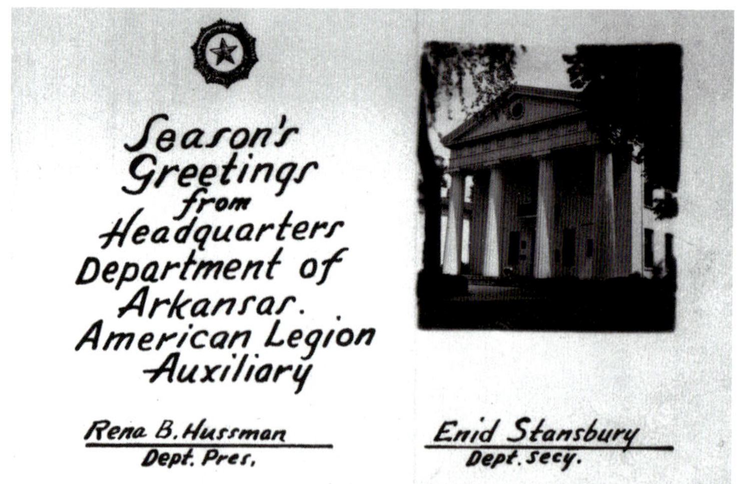

Fig. G.59: Although not a postcard, this ca. 1940 holiday greeting card was sent by the Arkansas American Legion Auxiliary, which had its headquarters at the Old State House when it was the War Memorial Building. *Old State House Museum Collection.*

Souvenirs and Promotions

As one of Arkansas's most historically prominent buildings, the Old State House was featured on souvenirs and collectibles as far back as the nineteenth century. Its image was also used to promote the state on various printed materials, including as a museum on tourism brochures.

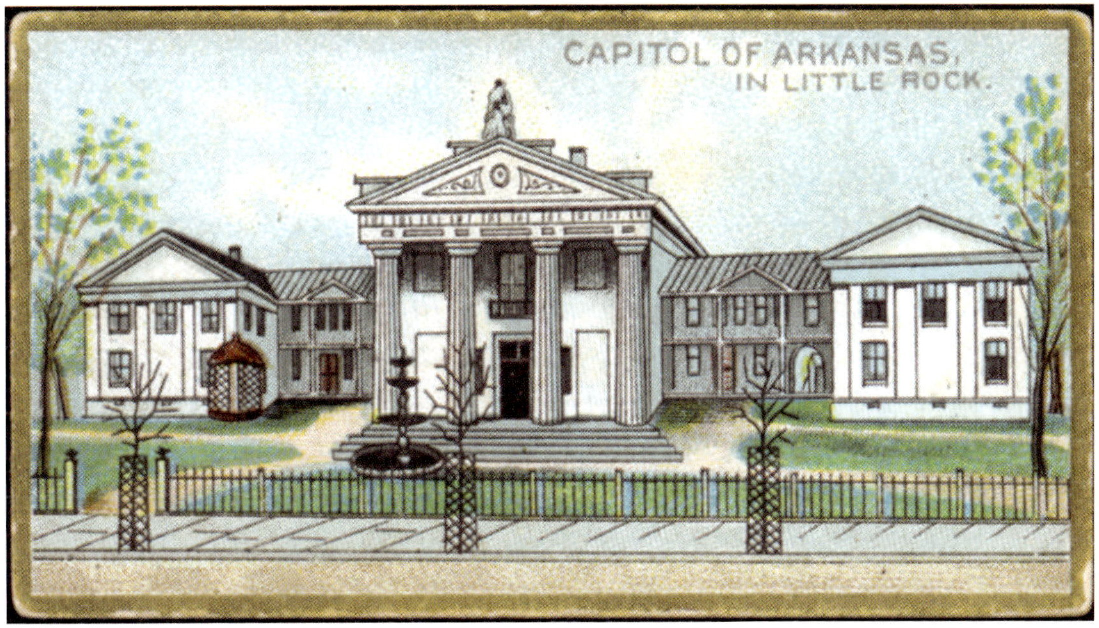

Fig. G.60: The tobacco company of (John) Allen and (Lewis) Ginter of Richmond, Virginia, established in 1875, was the first to place trading cards in their packs of cigarettes. The cards were very popular at the turn of the twentieth century; Lewis & Ginter alone produced over 80 sets. This small, colorful card of the Old State House, which measures 1½ x 2¾ inches, was part of a series on General Government and State Capitol Buildings of the United States, released ca. 1890. *Old State House Museum Collection.*

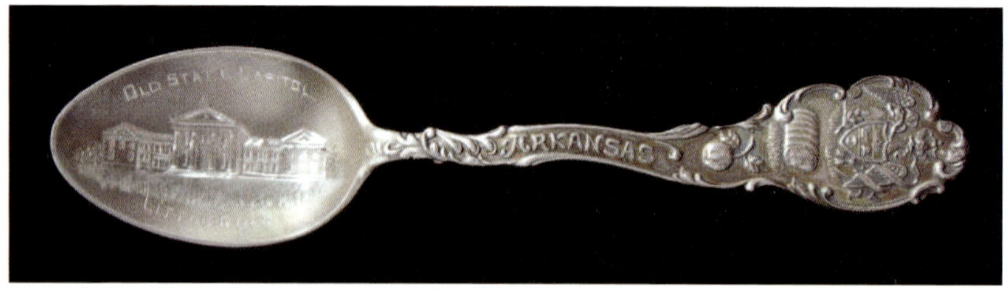

Fig. G.62: The Old State House is featured in the bowl of this silver souvenir spoon. The craze for souvenir spoons spanned about thirty years, from about 1890 to 1920. The spoon, which features the state seal, an apple, a bale of cotton, and the state name on the handle, probably dates to the 1910s, after the new Capitol was under construction or completed. *Courtesy of Gail Moore Stephens.*

Fig. G.61: A pin-back button celebrating Arkansas's centennial features the Old State House. The button was manufactured by the Whitehead and Hoag Company, Newark, New Jersey, one of the world's largest producers of advertising and political products, including celluloid pin-back buttons. *Old State House Museum Collection.*

The following three commemorative plates feature the Old State House either as the sole image or in a group with other Arkansas buildings.

Fig. G.63: Commemorative plate issued by the United Daughters of the Confederacy in 1955. *Old State House Museum Collection.*

Fig. G.64: This blue transfer-print plate, produced for the Gus Blass department store, ca. 1955, features a variety of noted Little Rock buildings. The Old State House is located at the two o'clock position. *Old State House Museum Collection.*

Fig. G.65: Commemorative plate issued in 1972. *Old State House Museum Collection.*

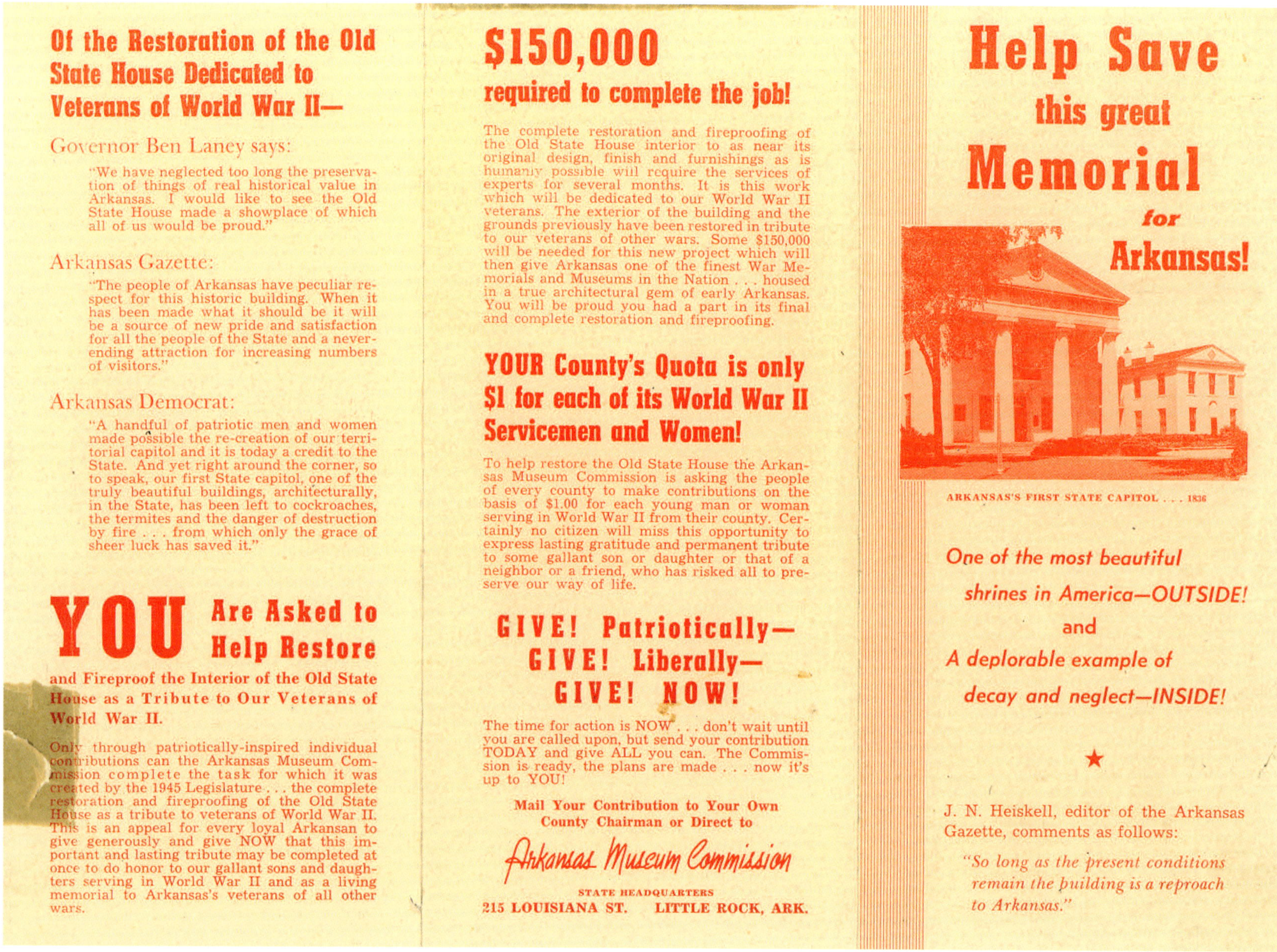

Of the Restoration of the Old State House Dedicated to Veterans of World War II—

Governor Ben Laney says:

"We have neglected too long the preservation of things of real historical value in Arkansas. I would like to see the Old State House made a showplace of which all of us would be proud."

Arkansas Gazette:

"The people of Arkansas have peculiar respect for this historic building. When it has been made what it should be it will be a source of new pride and satisfaction for all the people of the State and a never-ending attraction for increasing numbers of visitors."

Arkansas Democrat:

"A handful of patriotic men and women made possible the re-creation of our territorial capitol and it is today a credit to the State. And yet right around the corner, so to speak, our first State capitol, one of the truly beautiful buildings, architecturally, in the State, has been left to cockroaches, the termites and the danger of destruction by fire . . . from which only the grace of sheer luck has saved it."

YOU Are Asked to Help Restore

and Fireproof the Interior of the Old State House as a Tribute to Our Veterans of World War II.

Only through patriotically-inspired individual contributions can the Arkansas Museum Commission complete the task for which it was created by the 1945 Legislature . . . the complete restoration and fireproofing of the Old State House as a tribute to veterans of World War II. This is an appeal for every loyal Arkansan to give generously and give NOW that this important and lasting tribute may be completed at once to do honor to our gallant sons and daughters serving in World War II and as a living memorial to Arkansas's veterans of all other wars.

$150,000 required to complete the job!

The complete restoration and fireproofing of the Old State House interior to as near its original design, finish and furnishings as is humanly possible will require the services of experts for several months. It is this work which will be dedicated to our World War II veterans. The exterior of the building and the grounds previously have been restored in tribute to our veterans of other wars. Some $150,000 will be needed for this new project which will then give Arkansas one of the finest War Memorials and Museums in the Nation . . . housed in a true architectural gem of early Arkansas. You will be proud you had a part in its final and complete restoration and fireproofing.

YOUR County's Quota is only $1 for each of its World War II Servicemen and Women!

To help restore the Old State House the Arkansas Museum Commission is asking the people of every county to make contributions on the basis of $1.00 for each young man or woman serving in World War II from their county. Certainly no citizen will miss this opportunity to express lasting gratitude and permanent tribute to some gallant son or daughter or that of a neighbor or a friend, who has risked all to preserve our way of life.

GIVE! Patriotically— GIVE! Liberally— GIVE! NOW!

The time for action is NOW . . . don't wait until you are called upon, but send your contribution TODAY and give ALL you can. The Commission is ready, the plans are made . . . now it's up to YOU!

Mail Your Contribution to Your Own County Chairman or Direct to

Arkansas Museum Commission

STATE HEADQUARTERS
215 LOUISIANA ST. LITTLE ROCK, ARK.

Help Save this great Memorial for Arkansas!

ARKANSAS'S FIRST STATE CAPITOL . . . 1836

One of the most beautiful shrines in America—OUTSIDE! and A deplorable example of decay and neglect—INSIDE!

★

J. N. Heiskell, editor of the Arkansas Gazette, comments as follows:

"So long as the present conditions remain the building is a reproach to Arkansas."

Fig. G.66: Various brochures aimed to preserve the Old State House or advertise it as a museum. The 1946 brochure, produced by the Arkansas Museum Commission, sought to raise money for the restoration of the building and honor World War II servicemen and -women. *Old State House Museum Collection.*

Fig. G.67: The Arkansas Commemorative Commission produced the ca. 1955 brochure promoting the Old State House as a museum and tourist attraction. *Old State House Museum Collection.*

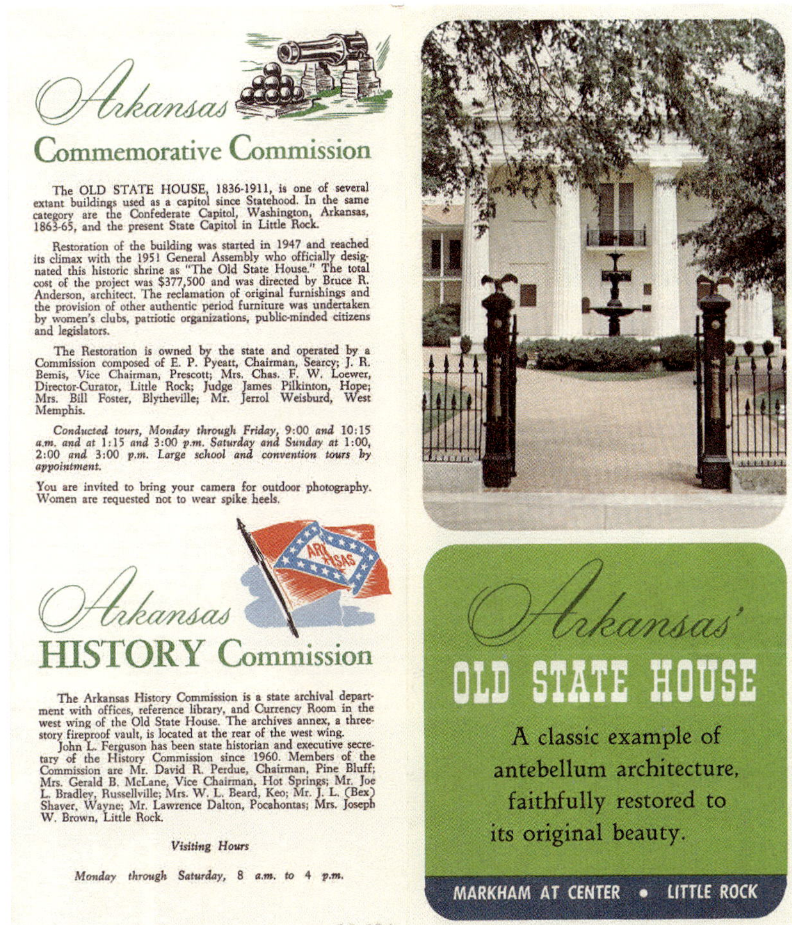

Fig. G.68: The same brochure in its redesigned 1963 version. *Old State House Museum Collection.*

Fig. G.69: This beautiful picture of the Old State House in the snow was featured on the cover of the *American Vocational Journal* for February 1953, highlighting an article titled "The Journal Salutes Arkansas." *Old State House Museum Collection.*

Fig. G.70: Southern belles and the Old State House graced the cover of the 1965 Arkansas state highway map. *Old State House Museum Collection.*

Re-Purpose for the Building

After state government moved to the new Capitol in 1911 and before the Old State House became a museum, the building survived by serving as office space for a number of smaller state and federal agencies and patriotic organizations. The most prominent tenant was the University of Arkansas Medical School, which occupied much of the building from 1912 to 1935. Numerous agencies of the WPA had office space during the 1930s. In addition, the building and grounds continued to be used for special events, such as the 1911 reunion of the United Confederate Veterans.

From May 15–18, 1911, 50 years after the beginning of the Civil War, the United Confederate Veterans held their reunion in Little Rock, an event that brought an estimated 106,000 visitors to the city, including some 12,000 veterans. It was the largest event in Little Rock history to that time. The Old State House served as headquarters for the reunion.

Fig. G.71: Only the statues on the roof of the Old State House are visible behind the banners and mobs of visitors in this photo postcard, taken on May 16, 1911. *Old State House Museum Collection.*

Fig. G.72: Another photo postcard from the United Confederate Veterans Reunion shows flags, banners, and reviewing stands for the reunion parade. *Old State House Museum Collection.*

Fig. G.73: This group of women, probably wives and daughters of Confederate veterans, may have been attending the reunion in 1911. They are posed in front of the east hyphen. The picture reveals the brickwork of the hyphen, the arched passage, and the Victorian rail on the balcony. *Old State House Museum Photo Collection.*

Fig. G.74: During the Arkansas State Reunion in 1909, a group of Confederate veterans and ladies posed in front of the Old State House with their guest, General Clement A. Evans (probably third from left in front row). Evans was commander-in-chief of the UCV that year. As a member of the UCV's Historical Committee, Evans edited the 12-volume *Confederate Military History,* published in 1899. This picture appeared in the *Confederate Veterans Magazine* in 1911. *Old State House Museum Collection.*

Fig. G.75: In September 1949, very few Civil War veterans were still alive to participate in the Sons of Confederate Veterans Reunion that year in Little Rock. In this publicity photo, W. W. Alexander, 100, and James Thrasher, 97, pose on the front lawn with the cannon. The image was published in the *Arkansas Democrat* on September 27, 1949. *Old State House Museum Collection.*

Fig. G.76: From 1912 to 1935, the University of Arkansas Medical School occupied much of the building, as noted in the sign over the door. This picture, ca. 1918, was probably taken just a few months later than the one shown in Fig. 8.3. The plaster on the exterior walls of the building was scored to resemble blocks of stone, which can be seen in this image and in a close-up in Fig. 9.10. *Courtesy of University of California, Riverside/California Museum of Photography, Keystone-Mast Collection.*

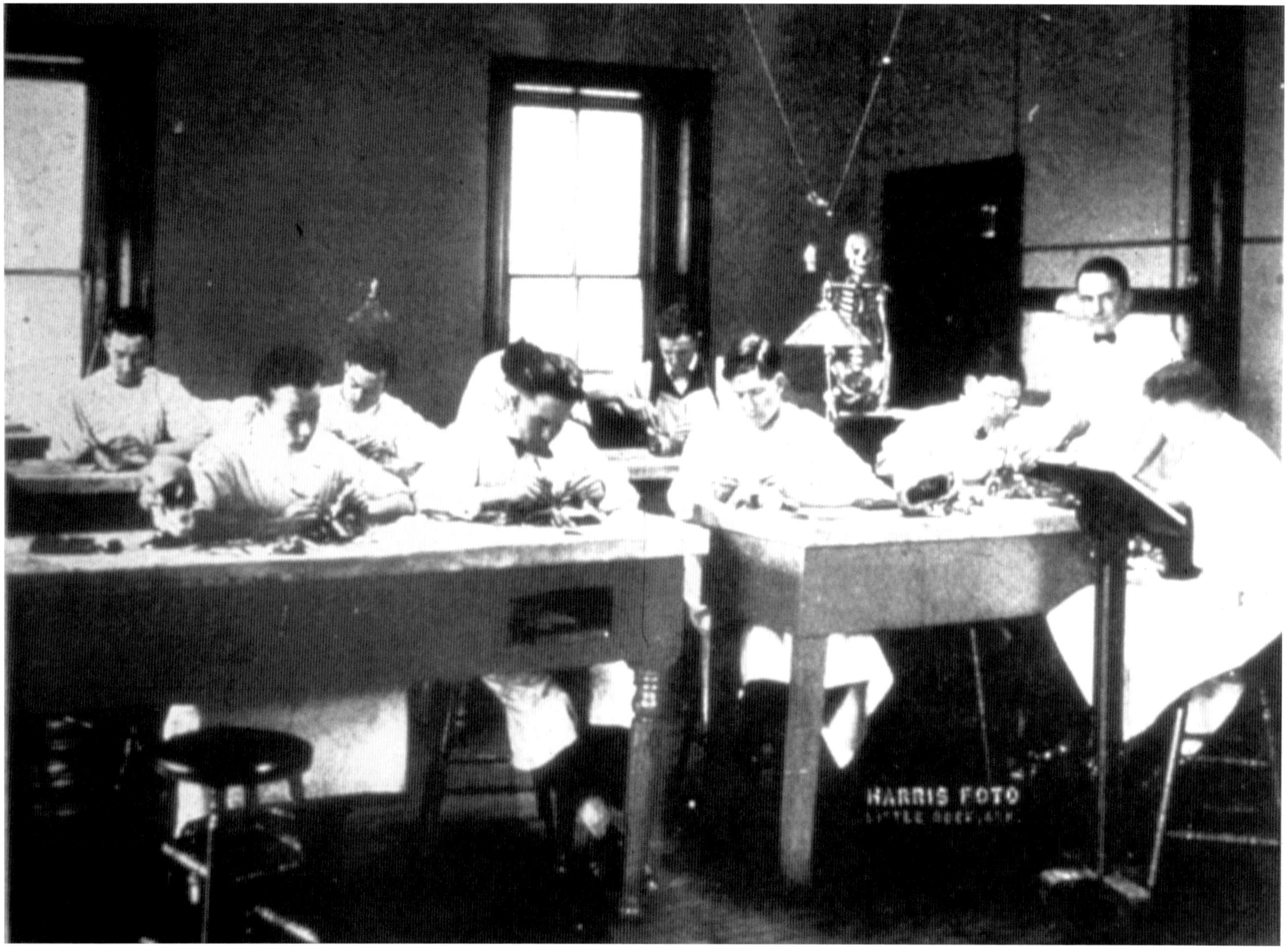

Fig. G.77: The Anatomical Laboratory was located in the north end on the second floor of the east wing. Because of the good light provided by the windows, the room was used for dissections. *Courtesy of University of Arkansas for Medical Sciences.*

Fig. G.78: Students received practical instruction in drug preparation in the Chemistry Laboratory, ca. 1925, located in the north end on the first floor of the main building, what is now the Riverfront Room. Remnants of chemical and pharmaceutical bottles used by the Medical School have been found in the Old State House grounds. *Courtesy of University of Arkansas for Medical Sciences.*

Fig. G.79: The gallery at the south end of the 1885–1886 House Chamber was used by the Medical School, beginning in 1915, as a laboratory for surgical technique. By 1923 it was being used as a laboratory of pharmacology, and by 1928 it had been converted to the Incinerator Room. *Courtesy of University of Arkansas for Medical Sciences.*

Fig. G.80: The original House Chamber, which was converted to the Senate Chamber in the 1885–1886 expansion, was used by the Medical School from 1915 as the Assembly Hall. It is located at the front of the main building on the second floor. This picture, which appeared in the 1924 *Caduceus,* the Medical School yearbook, shows the hall decorated with patriotic bunting. *Courtesy of University of Arkansas for Medical Sciences.*

Fig. G.81: During the 1930s, a number of state and federal agencies had offices in the Old State House, including the Arkansas State Rangers (precursor of the Arkansas State Police), a statewide law enforcement agency established in 1935. Ranger J. Earl Scroggin (in uniform) stands with two plainclothes officers in front of their headquarters at the Old State House. Scroggin organized the state's fingerprint files. *Old State House Museum Collection.*

Fig. G.82: Shown in this group photograph are the 13 original Rangers, 1935–1936, and various officials. Identification is left to right. *Front row:* Governor J. M. Futrell; board members W. V. Tomkins, J. P. Woods, and S. L. Cooke; Chief Gray Albright, and Assistant Chief Robert LaFollette. *Middle row:* Lieutenant J. Earl Scroggin, Ranger G. D. Morris, Ranger J. H. Sewell, Ranger Lindsey Hatchet, Lieutenant E. E. Frazier, and civilian employee Leon Gershner. *Back row:* Ranger Neal Shannon, Capt. Cliff Atkinson, Ranger John Hendricks, Ranger J. P. Hill, Ranger Gene Mooney, and Ranger J. Ed Clark. *Old State House Museum Collection.*

Fig. G.83: Captain Cliff T. Atkinson, one of the 13 original Rangers, poses in front of the Old State House fountain, ca. 1935. The Rangers were charged with enforcing criminal and traffic laws, including motor vehicle weights and standards, acting as state fire marshal and conducting arson investigations, and establishing and maintaining a bureau of criminal identification. *Old State House Museum Collection.*

Political Memorabilia

Photography was not invented nor in common usage until the latter years that the Old State House served as the seat of government, so images of the governors and legislators at work inside the building are extremely rare. Later politicians, however, have continued to make use of the Old State House as a symbol of Arkansas government and history.

Fig. G.84: Early photographs of the Legislature in the Old State House are very rare. This image was taken inside the hall of the House of Representatives during the inauguration of Governor Jeff Davis on January 18, 1901. Governor Davis served to 1907. Another early photograph of the House of Representatives, taken in 1909, can be seen in Fig. 7.7. *Old State House Museum Photo Collection.*

Fig. G.85: Governor George Donaghey (*seated on right*) was photographed with his staff in his office at the Old State House, ca. 1910. Donaghey, who served from 1909 to 1913, was the last governor to serve in the Old State House before moving to the new Capitol building. *Courtesy of Arkansas History Commission.*

On May 2, 1914, the Political Equality League of Little Rock joined suffragists throughout the nation in sponsoring Suffrage Day with a program of speakers at the Old State House.

Fig. G.86: Among the women who spoke that morning were Mrs. George E. Cunningham, Miss Josephine Miller, Mrs. S. S. Wassell, Mrs. C. E. Rose, Mrs. T. T. Cotnam, Mrs. Minnie U. Rutherford, Miss Frances Edmondson, and Miss Julie Warner. Mrs. O. F. Ellington, president of the League, presided over the meeting and introduced the speakers. *Courtesy of Arkansas History Commission.*

Fig. G.87: A number of men also participated in Suffrage Day, including Dr. L. P. Gibson, attorney John W. Blackwood, Rabbi Louis Wise, C. C. Kirkpatrick, George R. Brown, George W. Jones, and Henry C. McCain. *Courtesy of Arkansas History Commission.*

Fig. G.88: On June 10–12, 1949, President Harry S. Truman visited Little Rock for a reunion of World War II veterans of the Thirty-fifth Infantry Division, which had trained in Arkansas, and to dedicate War Memorial Stadium. President Truman and officials pose at the reviewing stand in front of the Old State House on the day of his arrival in Little Rock, June 10, 1949. Of the nonmilitary men, Truman is third from the right in the dark suit and wearing a hat. To the left of Truman is Orval Faubus (with hat in hand) who would become Arkansas governor in 1955, and on the far left (in the dark suit) is Governor Sid McMath, who served from 1949 to 1953. *Old State House Museum Collection.*

Fig. G.89: President Harry Truman, looking dapper in his white suit, spectator shoes, and walking cane, leaves the parade reviewing stand in front of the Old State House on June 11, 1949. Behind him is Governor Sid McMath. In the afternoon, Truman made a speech at the dedication of War Memorial Stadium. Truman served as the thirty-third president, from 1945 to 1952. *Courtesy of Butler Center for Arkansas Studies, Central Arkansas Library System.*

Fig. G.90: By 1971 the new Capitol had long been the seat of state government, but the Old State House remained an important political symbol for new governors. Here, Governor Dale Bumpers, in the light coat sitting beside First Lady Betty Bumpers, enjoys his inauguration day parade. Bumpers served from 1971–1975. *Old State House Museum Collection.*

Fig. G.91: Barely visible in the center of the picture, Governor David Pryor delivers his inaugural address in January 1975. Pryor served to 1979. *Photograph by Captain Bill Lawson, 176th PI Det Arkansas National Guard, Old State House Museum Collection.*

In a wonderfully symbolic gesture, Arkansas governor Bill Clinton chose the Old State House as election night headquarters for his 1992 presidential campaign, thus focusing the eyes of the nation and the world on Arkansas and the Old State House. President Clinton repeated the winning location in 1996 for his re-election campaign.

Fig. G.92: Press passes for election night 1992 feature an image of the Old State House. *Courtesy of Randy Dixon.*

Fig. G.93: Pin-back button celebrates Clinton's inauguration day, January 20, 1993, although the photograph was taken in front of the Old State House on election night, November 3, 1992. From left to right are First Lady Hillary Clinton, President Bill Clinton, Vice President Al Gore, and Second Lady Tipper Gore. Clinton served as the forty-second president from 1993 to 2001. *Old State House Museum Collection.*

.

Fig. G.94: This pin-back button celebrates President Clinton's second-term election night, with the Old State House bedecked in political finery. *Old State House Museum Collection.*

Images through the Years

Images of the Old State House began appearing first in drawings from the nineteenth century and later in photographs beginning during the Civil War and continuing to today. These drawings and photographs capture the architectural changes to the building, as well as the succession of plantings and objects on the grounds. The images also are interesting in showing the progression of clothing styles, technological evolution of transportation, and changes in the Little Rock cityscape.

Fig. G.95: The Old State House as it appeared ca. 1870. The view from the east wing hides the colonnades between the buildings, but provides a good view of the east elevation, showing two entrances on the side. The front fence and east retaining wall can also be seen. The illustration was made by Frank Hamilton Taylor (1846–1927), a Philadelphia artist who illustrated articles for the pictorial press. His drawing was based on a photograph taken by Byron S. Alford (b. ca. 1840), a Little Rock photographer operating just after the Civil War. His studio was located at 204 East Markham Street. *Old State House Museum Collection.*

Fig. G.96: This view of the Old State House dates prior to 1878, when the fountain was added. Clearly seen, *from left to right,* is the well house, a flagpole on the main building, the east colonnade, and an awning on one window of the east wing. The print was published by D. Appleton Co., a large New York book publisher, known for their *New American Cyclopedia, Picturesque* series, and many others. *Old State House Museum Collection.*

Fig. G.97: This engraving of the Old State House was published in March 1880 in the New York *Daily Graphic,* the first American newspaper with daily illustrations. It clearly shows the configuration of the two hyphens, although the artist added an extra tier to the fountain. Note the horse-drawn streetcar on the right. *Old State House Museum Collection.*

Fig. G.98: Although this illustration bears an 1890 date, it actually shows the Old State House as it appeared prior to the 1885–1886 expansion. It is obvious that the artist used the 1880 *Daily Graphic* engraving as a model, but apparently did not know the Old State House had changed by 1890. This suggests that the artist was unfamiliar with Little Rock and lived out of state. *Old State House Museum Photo Collection.*

Fig. G.99: This reproduction of a 1903 print by F. B. Sandusky shows the Old State House as it appeared after the 1885–1886 expansion, with the colonnades now enclosed and enlarged into the hyphens. The well house, fountain, and statues on the roof are visible, as is the fence and protective latticed framework around the street-side trees. *Courtesy of Arkansas Arts Center Foundation Collection: Gift of Mr. Thompson.*

Fig. G.100: Three young men pose jauntily with the fountain about 1890. Plantings of trees and shrubs, as well as the placement of flowerpots and a decorative bench, fill the grounds. Another photograph from the same period can be seen in Fig. 5.17. *Old State House Museum Collection.*

Fig. G.101: Changes to the street in front of the Old State House can be seen in this photograph, ca. 1900. Utility poles and streetlights fill the scene, while young trees along the street are protected from hungry horses by the latticed framework. *Old State House Museum Collection.*

Fig. G.102: This ca. 1910 photograph provides an unusual view from the west wing. Not only is the well house visible, but the pump handle of the well also can be seen. *Old State House Museum Photo Collection.*

Fig. G.103: Early-model cars are parked along the street in front of the Old State House in this photograph from the mid-1920s. *Old State House Museum Collection.*

Fig. G.104: This beautiful scene, taken about 1935, captures the Old State House after a snowfall, with the flow from the fountain frozen into icicles. The photo was taken by Howard S. Stern (1910–2002), a Little Rock physician, award-winning artist, and noted photographer, who helped organize the Little Rock Camera Club in 1935. *Old State House Museum Collection.*

Fig. G.105: What looks like ice in the trees is, in fact, an unusual lighting effect produced by the sun. The stunning image was captured in 1942 by Little Rock resident Frank Fredeman (1895–1982). *Old State House Museum Collection.*

Fig. G.106: This bird's-eye view shows the Little Rock cityscape around the Old State House as it appeared about 1978. The Law Library on the left has been replaced by the Doubletree Hotel, condos, and a parking garage; the Peabody Hotel now stands on the right, and the Stephens Building now stands where the parking lot is. *Old State House Museum Photo Collection.*

Fig. G.107: After restoration of the Old State House was complete, a Grand Reopening Gala was held on June 12, 1999. *Old State House Museum Photo Collection.*

Fig. G.108: The Grand Reopening Gala concluded with a fireworks display. *Courtesy of* Arkansas Democrat-Gazette, *Karen E. Segrave, photographer.*

Contemporary Artists' Interpretations

Twentieth-century artists have continued to be interested in the Old State House as a beautiful historic structure and a symbol of Arkansas history. Several pieces of art from the museum's collection are illustrated below.

Fig. G.109: Watercolor by David Greene (1939–2006), painted in 1972, depicts the Old State House in a winter scene beneath the Christmas star. Greene was a California native, but spent much of his life in Arkansas, his last home being in North Little Rock. He studied at the Los Angeles Art Institute and worked in a variety of media, including sculpture and animation. He won awards for a mural at the Arkansas Territorial Restoration, for graphic design, and for animated commercials. *Old State House Museum Collection.*

Fig. G.110: Charlene Shryock, a descendant of Old State House architect Gideon Shryock, commemorated the work of her ancestor, ca. 1980, through the needlework technique called "counted cross stitch." *Old State House Museum Collection.*

Fig. G.111: A 2003 pen-and-ink drawing by Searcy artist Bill Reames (b. 1961) shows the Old State House as it might have looked shortly after completion in 1842. *Old State House Museum Collection.*

Fig. G.112: Etching of the Old State House by J. Carl Hancock (1898–1966). Hancock, who lived in North Little Rock, was a self-taught etcher, designer, painter, and commercial artist. He sketched many architectural subjects in Little Rock, Memphis, New Orleans, and elsewhere in the South, and was noted for his book *New Orleans Etching, Drypoints and Sketches,* published in 1938. *Old State House Museum Collection.*

Fig. G.113: Oil painting of the Old State House by Fern Edie Knecht (1888–1979) appeared on the cover of the *Arkansas Gazette* State Centennial Edition, June 15, 1936. Born in Nebraska and raised in Kansas, Knecht lived in Little Rock during the 1930s and from 1947 to 1957. She studied at the University of Kansas, the St. Louis School of Fine Art, and with Taos, New Mexico, artist Ernest Blumenschein, among others. She painted the Mother Goose mural in the Little Rock Public Library in 1934, as well as murals in the Woman's City Club of Little Rock. She also taught art for a short time at Little Rock Junior College. *Courtesy of Butler Center for Arkansas Studies, Central Arkansas Library System.*

Fig. G.114: Woodcut print by Adrian Brewer (1891–1956) shows the Old State House as it appeared after the 1885–1886 expansion. Born in Minnesota, Adrian Brewer was the son of artist N. R. Brewer. In the early years, Adrian traveled extensively, painted landscapes, and managed his father's exhibitions. Adrian visited Arkansas in the 1920s, married a Hot Springs woman, and eventually established an art school in Little Rock in 1933. He was particularly known for his patriotic artwork during the World Wars and for his portraits of Arkansans. During the 1940s he created a series of woodcuts of Arkansas landmarks as a project to bring art to average people. With his son Edwin, also an artist, Adrian organized the Arkansas Art League in 1953. *Old State House Museum Collection.*

Fig. G.115: Watercolor of the Old State House by Edwin Brewer (1927–2002). Born in Little Rock, Edwin Brewer was the son of noted artist Adrian Brewer. In 1953 he and his father organized the Arkansas Art League, and in 1970 Edwin was one of the founders of the Mid-Southern Watercolorists. Besides painting in oils and watercolors, Edwin also worked as an art teacher at the Arkansas Arts Center and the University of Arkansas-Little Rock, and as an art specialist at the Arkansas Department of Education, where he wrote two books on art education. *Courtesy of Butler Center for Arkansas Studies, Central Arkansas Library System.*

Fig. G.116: Numbered artist's proof of a pen-and-ink drawing made by Arkansas artist Richard DeSpain for the Arkansas sesquicentennial. DeSpain was born in Marked Tree in 1946, retired from the University of Arkansas Cooperative Extension Service where he worked as an artist and draftsman, and resides in North Little Rock. *Old State House Museum Collection.*

Acts of Arkansas

1838 *Acts Passed at a Special Session of the General Assembly of the State of Arkansas.* Woodruff & Pew, Printers to the State, Little Rock, Ark.

1885 *Acts and Resolutions of the General Assembly, of the State of Arkansas.* A. M. Woodruff, State Printer, Little Rock, Ark.

Ahart, Larry

n.d. A Brief Informal "History" of the Old State House Museum. Manuscript on file, Old State House Museum, Little Rock, Ark.

Allard, Chester C. (compiler)

1959 *Who is Who in Arkansas, Volume 1 (Arkansans of the Years Volume Five).* Allard House Publishers, Little Rock, Ark.

Allsopp, Fred W.

1907 *Twenty Years in a Newspaper Office.* Central Printing Co., Little Rock, Ark.

1922 *History of the Arkansas Press for a Hundred Years and More.* Parke-Harper Publishing Co., Little Rock, Ark.

Anderson, Bruce R.

1950 Report on the Restoration of Arkansas's First State Capitol, Little Rock, Arkansas. Report by the architect, on file, Old State House Museum.

Andrews, Alfred J.

1944 Gideon Shryock, Kentucky Architect, and Greek Revival Architecture in Kentucky. *Filson Club History Quarterly* 18(2):67–77.

1945 Gideon Shryock: Kentucky Architect. *Magazine Antiques* 58(1):35–37.

Anonymous

1920 New Home of Historical Society. *Register of the Kentucky State Historical Society* 18(54):5–6.

1974 *Charleston, Arkansas Centennial Yearbook: A Time of Change.* On-line excerpt, http://users.rootsweb.com/~arfrankl/Town/towns.htm (accessed April 17, 2007).

Arkansas Reports

1841 The State Against William W. Stevenson. *Arkansas Reports, Vol. 2: Cases Argued and Determined in the Supreme Court of Arkansas During the July Term, 1839, and January and July Terms, 1840, in Law and Equity.* State of Arkansas, Little Rock, Ark., pp. 260–281.

Armistead, H. B.

1895 *Biennial Report of the Secretary of State of the State of Arkansas, February 20, 1895.* Brown Printing Company, Little Rock, Ark., 1895.

1896 *Biennial Report of the Secretary of State of the State of Arkansas, December 1896.* Tunnah & Pittard, Printers, Little Rock, Ark.

Arnaud, Leopold

1944 Foreword. In *Greek Revival Architecture in America* by Talbot Hamlin. Oxford University Press, New York.

Atkinson, James H.

1945 The Brooks-Baxter Contest. *Arkansas Historical Quarterly* 4(2):124–149.

Baird, W. David

1979 *Medical Education in Arkansas, 1879–1978.* Memphis State University Press, Memphis, Tennessee.

Baker, Russell P.

1998 Arkansas's Major Joseph J. Anthony. *Pulaski County Historical Review* 46(4):74–79.

2006a Arkansas History Commission and State Archives. On-line source, Encyclopedia of Arkansas History and Culture, www.encyclopediaofarkansas.net/.

2006b Dallas Tabor Herndon. On-line source, Encyclopedia of Arkansas History and Culture, www.encyclopediaofarkansas.net/.

Banks, W. N.

1997 Letter from W. N. Banks, Newnan, Ga., to Mary L. Kwas, Arkansas Archeological Survey, Fayetteville, September 2, 1997.

Barnes, Kenneth C.

2000 The Old State House and the Brooks-Baxter War. In *Sentinels of History: Reflections on Arkansas Properties on the National Register of Historic Places,* edited by Mark K. Christ and Catheryn H. Slater. University of Arkansas Press, Fayetteville, pp. 50–54.

Baylor, Orval W.

1943 *John Pope, Kentuckian: His Life and Times, 1770–1845.* Hobson Press, Cynthiana, Ky.

Beavers, B. B.

1878 *Report of the Secretary of State of the State of Arkansas, October 1st, 1878.* A. H. Sevier, "Gazette" Book and Job Printing House, Little Rock, Ark.

Benjamin, Asher

1969 *The American Builder's Companion.* 6th edition (originally published 1827 by R. P. & C. Williams). Dover Publications, New York.

Bowman, Michael
2006 Stopover of the Beatles. On-line source, Encyclopedia of Arkansas History and Culture, www.encyclopediaofarkansas.net/.

Boyd, Gregory A.
2006 *Family Maps of Pike County, Arkansas, Deluxe Edition.* Alphax Publishing Co., Norman, Okla.

Brittain, Bertie
1997 Letter from Bertie Brittain, Mineola, Texas, to Mary L. Kwas, Arkansas Archeological Survey, Fayetteville, September 27, 1997.

Brough, Charles Hillman
1906 Historic Homes. In *Publications of the Arkansas Historical Association, Vol. 1*, edited by John Hugh Reynolds, pp. 286–293.

Brown, C. Allan
1984 History of the Old State House Grounds. In "Landscape Manual Old State House Museum," in the collection of the Old State House Museum, July 1984, pp. 1–16.

Brown, Donald Richard, Marvin Ray Franklin, and Michele Roussel Wasson
1978 *The Old State House: Its Survival and Contributions, 1911–1947.* Arkansas Commemorative Commission, Little Rock.

Bush, George F.
1911 Gideon Shryock: An Appreciation. *The Transylvanian* 19(4):104–106.

Calloway, Jan
1981 *The Trapnall Legacy.* Arkansas Commemorative Commission and Trapnall Hall, Little Rock.

Campbell, William S.
1928 *One Hundred Years of Fayetteville, 1828–1928.* William S. Campbell, publisher, Fayetteville, Ark.

Cantrell, Ellen Harrell (comp.)
1900 *The Annals of Christ Church Parish of Little Rock, Arkansas, from A.D. 1839 to A.D. 1899.* Arkansas Democrat Co., Little Rock, Ark.

Carter, Clarence Edwin (ed.)
1954 *The Territorial Papers of the United States,* Volume XXI (The Territory of Arkansas, 1829–1836, Continued). National Archives and Records Service, Publication No. 56–10, Washington, D.C.

Chism, B. B
1891 *Biennial Report of the Secretary of State of the State of Arkansas, September 30, 1890.* Press Printing Co., Little Rock, Ark.
1893 *Biennial Report of the Secretary of State of the State of Arkansas, September 30, 1892.* Press Printing Co., Little Rock, Ark.

City of St. Louis
1996 Period I: The Walking City, 1820–1869. City of St. Louis CDA/SLDC Web page (http://stlouis.missouri.org/government/heritage/buildtyp/p1-3.htm#government), pp. 1–5 (accessed June 12, 1996).

Clay, Charles A.
2006 My Son's and Their Heritage. http://worldconnect.rootsweb.com/~1800–2003&id=I3971 (search on Richard Clay Hawkins) (accessed July 20, 2006).

Collins, Lewis, and Richard H. Collins
1877 *History of Kentucky (Collins' Historical Sketches of Kentucky).* Published by Richard H. Collins, Louisville, Ky.

Cook, Michael L.
1996 *Jefferson County, Kentucky, Records, Vol. 7: Marriages, 1836–1845.* The Researchers, Indianapolis, Ind.

Counts, Mrs. William H. (comp.)
1977 *A Compendium of Arkansas Genealogy, Volume 1, Featuring Pulaski County, Arkansas.* No publisher listed, North Little Rock, Ark., p. 133.

Crawford, Sybil F.
1993 *Jubilee: Mount Holly Cemetery, Little Rock, Arkansas: Its First 150 Years.* Mount Holly Cemetery Association, Little Rock, Ark.

Crawford, Sybil F., and Mary Fletcher Worthen (comps.)
1993 *Mount Holly Cemetery, Little Rock, Arkansas: Burial Index, 1843–1993.* Mount Holly Cemetery Association, Little Rock, Ark.

Crockett, John W.
1903 *Arkansas Biennial Report of the Secretary of State, 1901–1902.* Tunnah & Pittard, Little Rock, Ark.
1905 *Arkansas Biennial Report of the Secretary of State for the Years 1903–1904.* Tunnah & Pittard, Printers, Little Rock, Ark.

Cummings, Hubertis
1953 Stephen Hills and the Building of Pennsylvania's First Capitol. *Pennsylvania History* 20(October):417–437.

Dalton, Lawrence
1981 *History of Randolph County Arkansas.* Originally published 1946, Democrat Printing and Lithographing Company, Little Rock, Ark.

DeBlack, Thomas A.
2010 Civil War Through Reconstruction, 1861 Through 1864. On-line source, Encyclopedia of Arkansas History and Culture, www.encyclopediaofarkansas.net/ (accessed August 5, 2010).

Dekle, Clayton B.
1966 The Tennessee State Capitol. *Tennessee Historical Quarterly* 25(3):213–238.

Dodd, Jordan R. (ed.)
1990 *Missouri Marriages Early to 1825.* Precision Indexing, Bountiful, Utah.

Donaghey, George W.
1937 *Building a State Capitol.* Parke-Harper Co., Little Rock, Ark.

Donovan, Timothy P., Williard B. Gatewood Jr., and Jeannie M. Whayne (eds.)
1995 *The Governors of Arkansas: Essays in Political Biography,* 2nd edition. University of Arkansas Press, Fayetteville.

Dougan, Michael B.

1994 *Arkansas Odyssey.* Rose Publishing Co., Little Rock, Ark.

Easley, Barbara Pickering, and Verla Pickering McAnelly (comps. and eds.)

1996 *Obituaries of Washington County, Arkansas, Volume 2, 1893–1902.* Heritage Books, Bowie, Md.

Ellesin, Dorothy E. (ed.)

1974 Collectors' Notes. *Magazine Antiques* 106(4):602.

Eno, Clara B.

1945 Old and New Capitols of Arkansas. *Arkansas Historical Quarterly* 4(3):241–249.

Evans, Mrs. E. E., and Mrs. J. Frank Thompson

1992 *Tombstone Records of Boone County, Missouri.* Reprint of 1934 edition, Genealogical Society of Central Missouri, Columbia.

Ewbank, Lynn

1986 "Doctor, Lawyer, Merchant, Chief": The History and Contributions of the Lorenzo Gibson Family. *Pulaski County Historical Review* 34(2):30–37.

Fagan, S.

1838 Miscellaneous. In *Journal of the Second Session of the General Assembly of the State of Arkansas (House Journal).* Woodruff & Pew, Printers to the State, Little Rock, Ark., p. 360.

Featherstonhaugh, G. W.

1844 *Excursion Through the Slave States, From Washington on the Potomac to the Frontier of Mexico; with Sketches of Popular Manners and Geological Notices, Vol. 2.* John Murray, London.

Feld, Stuart P.

1997 Letter from Stuart P. Feld, Hirschl & Adler Galleries, New York, to Mary L. Kwas, Arkansas Archeological Survey, Fayetteville, September 16, 1997.

Ferguson, John L.

1968 *The Old State House—Some Questions and Answers.* Arkansas Commemorative Commission, Little Rock.

Field, Ben J.

1951 The Weaver Homestead in Little Rock. *Arkansas Historical Quarterly* 10(4):328–338.

Field, Elizabeth S.

1923 Letter from E. S. Field to R. Newcomb, March 8, 1926. University of Illinois Archives, Rexford Newcomb Papers, Record Series 12/2/23.

1952 Gideon Shryock: His Life and His Work. *Register of the Kentucky Historical Society* 50(171):110–129.

Floyd, William Barrow

1978 The Restored Old Capitol, Frankfort, Kentucky. *Magazine Antiques* 114(1): 106–116.

Flynn, Elisabeth Louise

1971 *Gideon Shryock, 1802–1880: Greek Revival Architect in Kentucky.* Northwestern University Ph.D. dissertation in Fine Arts, University Microfilms, Ann Arbor, Mich.

Frolich, Jacob

1880 *Report of the Secretary of State of the State of Arkansas, October 1st, 1880.* James Mitchell, State Printer, Little Rock, Ark.

1882 *Biennial Report of the Secretary of State of the State of Arkansas, October 1st, 1882.* Mitchell & Bettis, State Printers, Little Rock, Ark.

1884 *Biennial Report of the Secretary of State of the State of Arkansas, October 1st, 1884.* Mitchell & Bettis, Printers and Binders, Little Rock, Ark.

Garrett, Wendell (ed.)

1972 Clues and Footnotes. *Magazine Antiques* 102(4):598, 602.

Gems of Pike County

1995 Records of the Antioch Church of Christ, Delight, Arkansas 1933–1884. *Gems of Pike County Arkansas* 6(1):1–2.

General Assembly

1838 *Acts Passed at a Special Session of the General Assembly of the State of Arkansas* (November 6, 1837–March 5, 1838). Woodruff & Pew, Little Rock, Ark.

Gilchrist, Agnes Addison

1969 *William Strickland: Architect and Engineer, 1788–1854.* Da Capo Press, New York.

Goodspeed

1889a *Biographical and Historical Memoirs of Pulaski, Jefferson, Lonoke, Faulkner, Grant, Saline, Perry, Garland and Hot Spring Counties, Arkansas.* Goodspeed Publishing Co., Chicago, Ill.

1889b *History of Benton, Washington, Carroll, Madison, Crawford, Franklin, and Sebastian Counties, Arkansas.* Goodspeed Publishing Co., Chicago, Ill.

1890 *Biographical and Historical Memoirs of Southern Arkansas.* Goodspeed Publishing Co., Chicago, Ill.

1894 *A Reminiscent History of The Ozark Region.* Goodspeed Brothers, Publishers, Chicago, Ill.

1978 *Biographical and Historical Memoirs: History of Arkansas.* (Reprint of 1889 edition.) Southern Historical Press, Easley, S.C.

Greer, D. B.

1858 Report of the Commissioner of Public Buildings. In *Message of Elias N. Conway, Governor of Arkansas, to Both Houses of the General Assembly, November 3, 1858* (bound in *Message and Documents, 1858–1859, Arkansas).* Johnson & Yerkes, State Printers, Little Rock, Ark., p. 29.

Guendling, Randall L., and Mary L. Kwas

1997 *The Historical Archeology of Arkansas' Old State House.* Project 954 Draft Report, submitted to Department of Arkansas Heritage, Arkansas Archeological Survey, Fayetteville.

Haggard, John C.

1971 *The Architecture of Gideon Shryock.* Unpublished master's thesis, School of Architecture, University of Virginia.

Hallum, John

1887 *Biographical and Pictorial History of Arkansas, Vol. 1.* Weed, Parsons, and Co., Printers, Albany, New York.

Hamlin, Talbot

1940 The A.I.A. Meets in Kentucky. *Pencil Points* 21(5):276, 279–294.

1944 *Greek Revival Architecture in America: Being an Account of Important Trends in American Architecture and American Life Prior to the War Between the States.* Oxford University Press, New York.

Hanger, Mrs. Frederick, and Miss Clara B. Eno

1935 *History of the Arkansas Federation of Women's Clubs, 1897–1934.* Press-Argus Printers, Van Buren, Ark.

Hardin, Bayless E.

1945 The Capitols of Kentucky. *Register of the Kentucky State Historical Society* 43(144):173–200.

Harding, T., and A. M. Bailey

1885 Specifications of Work to be Done on the State House. Manuscript dated August 4, 1885. University of Arkansas at Little Rock Archives, J. N. Heiskell Historical Collection H-17, Series V, Box 1, File 6.

Hathaway, Gilbert

1973 Travels in the Southwest. In *Travels in the Old South, Selected from Periodicals of the Times,* Vol. 2, edited by Eugene L. Schwaab, University Press of Kentucky, Lexington.

Hawkins, Richard C.

1843 Report of the Commissioner of Public Buildings. In *Journal of the House of Representatives for the Fourth Session of the General Assembly of the State of Arkansas* (1842). Eli Colby, printer, Little Rock, Ark., pp. 40–48.

Heath, Patricia

2007 The History of the Heath Family. http://worldconnect.rootsweb.com/~prheath&id=I30574 (search on John Wilson, born 1787) (accessed January 30, 2007).

Hempstead, Fay

1890 *A Pictorial History of Arkansas From Earliest Times to the Year 1890.* N. D. Thompson Publishing Co., St. Louis, Mo.

1911a *Historical Review of Arkansas: Its Commerce, Industry and Modern Affairs. Vol. 1.* Lewis Publishing Co., Chicago, Ill.

1911b *Historical Review of Arkansas: Its Commerce, Industry and Modern Affairs. Vol. 2.* Lewis Publishing Co., Chicago, Ill.

Herndon, Dallas T.

1922a (ed.) *Centennial History of Arkansas, Volume 2.* S. J. Clarke Publishing Company, Little Rock, Ark.

1922b The Site of Little Rock Laid Out for a Town (1820). In *The Highlights of Arkansas History.* Arkansas History Commission, Little Rock.

1933 *Why Little Rock Was Born.* Central Printing Co., Little Rock, Ark.

1947 *Annals of Arkansas, 1947.* Historical Record Association, Little Rock, Ark.

Hinkle, Kebel W., Mrs.

1974 Letter from Mrs. Kebel W. Hinkle (nee Dorothy Weigart), Mountain View, Ark., to Curator, Old State House, Little Rock, Ark., January 30, 1974, in the files of the Old State House Museum, Little Rock.

Hitchcock, Henry-Russell, and William Seale

1976 *Temples of Democracy: The State Capitols of the USA.* Harcourt Brace Jovanovich, New York.

Hodges, Earle W.

1913 *Arkansas Biennial Report of the Secretary of State for the Years 1909–10–11–12.* Tunnah & Pittard, Printers, Little Rock, Ark.

1915 *Syllabus of Biennial Report of Earle W. Hodges, Secretary of State, 1913–1914.* No publisher or printer listed.

Hopper, Ira C.

1924 *Arkansas Biennial Report of the Secretary of State for the Years 1921–1924.* H. G. Pugh & Co., Little Rock, Ark.

House Journal

1837 Journal of the House of Representatives. In *Journals of the Special Session of the General Assembly of the State of Arkansas, 1837–1838.* Little Rock, Ark. (No printer or publication information provided.)

1840 *Journal of the House of Representatives of the General Assembly of the State of Arkansas.* (No printer or publication information provided.)

1861 *Journal of the House of Representatives for the Thirteenth Session of the General Assembly of the State of Arkansas.* Johnson & Merkes, State Printers, Little Rock, Ark., p. 660.

Hudson, Ralph M.

1944 Art in Arkansas. *Arkansas Historical Quarterly* 3(4):312–215.

Hull, Alex. C.

1898 *Biennial Report of the Secretary of State of Arkansas, for the Years 1897–98.* Little Rock Printing Co., Little Rock, Ark.

1900 *Arkansas Biennial Report of the Secretary of State, 1899–1900.* Tunnah & Pittard, Printers, Little Rock, Ark.

Jacoway, Peggy

1941 *First Ladies of Arkansas.* Southern Publishers, Kingsport, Tenn.

Jones, Ruth Irene

1955 Hot Springs: Ante-bellum Watering Place. *Arkansas Historical Quarterly* 14(1):3–31.

Jordan, B. Gail

2006 Jerry Jordans Family. http://worldconnect.rootsweb.com~:3198177&id=I173 (search on William Wilson Stevenson) (accessed July 14, 2006).

Kannaday, Nixby Daniel, and Loreda Hicks Daniel (comps.)

1984 *Cemetery Inscriptions of Polk County, Arkansas.* Copyright by authors, no publication place.

Kennan, Clara B.

1950 Arkansas's Old State House. *Arkansas Historical Quarterly* 9(1):33–42.

Klein, Dee, and Chriss Chapman

2006 Thorn Cemetery Index, Mariposa County, California. On-line: www.mariposaresearch.net/THORN.html (accessed October 6, 2006).

Laist, Theodore

1926 Two Early Mississippi Valley State Capitols. *Western Architect* 35(5):53–58.

Lancaster, Clay
1943 Gideon Shryock and John McMurtry: Architect and Builder of Kentucky. *Art Quarterly* 6(4):257–275.

Leonard, Cynthia Miller (comp.)
1978 *The General Assembly of Virginia, July 30, 1619–January 11, 1978: A Bicentennial Register of Members.* Published for the General Assembly of Virginia by the Virginia State Library, Richmond.

Leonard, John W. (ed.)
1901 *Who's Who in America, 1901–1902.* A. N. Marquis & Co., Pub., Chicago, Ill., p. 30.

Lewellyn, Laura
1947 The Pulaski County Hospital. *Arkansas Historical Quarterly* 6(2):145–154.

Ludwig, O. C.
1906 *Arkansas Biennial Report of the Secretary of State for the Years 1905–1906.* Tunnah & Pittard, Printers, Little Rock, Ark.
1909 *Arkansas Biennial Report of the Secretary of State for the Years 1907–1908.* Tunnah & Pittard, Printers, Little Rock, Ark.

MacDuff, Inez Hale
1949 Old Statehouse Cornerstone Gives Up Ill-Kept Documents. *Arkansas Gazette,* undated clipping from Old State House Vertical File, Special Collections Division, University of Arkansas Libraries, Fayetteville.

Mahoney, Nell Savage
1945 William Strickland and the Building of Tennessee's Capitol, 1845–1854. *Tennessee Historical Quarterly* 4(2):99–153.

McArthur, Priscilla
1986 *Arkansas in the Gold Rush.* August House Publishers, Little Rock, Ark.

McVicar, James
1838 Miscellaneous. In *Journal of the Second Session of the General Assembly of the State of Arkansas (House Journal).* Woodruff & Pew, Printers to the State, Little Rock, Ark., pp. 360–361.

Moneyhon, Carl H.
1996 The Creators of the New South in Arkansas: Industrial Boosterism, 1875–1885. *Arkansas Historical Quarterly* 55(4):383–409.

Moore, E. B. (Elias B.)
1886 *Biennial Report of the Secretary of State of the State of Arkansas, October 1st, 1886.* A. M. Woodruff, State Printer, Little Rock, Ark.
1888 *Biennial Report of the Secretary of State of the State of Arkansas, October 1st, 1888.* Press Printing Co., Little Rock, Ark.

More, E. A. (Elijah A.)
1837 Report of Elijah A. More, Commissioner of Public Buildings. In Journal of the House of Representatives, *Journals of the Special Session of the General Assembly of the State of Arkansas* (1837). Woodruff & Pew, Little Rock, Ark., pp. 201–203.
1838a Report of the Commissioner of Public Buildings. In *Journals of the Second Session of the General Assembly of the State of Arkansas* (1838). Woodruff & Pew, Printers to the State, Little Rock, Ark., pp. 331–338.
1838b Miscellaneous. In *Journal of the Second Session of the General Assembly of the State of Arkansas (House Journal).* Woodruff & Pew, Printers to the State, Little Rock, Ark., pp. 356–358.

Morgan, James Logan
1992 *Arkansas Marriage Notices 1819–1845.* Reprint of 1984 edition. Arkansas Research, Conway.

Nail, Alison
1995 The Preservation & Restoration of the Old State House and the Women Who Made it Possible. Unpublished student paper, which includes an interview with John Ferguson, in collection of Old State House Museum.

Newcomb, Rexford
1927 Benjamin Henry Latrobe, Early American Architect. *Architect* 9(2):173–177.
1928a Gideon Shryock: Pioneer Greek Revivalist of the Middlewest. *Register of the Kentucky State Historical Society* 26(78):220–235.
1928b Gideon Shryock—Pioneer Greek Revivalist of the West. *Architect* 11(1):41–46.
1930 Transylvania College and Her Century-Old Greek Revival Building. *Art and Archaeology* 29(6):250–255, 285.
1940 *Old Kentucky Architecture.* Bonanza Books, New York.
1953 *Architecture in Old Kentucky.* University of Illinois Press, Urbana.

Nuttall, Thomas
1821 *A Journal of Travels Into the Arkansas Territory.* Thomas Palmer, Philadelphia, Pa. (University Microfilms, 1966).

O'Donnell, Susannah Cassedy
1996 AAM Accreditation: Celebrating 25 Years. *Museum News* (May/June):42–46.

Pendleton, Henry F.
1845 Report of the Commissioner on Public Buildings (1844). In *Journal of the House of Representatives for the Fifth Session of the General Assembly of the State of Arkansas.* S. Borland & Co., Little Rock, Ark., pp. 135–146.

Pendleton & Wassell
1838 Miscellaneous. In *Journal of the Second Session of the General Assembly of the State of Arkansas (House Journal).* Woodruff & Pew, Printers to the State, Little Rock, Ark., pp. 356, 360.

Peter, Robert, and Johanna Peter
1896 *Transylvania University: Its Origin, Rise, Decline, and Fall.* Filson Club Publications No. 11, Louisville, Ky.

Pike, Albert
1973 Letters from Arkansas. In *Travels in the Old South, Selected from Periodicals of the Times,* Vol. 1, edited by Eugene L. Schwaab, University Press of Kentucky, Lexington.

Pope, William F.
1895 *Early Days in Arkansas.* F. W. Allsopp, Little Rock, Ark.

Poppeliers, John C., S. Allen Chambers Jr., and Nancy B. Schwartz
1983 *What Style is It?: A Guide to American Architecture.* Preservation Press, Washington, D.C.

Priest, Sharon
1998 *Historical Report of the Secretary of State, 1998.* Little Rock, Ark.

Puryear, Jerry
2006 *University of Arkansas for Medical Sciences (UAMS).* Encyclopedia of Arkansas History and Culture, www.encyclopediaofarkansas.net (accessed October 16, 2006).

Quapaw Quarter
1976 *The Quapaw Quarter: A Guide to Little Rock's 19th Century Neighborhoods.* Quapaw Quarter Association, Little Rock, Ark.

Quartzburg
2006 Quartzburg—California Ghost Town. On-line: www.ghosttowns.com/states/ca/quartzsburg.html (accessed October 6, 2006).

Ramsaur, L. M.
1870 Report of the Committee on Public Buildings. In *Journal of the House of Representatives, Arkansas, Seventeenth Session.* Price & Barton, Public Printers, Little Rock, Ark., pp. 132–136.

Reynolds, John Hugh, and David Yancey Thomas
1910 *History of the University of Arkansas.* University of Arkansas, Fayetteville.

Richter, Wendy (ed.)
1992 *Clark County Arkansas: Past and Present.* Clark County Historical Association, Arkadelphia, Ark.

Rose, U. M.
1917 John Pope: An Unfinished Sketch. *Publications of the Arkansas Historical Association* 4:284–292.

Ross, Margaret
1966a Historical Association's Meeting Here Will Explore the Group's Predecessors. *Arkansas Gazette,* May 1, 1966.
1966b The Homes of the *Arkansas Gazette* at Little Rock, 1821–1866. *Arkansas Historical Quarterly* 25(2):128–141.
1967 Elijah A. More is Elected Commissioner of Public Buildings by Legislature in 1836. *Arkansas Gazette,* September 17, 1976.
1969 *Arkansas Gazette: The Early Years 1819–1866.* Arkansas Gazette Foundation, Little Rock, Ark.
1971 The Hinderliter House: Its Place in Arkansas History. *Arkansas Historical Quarterly* 30:181–192.
1972 Retaliation Against Arkansas Newspaper Editors During Reconstruction. *Arkansas Historical Quarterly* 31(2):150–165.

Ross, Margaret Smith
1954 The Watkins-Stevenson Family, Pulaski County Pioneers. *Pulaski County Historical Review* 2(1):5–16.

Rothrock, Thomas
1975 The Arkansas State Horticultural Society. *Arkansas Historical Quarterly* 34(3): 242–267.

Roy, F. Hampton Sr., and Charles Witsell Jr.
1984 *How We Lived: Little Rock as an American City.* August House, Little Rock, Ark.

Schwitalla, Alexis Wade
1921 *Who's Who in Little Rock, 1921: An Accurate Biographical Record of Men and Women of Little Rock, Ark., Prominent in Various Lines of Civic Activity.* Who's Who Publishers (New Era Press), Little Rock, Ark.

Select Committee
1845 Report of Select Committee, in Relation to Hon. John Pope. In *Journal of the House of Representatives for the Fifth Session of the General Assembly of the State of Arkansas.* S. Roland & Co., printers, Little Rock, Ark., pp. 141–146.

Scully, Arthur Jr.
1973 *James Dakin, Architect: His Career in New York and the South.* Louisiana State University Press, Baton Rouge.

Shank, Ned
1977 *Arkansas' First State Capitol, 1885–1947.* Arkansas Commemorative Commission, Little Rock.

Sherwood, Diana
1938 Horse Racing in Arkansas. *Arkansas Gazette,* Magazine Section, February 13, 1938.
1952 Historical Societies in Arkansas. *Arkansas Historical Quarterly* 11(2):131–136.

Shiras, Frances H.
1939 *History of Baxter County.* Printed by J. W. Daniel and Shiras Brothers Print Shop, Mountain Home, Ark.

Shryock, Gideon
ca. 1839 Letter from G. Shryock to E. A. More, postmarked January 4, Louisville, Ky. University of Arkansas at Little Rock Archives, J. N. Heiskell Historical Collection H-17, Series V, Box 1, File 7.
1846a Letter from Gideon Shryock, Louisville, to John Bass, Nashville, May 12, 1846. Tennessee State Library and Archives, Capitol Construction File, John Bass, Incoming Correspondence, Box 2, Folder 6.
1846b Letter from Gideon Shryock, Louisville, to John Bass, Nashville, November 26, 1846. Tennessee State Library and Archives, Capitol Construction File, John Bass, Incoming Correspondence, Box 2, Folder 6.

Smyer, Susan
1976 First State Capitol in Transition, 1833–1885. Unpublished mss. in the files of the Old State House Museum, Little Rock, Ark.

Speer, William S., and John Henry Brown
1881 *The Encyclopedia of The New West.* Arkansas volume. United States Biographical Publishing Co., Marshall, Tex. (1978 reprint, Southern Historical Press, Easley, S.C.)

Stevenson, W. W.
1840 Report of the Commissioner of Public Buildings. In *Journals of the Third Session of*

the General Assembly of the State of Arkansas (1840). No publisher listed, pp. 553–559.

Stiles, Wilson

1978 Restoration Study for the Old State House, Little Rock, Arkansas. Dated July 20, 1978. On file, Old State House Museum, Little Rock, Ark.

Sutton, Robert K.

1992 *Americans Interpret the Parthenon: The Progression of Greek Revival Architecture from the East Coast to Oregon, 1800–1860.* University Press of Colorado, Niwot.

Thomas, David Y. (ed.)

1930 *Arkansas and Its People: A History, 1541–1930.* Biographical and Genealogical, Vol. 4. American Historical Society, New York.

Thorn, Thomas

1837 Entry. *Journals of the First Session of the General Assembly of the State of Arkansas.* Woodruff & Pew, Little Rock, Ark., pp. 179–181.

Thornton, A. E.

1838 Report. In *Journals of the Second Session of the General Assembly of the State of Arkansas, Journal of the Senate* (no publisher listed, prob. Woodruff & Pew, Little Rock, Ark.), pp. 94–97.

Tintner, Adeline R.

1946 The City of Three Capitols. *Magazine of Art* 39(1):9–11.

Treon, John A.

1972 Politics and Concrete: The Building of the Arkansas State Capitol, 1899–1917. *Arkansas Historical Quarterly* 31(2): 99–149.

Tunnah, Fanny Stevenson

1913 Pioneer Preacher. *Arkansas Pioneers* 1(2): 23–26.

VMI

2007 Virginia Military Institute Archives. Online Rosters Database. www.vmi.edu/archives/archiverosters/Search.asp (accessed 2007).

Walden, Edward H.

1954 An Account Book of the 1840s, Edward H. Walden, Brick Contractor. *Pulaski County Historical Review* 2(2):9–11.

Washburn, Reverend Cephas

1869 *Reminiscences of the Indians.* Presbyterian Committee of Publication, Richmond, Va. (Johnson Reprint Corp., New York, 1971).

Weaver, S. M.

1860 Report of the Commissioner of Public Buildings. May be part of: *Message of Elias N. Conway, Governor of Arkansas, to Both Houses of the General Assembly; November 6, 1860.* Johnson & Yerkes, State Printers, Little Rock, Ark. (Bound in: "Messages and Documents, 1859–1860"; Special Collections Division, University of Arkansas Libraries, Fayetteville.)

Weigart, Mr. and Mrs. Larry D.

1997 Letter from Mr. and Mrs. Larry D. Weigart, Roach, Missouri, to Mary L. Kwas, Arkansas Archeological Survey, Fayetteville, July 6, 1997.

Western Historical Company

1882 *History of Boone County, Missouri, Written and Compiled From the Most Authentic Official and Private Sources; Including a History of Its Townships, Towns and Villages.* Western Historical Co., St. Louis, Mo., pp. 777–778.

Whayne, Jeannie M., Thomas A. DeBlack, George Sabo III, and Morris S. Arnold

2002 *Arkansas: A Narrative History.* University of Arkansas Press, Fayetteville.

White, Lonnie J.

1964 *Politics on the Southwestern Frontier: Arkansas Territory, 1819–1836.* Memphis State University Press, Memphis, Tenn.

White, Robert J. T.

1866 *Report of the Secretary of State of the State of Arkansas, Accompanying the Message of the Governor, to the General Assembly, Session of 1866.* Arkansas Gazette Print., Little Rock, Ark.

1870 Report of the Secretary of State. In *Journal of the House of Representatives, Arkansas, Seventeenth Session.* Price & Barton, Public Printers, Little Rock, Ark., pp. 125–127, 129–131.

1873 *Report of the Secretary of State of the State of Arkansas, December, 1872.* Little Rock Printing and Publishing Co., Little Rock, Ark., pp. 8–9.

Wiedeman, Ruby Johnson

1984a Colonel James M. Johnson. *Madison County Musings* 3(1):30–31.

1984b Colonel James Madison Johnson and His Family. *Madison County Musings* 3(2): 91–102.

Williams, Nancy A., and Jeannie M. Whayne (eds.)

2000 *Arkansas Biography: A Collection of Notable Lives.* University of Arkansas Press, Fayetteville.

Wishard, R. W.

1870 Resolution. In *Journal of the House of Representatives, Arkansas, Seventeenth Session.* Price & Barton, Public Printers, Little Rock, Ark.

Woodward, Mrs. C. G.

1960 The Wassell Family of Little Rock. *Pulaski County Historical Society Review* 8(2):19–22.

Worley, Ted R.

1950 The Control of the Real Estate Bank of the State of Arkansas, 1836–1855. *Mississippi Valley Historical Review* 37(3):403–426.

Worthen, William B.

1987 Municipal Improvement in Little Rock: A Case History. *Arkansas Historical Quarterly* 46(4):317–347.

1992 Louise Loughborough and Her Campaign for "Courage and Fineness." *Pulaski County Historical Review* 40(2):26–33.

INDEX

Mary L. Kwas is a research associate for the Arkansas Archeological Survey. Her recent work includes an article on the Abraham Block family of Washington, Arkansas, for the journal *Southern Jewish History* and a special issue on historical archeology in Arkansas for the *Arkansas Historical Quarterly*, for which she served as editor. She is the author of *Digging for History at Old Washington* published by the University of Arkansas Press.

Bill Gatewood is executive director of the Old State House Museum, an agency of the Department of Arkansas Heritage. He previously served as the museum's curator and deputy director.